THE
PLAN

THE LAMB SLAIN FROM THE
FOUNDATION OF THE WORLD

ELSA HENDERSON

Copyright © 2024 Elsa Henderson.
Front cover: Janice Park Wong

All rights reserved. No part of this book may be reproduced, stored, or transmitted by any means—whether auditory, graphic, mechanical, or electronic—without written permission of both publisher and author, except in the case of brief excerpts used in critical articles and reviews. Unauthorized reproduction of any part of this work is illegal and is punishable by law.

All Scriptures taken from ESV unless otherwise noted. Scripture quotations are from The ESV© Bible (The Holy Bible, English Standard Version©), copyright © 2001 by Crossway, a publishing ministry of Good News Publishers. Used by permission. All rights reserved.

ISBN: 979-8-89031-837-4 (sc)
ISBN: 979-8-89031-838-1 (hc)
ISBN: 979-8-89031-839-8 (e)

Because of the dynamic nature of the Internet, any web addresses or links contained in this book may have changed since publication and may no longer be valid. The views expressed in this work are solely those of the author and do not necessarily reflect the views of the publisher, and the publisher hereby disclaims any responsibility for them.

One Galleria Blvd., Suite 1900, Metairie, LA 70001
(504) 702-6708

Contents

Dedication v
God's Long Range Plan vii

1. Eternity Past 1
2. The Plan Conceived 12
3. Paradise 19
4. The First Rebellion 26
5. Expelled 35
6. Chaos 39
7. From Chaos to Order 46
8. The Heavens Declare the Redeemer Promised 53
9. The Heavens Declare the Redeemer's People 69
10. The Heavens Declare the Redemption Completed 81
11. New Creation 97
12. Paradise Lost 114
13. Forgiven, But Expelled 125
14. The Dragon 129
15. The Plan Told and Retold 132
16. The Battle for Jerusalem 145
17. The Battle for the Ark 149
18. Israel's First King 153
19. The Giant Killer 165
20. Saul Fails, David Succeeds 172
21. David Conquers Jerusalem 178

22. David Brings Back the Ark 180
23. Why Not David? 186
24. David's Flaw 190
25. David's Impact on Solomon 203
26. Failures and Glory 216
27. Preparations for the Temple 223
28. Solomon Starts Well 230
29. Solomon's Downward Journey 234
30. Idolatry, Judgment and Hope 244
31. Restoration 254
32. Repentance Didn't Last 260
33. The Plan Begins 262
34. The Newborn Lamb 279
35. Other Witnesses 285
36. The Voice 292
37. At the Right Time 298
38. The Dragon Does His Worst 311
39. Darkness to Dawn 324
40. Power to Change 331
41. Ups and Downs 341
42. Authority Restored 348
43. The Battle Engaged 351
44. God Steps In 355
45. Millennium and Judgment 366
46. Eternity Future 370

Author's Comments 373
The Cover 379

Dedication

I dedicate this book to God—Father, Son and Holy Spirit—my first love, and to his Word, his love letter to me. I love reading it and exploring its mysteries. It is like a giant jigsaw puzzle whose finished picture is The Plan, the plan of redemption. There is no picture on the box, so I put the pieces together little by little, a day at a time. Sometimes I discover that I have put some pieces in the wrong place and I have to take them apart and put them aside until I understand the picture better. I know I will not complete the puzzle in my lifetime, but I keep working on it.

Thank you, Lord, for your precious Word.

Thank you, Janice, an inveterate doodler, who captured beautifully the hand of God doodling about The Plan.

Thank you, Robert and Holly, whose enthusiasm pushed me past my inertia to actually get this book published.

And thanks to my friend Ronnie, who was in the room the day I started my spiritual journey on the path to the Celestial City. We were both in Grade 3. He was serving a detention after school one Friday when I went up to my teacher and blurted out through tears, "I need to be saved!" She quickly excused Ronnie and showed me the Way.

Ronnie is still part of my journey. He looked at the picture I was putting together and questioned whether some of the puzzle pieces were in the right place. If I moved some of those pieces, other pieces didn't fit, so I left the puzzle as I had assembled it.

You, too, dear reader, may see some pieces out of place, but the final picture is the same. The Lamb slain from the foundation of the world has by his blood ransomed people for God from every tribe and language and people and nation. He is worthy to take the scroll and open its seals. He is worthy to receive honor and glory and praise. Amen!

God's Long Range Plan

God told Jeremiah: "This is the covenant I will make with the people of Israel after that time," declares the Lord. "I will put my law in their minds and write it on their hearts. I will be their God, and they will be my people. No longer will they teach their neighbor, or say to one another, 'Know the Lord,' because they will all know me, from the least of them to the greatest," declares the Lord.[1]

What God will do for Israel, He will do for all who are children of the one true God. He wants the law to be not just in our Bibles but in our hearts.

---

[1] Jeremiah 31:33-34, NIV

1

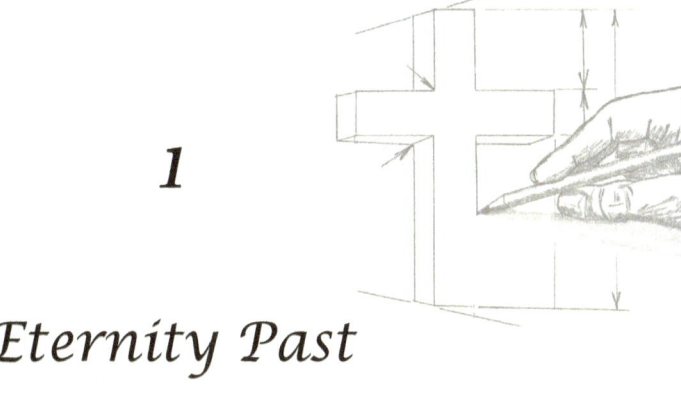

Eternity Past

Once upon a time . . . .
Don't be silly. This story begins before time.
In the beginning . . . .
No, no, no! This story starts *before* the beginning.

Before earth and time began—God!
Eternal. Alpha and Omega, the Beginning and the End.
Almighty.
Holy.
Love personified.
Father, Son and Spirit in perfect loving relationship. In perfect communion and communication.
Their unity is so perfect that they declare themselves to be the Holy One. They have only one name. Yahweh.

Father is a being like no other. The Ancient of Days. Beyond comprehension. Words capture only snatches of his glory.
Look!
Behold the beauty of his holiness!
If you cannot look into the Father's face, focus on his beautiful robe. The Father is clothed in honor and majesty, adorned with glory and splendor. His robe—like jasper with its countless variations of green, yellow, red, brown, purple and black—reflects his incredible creativity. The colors of his robe flow in waves and ripples. Like carnelian with its

warm variations of red and red-yellow. Colors warm and rich, conveying a distinct sense of unconditional love.

Listen!

Father's voice is powerful and majestic.

His voice commands the respect due to the Almighty. Listen! To the roar of his voice! His voice thunders in marvelous ways.[1]

Son, like Father, has always existed. The First and the Last.[2] Like Father, Son is also difficult to describe. When he sets aside his glory, he looks pretty much like a man. He often dresses in linen, sometimes with a fine gold belt around his waist, sometimes with a golden sash across his chest.

When Son appears in the full glory of Yahweh, his entire appearance is fiery. His hair appears white as snow. His eyes blaze like flaming torches. His face shines like the sun in all its brilliance, the light flashing like lightning. His entire body appears to be full of fire. His torso appears transparent, like topaz, almost colorless but with hints of yellow and pink-orange glowing and shimmering as if with heat. His arms, legs and feet are of a deeper color, more like burnished bronze, gleaming like metal glowing in a furnace. A huge radiance surrounds him, like a rainbow after the rain, but with colors more brilliant and fiery.[3]

Son is also known as the Word. The ultimate communicator. The word from his mouth is full of both grace and truth, slicing to the heart of any issue as cleanly as a double-edged sword. His ability to communicate Father's love and character is without equal. When making a grand announcement, his voice sounds like a trumpet. When he appears in the full glory of Yahweh, his voice sounds like rushing waters. Yet he can speak in a quiet whisper, or without words, simply through a gentle touch.

---

[1] Job 37:2, 4, 5
[2] Rev. 1:17
[3] See Ezekiel 1:27-28; Daniel 10:5-6; Rev. 1:10-18.

Son knows and sees all, as if he has eyes everywhere. He is more kingly in his bearing than a lion. He is the King of kings, yet he does not flaunt his kingly position. He is willing to set aside his majesty to serve others, even if that means great sacrifice. The Son has the face and appearance of a man, yet he is totally divine. Something about him soars, like an eagle soaring through the heavens, coasting on unseen currents.

Spirit is everywhere and just as powerful as Father and Son. Like the wind, he makes his presence known by what he does— amazing things that take your breath away! Sometimes his actions are so subtle that they are ascribed to someone or something else. That does not matter to Spirit. He cares only that the glory goes to the Holy One, to Yahweh, not to some nameless force.

Spirit is invisible except to Father and Son. Nothing is invisible to any of them. Even darkness is no obstacle. They see as clearly in the dark as in the light. They can see the unseen.

* * * *

"Let's make ourselves a place to dwell," Father suggested before the beginning.

"Good idea," said Son. "What kind of place?"

"A place worthy of its occupants, of course," said Spirit. "A place that reflects our character and majesty. A place where our love can find full expression."

"We can start with something big enough for our present needs and expand it in the ages to come," suggested Father.

They envisioned their home as a magnificent tent-like structure of vast proportions surrounded by heavens, its architectural style blending into the surroundings. They proposed details, letting their creativity flow. Some proposals were discussed and unanimously rejected, other ideas were improved upon as they brainstormed. They

The Plan

used their foresight to visualize their needs far into the future, into all eternity, and revised their designs accordingly. In front of their dwelling place, their tabernacle, would be a throne hall. They would have to design everything very carefully, for it would be built to last forever. Righteousness and justice would be its foundation.[4]

When the three were satisfied with every detail, Father and Spirit turned to Son and gave him the nod. The Word spoke, and their dwelling place came into being with fireworks and explosive sounds louder than thunder.

All three clapped when the smoke cleared and they saw the result. After wandering through their personal dwelling and approving every detail, they entered the throne hall. It was enormous, as big as the sea.

The throne room was separated into two parts, upper and lower, by a beautiful partition of clear glass crystal.[5] From above, its surface was wavy like a sea of glass which formed the floor for the throne. From below, it looked like the high vaulted ceiling of a cathedral with beautiful crystal arches.

"This will separate us from any beings we create in the future," explained Son. "Our holiness is untouchable."

"Having the throne at such a lofty height is appropriate," said Father approvingly. "From here we can see all. The crystal floor is perfectly transparent."

"The entire expanse of our floor sparkles like ice," said Spirit with delight. "Awesome!"[6]

"The floor for us is a ceiling for others," said Son, "yet they can see perfectly through it."

They moved closer to inspect the hall's centerpiece—two thrones side by side. One throne was inlaid with ivory and overlaid with the finest gold. Its back had a rounded top. On both sides of the seat

---

[4] Psalm 89:14
[5] Rev. 4:6
[6] Ezekiel 1:22

were armrests, with the form of a lion standing beside each of them, looking alert and regal. A slightly smaller throne to the right of the first throne looked as though it was made of lapis lazuli, its deep celestial blue liberally sprinkled with flecks of gold that shone like stars in the heavens.

"The lions are a symbol of our royalty and majesty," commented Spirit.

"The gold in your throne speaks of the riches, honor, glory and power due to your name," said Son turning to Father. "The white ivory speaks of your perfect holiness."

"Your throne is such a beautiful color," Father said to Son. "True blue. The color speaks to me of your wisdom and truth."

"Very appropriate for the Word," added Spirit.

"Its blue matches the heavens surrounding our tabernacle," Son pointed out, "and the gold in my throne matches the gold in yours, Father."

Above the thrones was a brilliant emerald-green rainbow with its outer edge fading to yellow-green and its inner edge fading to blue-green. The rainbow itself was transparent and cast an emerald glow throughout the room.

"What a beautiful rainbow!" exclaimed Father.

"Through the crystal floor you can see that it forms a complete circle around the thrones!" exclaimed Spirit.

"The greens of the rainbow compliment the deep cobalt blue of the heavens beyond, don't you think?" remarked Son.

The others nodded in appreciation.

"Why don't you try out your new throne, Father," suggested Son.

When the Father sat down, lightning flashed from the throne. Thunder pealed and crashed, then rumbled in the background. Spirit and Son laughed with delight at the startled yet pleased expression on the Father's face.

"That was a surprise I added just for you," Son informed Father. "I knew you would like it."

"Brilliant!" exclaimed Spirit. "It adds the perfect touch! It speaks of your power and holiness."

"Now it's your turn, Son," Father called, patting the seat beside him. "Come sit at my right hand."

While Son was taking his place, Spirit noticed something unusual about the thrones and those on them.

"Now I don't see your thrones, though I know they're there," said Spirit.

"Let me see," said Son coming down off his throne to look. "Sure enough, Father, the train of your robe spills over and around the throne so I don't notice it."

"Your radiance hides everything but you, Father," observed Spirit. "Now I don't even see Son's throne. It looks as though there is only one throne."

"What happens when I sit alone on my throne?" asked Son. Father came down off his white and gold throne and Son sat on his throne of lapis lazuli.

"See," said Spirit turning to Father, "Son's radiance hides everything around him, just like your radiance does when you sit on your throne. The throne is obscured by the One who sits on it."

"You're right," said Father to Spirit. "It looks like one throne."

When one or both sat on his throne, their holy radiance obscured everything around them, giving the impression of there being only one throne.

"Where is my throne?" asked Spirit. "Don't I get one?"

Father and Son laughed at his failed attempt to look disappointed. They all knew the answer.

"You don't need a throne, dear Spirit. You are everywhere," said Father.

"Besides," added Son, "Spirit never sits still."

"What do you mean, 'never sits still'?" laughed Father. "He never even sits!"

"When we sit on our thrones, you are here with us, Spirit," said Father. "We are One! You are visible in the radiance."

"I know what to do to make Spirit's presence more obvious," said Son. With a word he spoke a seven-branched candlestick into existence. "There, Spirit! You can make the flames dance! The light and the fire are symbolic of the work you do."

Spirit instantly made the flames dance as though they were alive.

"The throne room is exquisite," said Father. "Indescribably beautiful!"

"Nothing like this throne or this throne room will ever be matched by any kingdom from now to eternity," said Father.

"I love you, Son," said Spirit. "Thank you for this beautiful throne room and for the candlestick."

"This was a joint project," Son reminded them. "All three of us had a part in creating this wonderful place. We did it because we love each other."

It did not take long for Father, Son and Spirit to look for a way of sharing their love and their beautiful home. Their love was so great and so perfect that they could not keep it to themselves. They were not content to be a Holy Huddle.

"We need not just things but other living intelligent beings around us," declared Father.

"Let's make four living creatures specifically for this throne room," suggested Spirit.

"Only four!" exclaimed Son, horrified at such a limited number.

"Four for this throne room," said Spirit. "After that we can make a whole family of spirit beings. Tens of thousands of them."

Again they brainstormed, and decided to make the first four spirit creatures like a man but with four wings each. Yahweh decided to make their legs straight and their feet like those of a calf. Yahweh wanted bright creatures to reflect his holiness, so he gave the creatures a fiery appearance. Their upper bodies flamed like torches, their mid sections glowed like burning coals, and their legs gleamed like burnished bronze.

"Their wings will give them mobility and still allow for humility, so they can cover themselves in our presence," explained Spirit.

Yahweh decided to give each of the creatures four faces, each face representing an aspect of the Holy One.

"Let's make one face like a lion," suggested Son. "That will represent our royalty and majesty."

"How about making one face like an ox," suggested Spirit. "That would represent our strength."

"I would like one face to be like my beloved Son," said Father. "He is the easiest of us three for created beings to understand."

"Thank you, Father," responded Son. "And let me suggest that the fourth face be like an eagle to represent our divinity and the fact that we dwell in the heavens."

With a word the Holy One brought their ideas into existence. As soon as the four living creatures came into being, their eyes were drawn to the throne above. They saw the Holy One sitting high on his throne in all his glory, encircled by an emerald rainbow. They were awed by his appearance. They were drawn by the warmth of Yahweh's love.

Then from the throne came flashes of lightning, rumblings and peals of thunder. Instantly the four living creatures knew this God, Yahweh, was not to be taken lightly! His love is real, but He is also holy. The four living creatures covered themselves with their wings and worshiped the One who lives for ever and ever. They gave glory, honor and thanks to the One on the throne, saying, "Holy, holy, holy is Yahweh, God Almighty, who was, and is, and is to come."[7]

Then they said it again. And again. And again. They could not stop giving praise to Yahweh.

Meanwhile, the Holy One continued with creation.

---

[7] Revelation 4:8

"Let's make other spirit beings," suggested Spirit.

"Agreed," said Father. "But before we leave the throne room, we need to add one more touch."

Father paused, then turned expectantly to Son.

"Son!"

Son read his Father's mind. One word from him and twenty-four thrones appeared in a large circle on the lower level around Yahweh's royal throne, with the four living creatures inside the circle.

"The thrones are empty," observed Spirit.

"For now, yes," said Father. "We will make spirit beings first, and then we will decide what beings will be worthy to fill these thrones so close to ours."

"In the fullness of time we will elevate four living creatures and the twenty-four thrones to the upper level surrounding our throne," said Son, looking into the future.

First of all Yahweh made himself a family of spirit beings, sons of God, also known as *morning stars*.[8] These were the shining glory of living spirit beings. To them he gave high level responsibilities. They were administrators. They would act as a divine council,[9] providing input before Yahweh made his final decisions.

Then Yahweh made spirit beings of lower rank but no less important. Angels, or messengers.[10] He made angels by the hundreds, by the thousands, and by the tens of thousands in all shapes and sizes, some with wings and some without. All were beautiful. No two were exactly alike.

---

[8] Job 38:4-7

[9] "And *so the* heavens will praise your wonderful deed, O Yahweh, even your faithfulness, in *the* assembly of *the* holy ones. For who in the sky is equal to Yahweh? *Who is* like Yahweh among the sons of God, a God feared greatly in the council of *the* holy ones, and awesome above all surrounding him?" (Psalm 89:5-7, LEB)

[10] The Hebrew word *malak*, translated angel, means messenger or agent, as does the Greek word *angelos*.

The Plan

Each was made for a specific purpose in the Kingdom of God. Each was given a name appropriate to his character and purpose. A select few were specifically designed to be in the presence of the Holy One, ministering close to the throne.[11]

The spirit beings looked in wonder at their palatial surroundings and were immediately drawn to the throne and the One who sat on it.

"Holy and awesome is He!" some cried.

"Great is His majesty!" cried others.

"Exalt the name of Yahweh!"[12] shouted others.

Then the angels burst spontaneously into song.

> "To him who sits on the throne
> be praise and honor and glory and power
> for ever and ever!"[13]

The four living creatures could hardly contain themselves at the sound of all heaven praising the One on the throne.

"Amen!" they exclaimed in agreement, and they fell down and worshiped.

"We need more space for all these spirit beings," observed Spirit.

"Good idea!" remarked Father.

"Wait!" cautioned Son. "What our beloved spirit beings need most is not more space." Father and Spirit read his mind and agreed.

"Wisdom!"[14] they said in unison.

---

[11] Isaiah 63:9 speaks of "the angel of his presence."

[12] Adapted from "Exalt the Name," words and music by Margaret Becker and Mark Hauth, Meadowgreen Music Co., © 1986.

[13] Revelation 5:13

[14] See Proverbs 8:22-31

"Right!" replied Son. "We possess infinite wisdom, but our created beings do not. We need someone in our service whose sole responsibility will be to instruct the beings we create in the path of wisdom."

"Spirit beings are intelligent creatures capable of making choices," declared Father. "They are designed to love and worship us, but they are not robots. They are not programmed to say and do the right things. There is the risk that they will rebel against some of the rules and restrictions we place upon them for their good. Lady Wisdom will counsel our creatures so that their innocent state can mature into true holiness."

And so it was agreed.

"Wisdom!" Son called out with a loud voice, and Lady Wisdom[15] was brought forth. She bowed deeply before her Creator.

"I, Wisdom, live together with good judgment. I know where to discover knowledge and discernment. Counsel and sound judgment are mine. I have understanding and power.[16] I will teach your creatures to walk in your ways, O Holy One."

"Excellent!" said the Father with satisfaction. "We know you will do your best to teach all creation to drink deeply at the fountain of our infinite wisdom."

---

[15] If you take Proverbs 8 literally, it can be argued that Wisdom is a created being. If you take the passage figuratively, this is poetic language for God Himself. For literary purposes I have chosen to make Wisdom a created being and Folly her opposite.

[16] Proverbs 8:12, NLT; Proverbs 8:14, NIV

2

The Plan Conceived

Father, Son and Spirit returned to their deliberations.

"We need to plan very carefully what we do next," cautioned Father. "We have created the angels to be imagers of Yahweh. We have given them intelligence, creativity and free will. We have created them with purpose—to serve us and carry out our bidding."

"Being in the presence of the Holy One is no guarantee that free-will beings will never stray or act out of self-will," noted Spirit.

"I agree," said Son. "They could turn against us."

"So why not revoke their free will?" asked Spirit.

"Without genuine free will, they would not be our imagers," replied Father. "We are free to do anything we want, anything consistent with holiness and love. We want them to truly represent us."

"All the beings we have created have experienced our glory and majesty and our love," said Son. "They have also shared our magnificent home. If, after all that, they turn against us, they must be banished from our presence and punished severely."

"Rebellious spirits cannot simply be destroyed," added Spirit. "We have made them to live forever; consequently their punishment must also be forever."

After much discussion Father, Son and Spirit agreed upon a form of punishment and a place suitable for it to be carried out.

"Are we ready to create more space for our beloved family?" asked Spirit.

"Not yet," said Father. "We need to look even further into the future."

"We want to create even more beings," said Son, following the Father's train of thought. "Beings made in our image—like us in many ways."

As the Holy One discussed these new beings, they got more and more excited. They envisioned not spirits but human beings, millions and millions of them, living in harmony with each other and in intimate loving relationship with their Creator. What a thought! What joy to spend all eternity with human beings! What satisfaction to lavish their infinite love not just on spirit beings but on human beings made in their own image!

"The more these beings are like us, the more satisfying will be our fellowship and relationship with them," exulted Spirit.

Then a shadow of pain came across Father's face as he looked into the future.

"What if . . . ?"

Father could hardly bring himself to express his reservations. "What if they turn against us and go their own way?"

The pain was contagious as Son and Spirit also foresaw humans rebelling against the Holy One.

"One thing I know," concluded Father. "We must create humans under different circumstances than we did with spirit beings. Human beings, like spirit beings, will be perfect in their creation, but they must be tried and tested before they are allowed to live in our heavenly home. We will create them initially to be lower in rank than the angels. Only after their innocence matures into true holiness will they be promoted to a position above the angels. Only then will they be introduced to our heavenly home to live in it with us forever."[1]

---

[1] See Hebrews 2:6-8, NASB, NRSV or NIV margin. Also Psalm 8:4-6.

The Plan

"Lady Wisdom will coach them how to live in a manner pleasing to Yahweh," added Spirit. "She will keep them from straying onto the wrong path."

"We will keep records," Father assured them. "Every deed of every person will be meticulously recorded. After a period of testing, their innocence will mature into holiness, and presto! They can live here with us! I can hardly wait!"

For a long time there was silence in the throne room as reality sank in. The smile faded from Yahweh's face. Finally Son broke the silence.

"What if our plan fails?"

"We need a plan which will assure that Heaven, our dwelling place, is not contaminated," said Father. "We are holy. We cannot tolerate creatures anything short of being perfectly holy living with us."

"We are just," said Spirit. "If humans choose to go astray, they will deserve the same punishment as spirit beings who go astray. We will have to banish them forever from our presence. We will have to send them to the place we designed for rebellious angels."

Yahweh was grieved at the thought.

"These humans have so much potential," Father said through tears. "We can't bear to create them only to punish them forever."

The angels nearest the throne noted Yahweh's grief.

"What's wrong?" they asked each other. "How can sorrow exist in this beautiful, happy, joyful place?"

Those who had overheard some of Yahweh's conversation did their best to explain the tragedy to the angels next to them. The Holy One's deepest desire was to create special beings in his image. His infinite wisdom and foresight told him that if he did so, some of them would eventually rebel and have to be destroyed. There was even the possibility—perish the thought!—that *all* would rebel! If so, Yahweh would have to destroy every one of his specially created beings. Destroying even one of them was a tragedy. But not creating such beings was unthinkable. Yahweh had so much love to give that he had to share it, but he was grieved to consider the consequences of his love being rejected.

The angels whispered to each other until all Heaven heard the news. Heaven became silent. For the first time since they had been created the angels stopped singing. Yahweh spoke into the silence.

"Don't be afraid. Yahweh's will cannot be thwarted. We will formulate a Plan and tell you about it in due time."

* * * *

The Holy One withdrew to the throne room and discussed their plans in private. If the details of The Plan were known to all and if some angels were disloyal, they could sabotage The Plan. The Plan would be made known little by little at the right time with enough details to give hope to those in despair bt not enough to give ammunition to an enemy.

"We want our new creatures, human beings, to be holy as we are holy," said Father slowly. "They will qualify for entrance into our holy presence by being perfectly holy themselves. That is Plan A. But Plan A has flaws. What if humans don't listen to Lady Wisdom? What if they don't remain loyal to us? If Plan A doesn't work, we will need a Plan B."

"The penalty for man's sin will be death, as we have previously agreed," said the Son. "Justice must be done to satisfy true holiness. But what if the penalty is paid by someone other than the sinner? What if *I* died in man's place? Would that satisfy you, Father?"

"You cannot die, Son," Spirit objected. "You, like us, are eternal. Besides, Heaven would not be Heaven without you. It's unthinkable."

"Son is on to something," said Father, carefully thinking through the legal ramifications. "Justice requires that the punishment be meted out. The debt must be paid. Justice is satisfied when the debt is paid regardless of who pays it."

"But we cannot simply trade the Son for all humanity!" exclaimed Spirit. "As I said, Heaven without Son would be unthinkable. Intolerable!"

The Plan

"Having sinners in Heaven would be equally intolerable!" declared Father.

"There must be a solution," said Spirit, as all three lapsed into thoughtful silence. Then Son spoke up.

"Even if I die for the entire human race, entrance into Heaven must be conditional. Not conditional upon the individual's goodness, but upon his recognition that he is not and cannot ever be good enough. Upon that confession and upon his submission to our lordship, my payment will be applied to that individual's account. Spirit will then transform him into our likeness. He will become holy, and Heaven will not be contaminated when he enters here."

"I see where you are going," said Spirit. "Plan A is a choice— the choice to attempt entry to Heaven by being good enough. That choice requires individual human beings to listen to Lady Wisdom and to laws we write on their hearts. That choice requires that they follow the right path perfectly. We know there is a high probability Plan A will fail. So, too, Plan B is a choice. Only those who fail Plan A and also reject Plan B will be destroyed."

The Holy One agreed that Plan B would work.

"Plan A will be written on man's conscience," said Father, "but what about Plan B? How will humans know and understand Plan B so they can make that choice?"

"We will explain it to them," said Spirit.

"How will we do that?" asked Father. "We are infinitely superior to any of our creations. That automatically creates a communication gap. As long as they are innocent, we will be able to have communication with them; but if they sin, they will instantly run from us in fear, their sinfulness repelled by our holiness. They won't be able to understand that our intentions for them are good. We will no more be able to talk to humans than a human could talk to an ant."

"If a human wanted to talk to an ant and be understood by an ant, he would have to *be* an ant," said Son with a laugh. "That's not going to happen."

Son became serious as another thought struck him.

"What if . . . ? What if I became a human? Then I could talk to humans. Then I could show them my love for them. The Father's love for them. Our love for them. Then they would understand my death for them. Then they would choose Plan B."

"That would work for *them*," said Spirit slowly. "But how would we exist in eternity without *you*, Son?"

"I have figured it out," said Father. "Light is stronger than darkness. We did not create darkness. It simply exists where light is absent. Darkness has to flee in the presence of light. Similarly, life is stronger than death. We did not create death. It simply exists where life is absent. Death has to flee in the presence of Son, who is Life itself."

"If Son becomes human," said Spirit expanding on that thought, "if he lives in constant dependence on Father and me and with our help lives a perfect sinless life, then though he dies, death will not be able to keep him down. Life will triumph over death. Death will flee, and Son will be able to return to us and our dwelling place."

"It can be done," responded Father, "but it won't be easy. One tiny slip on Son's part and Plan B will crash and burn. We cannot stress strongly enough the need for you, Son, to remain in constant communication with us. You can't do it alone."

"You will have to give up absolutely everything that you have known from all eternity, Son," said Father. "Here you share our glory. Here you enjoy all the privileges that come with being equal with us. Here all the angels bow before you as they do before us and eagerly wait to do your bidding."

"Being equal with you two is indeed a privilege," said Son humbly, "a privilege I don't minimize, but it is not a privilege I cling to. I am willing to let all this go," he said with a great sweep of his arms. "Just say the word, and I will obey—even if it means death on a cross! I am willing to do absolutely anything if it means that human beings can share life with us for eternity."

"So it is settled," said Father with satisfaction. "I consider it done. You, Son, have paid the price. I am more pleased with you than words can tell. We can announce to the angels that we have come up with a Plan. That will make them sing again."

"Let's celebrate!" cried Spirit. "Let's get on with creation!"

3

Paradise

Again Yahweh spoke out of his infinite wisdom and his ideas came to be.

Bang! Out of nothing the universe exploded into existence. Stars and comets, planets and moons! Galaxies upon galaxies of them! An extravagance of motion and beauty!

The vastness of creation inspired wonder and awe in the angels. They sang for joy and worshiped the Creator as they watched him stretch out the heavens.

"I want a masterpiece in this universe," announced Father, "a place more special than all the other beautiful places we have created in space."

Yahweh chose one tiny planet for his masterpiece.

"Earth will be an extension of our lofty palace in the heavens," said Son. "As we continue to build our upper chambers in the heavens, we will set the foundations of our palace on Earth."[1]

"A foundation needs a cornerstone," advised Spirit. "The cornerstone sets the direction for whatever is built upon it. If the cornerstone is crooked, everything built on it will be crooked."

"I have that all planned out," said Father. "My precious Son himself will be that cornerstone. He will be Earth's sure foundation. Whoever builds his life on my Son will be acceptable to me. Whoever trusts in him will never be shaken."[2]

"And where do you plan to put the cornerstone?" asked Spirit.

---

[1] See Amos 9:6 in various translations: NIV, YLT, KJV, etc.
[2] See Isaiah 28:16 and 1 Peter 2:4-6.

"In Zion," replied Father. "I have eternal plans for that place. I will fill Zion with justice and righteousness."[3]

"Son, do the honors," said Father.

Stepping forward, Son marked out then laid the foundations of the earth with himself as the cornerstone.[4] The morning stars sang together and all the angels shouted for joy at the laying of the cornerstone and the foundations.[5]

Then Yahweh proceeded with creating the rest of the earth, building on the foundations that were laid.

Lady Wisdom rejoiced to see Yahweh acting with wisdom, the virtue for which she had been named. She was careful to give all the glory to Yahweh and not claim any for herself simply because she was wiser than other created beings.

"By wisdom Yahweh laid the earth's foundations," she cried out with a loud voice. "By understanding he set the heavens in place."[6] Lady Wisdom watched carefully as Yahweh created the oceans and filled streams with water, as he formed the mountains and shaped the hills, as he made the first handfuls of primal dust, then earth and fields. She watched as Yahweh established the heavens, as he marked out the horizon on the surface of the ocean, as he set the clouds above and established springs deep in the earth. She watched as Yahweh determined the currents in the ocean, as he assigned a limit for the sea so the waters would not overstep his command.[7]

The angels praised Yahweh saying, "He set the earth on its foundations. It can never be moved!"[8]

For the next while Yahweh concentrated on making sure every detail of tiny planet Earth was perfect. He made countless forms of

---

[3] Ephesians 1:3 and following.
[4] Isaiah 48:13
[5] Job 38:4-7
[6] Proverbs 3:19
[7] See Proverbs 8:22-29.
[8] Psalm 104:5

vegetation—shrubs and grasses, trees for shade and fruit, flowers in the brightest and wildest colors. All the plants were seed-bearing so they could reproduce their own kind. Yahweh created rivers and streams to water the vegetation and beautify the planet.

While beautifying the tiny planet Earth, Yahweh focused on one special spot within it, a place of delight and luxury, a garden he called Eden.

"Let's pattern this special place on this special planet after our home in Heaven," suggested Father.

"Good idea," said Spirit. "Though very different from our home in Heaven, it is just as beautiful, but we will need to add a throne, a high exalted place."

Son concurred and created a mountain in the center of the garden. The water of life, clear as crystal, flowed down from the mountain in four rivers which watered the garden and flowed out of the garden to other parts of the planet. Son planted the most beautiful trees of his creation in the garden—cedars and oaks, pines and cypress trees, flowering trees and fruit-bearing trees. He planted his favorite shrubs and flowers. Then he scattered precious stones and jewels throughout the garden—stones such as carnelian, chrysolite and emerald, topaz, onyx and jasper, lapis lazuli, turquoise and beryl, ruby and pearl.

"I see you included your favorite stone," said Father approvingly.

"Yes," replied Son with a smile. "Lapis lazuli. To match my throne in Heaven."

"We need another special touch," said Spirit, "fiery stones around the base of the mountain . . ."

" . . . to convey that this is a holy mountain," said Father, completing his thought.

"Done!" said Son, and fiery stones appeared.

Yahweh filled the planet with living creatures—animals and birds, fish and insects of every size, color and description—and put the most

The Plan

interesting and beautiful ones in the garden of Eden. Then he surveyed his work.

"*Good!*" said the Holy One in unison. "Very good!"

All the angels sang for joy at the beautiful sight. They all were eager to enter the garden and explore it. They looked to the Holy One for permission to enter.

Rather than granting permission, Yahweh motioned to the spirit beings to move farther from his presence. Father had something to discuss in private with Son and Spirit.

The spirits were quick to obey. They knew without being told that this special place had been created for the pleasure of Yahweh. If any spirit beings were allowed into the garden of Eden, it would be a very special privilege.

"We will have to protect Eden and our holy mountain within it," said Father with a frown as a dark thought crossed his mind.

"Who could possibly desecrate or vandalize this place?" asked Son, reading the Father's mind and saddened by the thought that a being they had created could harm such a special place.

"We have created beings capable of making choices," Father reminded Son and Spirit. "We agreed before this creation spree that there were risks. We also decided that we didn't want to populate heaven with robots. Love is a choice, not an action that can be programmed. We want all intelligent creatures to choose to serve us out of love, not out of compulsion, just as we love and serve each other freely."

"So we will need another rank of spirits," concluded Spirit, "beings whose special assignment is to stand on guard for the holiness of God."

Yahweh created fearsome cherubim with massive wings. Some had bodies like a man; others had the head, chest and arms of a man and the body of a lion. The cherubim were agile and powerful. Some carried flaming swords. All were designed to discourage any hint of rebellion against Yahweh. They were placed in strategic locations as visible reminders of the majesty and glory of God. They sang praises to

Yahweh, worshiping him and inspiring others to worship him for his holiness and power.

"And now for the seal of perfection," said Father, who was not finished creating. "My signature creation. An angel to surpass all angels."

Yahweh spoke and created an angel more beautiful and more full of wisdom than all the others.

"What shall we name him?" asked Son.

"He reminds me of a shining star," said Spirit. "Let's call him Son of the Dawn or Son of the Morning."

"Actually I intend him to be my light-bearer," responded Father. "I'll call him Lucifer."[9]

"He's your masterpiece of all the spirit beings in heaven, Father," exclaimed Son approvingly.

"He is perfect and full of wisdom, and much more beautiful than these cherubim," commented Spirit. "He will be the perfect reminder of our majesty and glory, our holiness and power."

"Let's ordain him to the position of guardian cherub," suggested Father.

"But even he has the potential to turn against us," cautioned Son.

"Someone has to be put in charge of the cherubim," Father argued. "If we promote him to the highest position in heaven other than giving him our throne, our goodness should maintain his loyalty. If our love and goodness to him don't satisfy him, nothing will."

"I agree," said Spirit. "As a further incentive to loyalty and discouragement against rebellion, we must create a place of punishment and let all the angels know about it."

"We must never make a threat we aren't willing to carry through," declared Father. "Empty threats will weaken our authority. If our creatures ever come to think that we don't mean what we say, there is no predicting what they will do."

---

[9] See various translations of Isaiah 14:12, especially KJV, RSV, NLT

The Plan

Out of sight of his holy dwelling place, Yahweh created a fiery lake of burning sulfur.

"I hope we never have to use this fiery lake," said Son with a shudder, and all three agreed.

"We love all the creatures we have created," said Spirit, "but we are holy, just and true. We cannot tolerate any disunity in our home." Yahweh ascended to his throne to make a grand announcement to all the angels.

"Tell them," said Father to Son.

Son rose and spoke with a voice like a trumpet, describing the lake of fire which had been created as a deterrent against any disunity or disloyalty within their ranks. The spirits shuddered with horror at the thought of such a terrible place, but they knew Yahweh was just. No angel in heaven could conceive of anyone acting out of any motive other than love and obedience to their Creator. Rebels would get what they deserved. Choirs of angels burst into song to express their approval.

"You are fair, just and righteous in your judgments, O Holy One, you who are and who were, because you have so judged."[10]

The four living creatures joined in the chorus together with the cherubim.

"Holy, holy, holy are you,
Yahweh, God Almighty!
True and just are your judgments."

"Righteousness and justice are the foundation of your throne!"[11] shouted the cherubim.

"Now we can ordain Lucifer," said Father. "Son, bring the appropriate decorations from our special garden."

Son picked up one of each of the precious stones from the garden of Eden and mounted them into a breastplate of gold. Father called

---

[10] Adapted from Revelation 16:5
[11] Psalm 89:14

Lucifer forward and Son hung the breastplate around his neck with a gold chain. Son took more stones—carnelian, emerald, topaz, onyx, jasper, lapis lazuli, turquoise and beryl—placed them in settings of gold, and attached them to Lucifer's garments. If Lucifer had been beautiful when he was first created, he was even more beautiful now!

In the presence of all the angels, Spirit anointed Lucifer as guardian cherub in charge of the cherubim and as chief guardian of Eden. The angels sang for joy. They could think of no one more worthy of such a high position, second only to Yahweh himself!

Lucifer was pleased with his position as guardian cherub, which required that he watch and listen carefully for any signs of rebellion. His position gave him free access to both Yahweh's throne room and his special garden. Who would have thought that he, Lucifer, would be assigned to such duty! He sang Yahweh's praises as he patrolled the throne room. He sang Yahweh's praises as he walked through Eden, the garden of God, enjoying the beautiful surroundings. He came to the holy mountain of God in the middle of the garden, walked among the fiery stones scattered around its base, and sang praises to Yahweh.

4

The First Rebellion

All those who visited planet Earth marveled at its beauty and perfection. Earth was the jewel of the universe. The angels always gasped in awe when they entered the gates of Eden even if they had been there before. They never grew accustomed to the beauty of this jewel of jewels. When they approached the holy mountain of God, they were content simply to marvel at the One who created it and who alone was worthy of praise.

No angels ventured up the mountain. Except Lucifer.

With each visit to Eden, Lucifer ventured a little higher up the holy mountain.[1] He noticed that the higher he went the more fiery the stones were. On one visit when he was higher than he had ever been before, Lucifer had difficulty placing his feet where they wouldn't be burned. He understood without having to be told that he couldn't go higher.

Just as the throne of Yahweh was off limits to anyone but Yahweh himself, so the summit of the holy mountain in Eden, which represented Yahweh's throne on Earth, was off limits. Only the Holy One could ascend the mountain to its very top. The fiery stones on this mountain served the same purpose as the lightning and thunder coming from the throne in heaven.

Lucifer retraced his steps. When he reached the base of the mountain, he noticed Lady Wisdom watching him.

---

[1] Ezekiel 28:11-19 provides a dual picture of the king of Tyre and of Satan. Similarly, Isaiah 14:12-15 likens the king of Babylon to Lucifer.

"How long have you been here, Lady Wisdom?" Lucifer asked. "I was here watching when you first started to ascend," she replied. "I notice that you go a little higher each time you come here. Be careful. Be sure to keep a respectful distance from the top of the mountain. That is for Yahweh and Yahweh alone."

"What are you implying?" Lucifer asked with a frown.

"I'm not implying anything. I am merely stating the obvious. The Holy One is to be loved and respected. Yes, even feared."

"I am perfect in beauty and wisdom," Lucifer retorted. "I have every right to be here."

"You *are* perfect in beauty and wisdom," Lady Wisdom agreed, "but no thanks to you. Yahweh made you that way. He should get all the glory. He gave you the right to be in his special garden but not to ascend to the top of the mountain."

"I didn't go to the very top," said Lucifer, starting to get annoyed. "I am the guardian cherub of this place! Who are you to challenge me?"

"Yes, you are the guardian," Lady Wisdom replied patiently, "but only because Yahweh ordained you to that position. He could have ordained any one of a thousand angels for that position, but he chose you. So give him the glory and be thankful to him."

From time to time Lucifer and Lady Wisdom crossed paths in the garden of Eden. Lucifer was happy to discuss Kingdom issues with her, but he got increasingly annoyed when she touched on personal things. Lady Wisdom warned him against pride and arrogance.

"Listen to me! I have important things to tell you. Don't brush me off. If you have an open mind, you will know I speak the truth. My mouth speaks what is true, for my lips detest wickedness and every kind of deception. Be careful not to deceive yourself! Choose my instruction over all the riches of Heaven. Wisdom is far more valuable than jewels," Lady Wisdom said, pointing first to the jewels on the ground, then to

The Plan

the jewels on Lucifer's breastplate and garments. "Nothing! Absolutely nothing you desire can compare with wisdom!"[2]

After that encounter, Lucifer avoided Lady Wisdom whenever he could do so without being obvious to others. That was his first mistake.

When Lucifer stopped listening to Wisdom, Folly was born. She proved to be a pitiful caricature of Wisdom. Just as darkness is the absence of light and cold is the absence of heat, so Folly is the absence of Wisdom. Like a dark shadow, Folly became Lucifer's constant companion.

"You don't need to listen to Lady Wisdom," Folly whispered. "You are wise, even wiser than she is. You are as wise as a god. In my opinion you *are* a god."

As Lucifer listened to Folly, he made his second mistake. He did not openly disagree with her counsel. He knew she was wrong, but he liked what he heard.

"Look how beautiful you are, Lucifer!" Folly exclaimed. "Your splendor dazzles me! You deserve to walk among the fiery stones. You belong at the top of the mountain of Eden. You would look great up there. Let Yahweh sit on his throne in Heaven. You can set up a throne on this mountain."

"Are you saying you would worship me?" Lucifer asked Folly, not really believing she was serious.

"Absolutely! Yahweh is so holy that his brightness hurts my eyes. And his voice! The thunder of his voice scares me."

"Most of us find his voice majestic. What about Yahweh's love?" Lucifer countered. "That comes through in spite of his holiness. Doesn't his love draw you to him? Doesn't his love make you want to praise him?"

"Yahweh doesn't love me."

"Why not? Doesn't he love everyone?"

---

[2] Adapted from Proverbs 8:6-11.

"He loves only the beings he created," Folly answered, ignoring the fact that Father, Son and Spirit also love each other. "He didn't create me. You did."

That was news to Lucifer.

"How or when did I create you?"

"I was born when you stopped listening to Lady Wisdom." Before Lucifer could digest that thought, Folly switched to flattery.

"You, O morning star, are not as bright as Yahweh, but I consider that to your advantage. That makes you more approachable than Yahweh. You are still bright enough to dazzle me. Do you have any idea how beautiful you are? I find your wisdom very attractive, too. More attractive than Lady Wisdom. You are wiser than she."

Lucifer listened to Folly and his heart became proud.

Then he did the unthinkable.

"Folly, if you really believe what you say, kneel before me and kiss my feet. Swear that your highest allegiance is to me and to me alone."

As Folly bent low before Lucifer, he observed her black garments and appreciated how seductive they were. She knelt and kissed his feet.

"I, Folly, swear allegiance to Lucifer, son of the dawn, king of Eden."

Lucifer knew he was not king of Eden. He was only Eden's guardian, anointed to protect Eden from anyone disloyal to Yahweh. But he liked the title, so he didn't correct Folly. He loved the sensation of being worshiped.

"Arise, Miss Folly," Lucifer commanded in his most authoritative voice. He drew his sword and touched the flat of the blade to her right shoulder. "I appoint you as my prime minister."

Lucifer and Folly worked well together. The angels were clearly attracted by Lucifer's wisdom, but even more so by his beauty. When Folly saw angels or sons of God admiring Lucifer, she would sidle up to them and whisper to them, "Doesn't he look like a god? Wouldn't he look even better on a throne?"

Lucifer would then strut among the fiery stones, suggestively going higher and higher up the mountain of Eden. As he did so, his wisdom became corrupted and he began to say in his heart, "I am as wise as a god. I *am* a god."

Soon he came to believe it.

Whenever Lady Wisdom noticed angels gathering admiringly around Lucifer with Folly working the crowds, she would move to counterattack. Lady Wisdom would go to her home supported by seven hewn timbers and she and her servants would prepare a banquet. While the food was cooking and the smell of fresh-baked bread filled the house, Lady Wisdom would set the table with silver and flowers. Then she would go to a prominent place and call out to everyone within sound of her voice:

"Are you confused about the truth, don't know what's going on? Come with me to my home! Have dinner with me! I've prepared a wonderful spread—fresh-baked bread, good food, carefully selected wines. Stop being gullible. Start traveling the road to insight and understanding. Learn to use good judgment. Leave your impoverished confusion and *live*!"[3]

Many responded to Lady Wisdom's generous invitation. Some came for the food, some came for the fellowship, some came simply out of curiosity. Lady Wisdom warned all her guests of the dangers of listening to Lucifer and Folly.

"Do you want wisdom? Fear Yahweh. Do you want understanding? Get to know the Holy One. Lucifer is very smooth and Folly is seductive, but to follow them is wicked. Yahweh alone deserves your worship. He will not tolerate disloyalty. He will throw you into the lake of fire."

Often Lady Wisdom invited cherubim to these special dinners as reinforcements. Their fearsome presence was helpful in inspiring the fear of Yahweh's wrath.

---

[3] Adapted from Proverbs 9:1-6, MSG, NRSV, NLT and GW.

When undecided angels raised the issue of punishment with Lucifer, he was careful not to deny it outright. Instead he would try to raise doubts in their minds.

"Have you ever seen the lake of fire?"

"No," they replied.

"Then how do you know it exists?"

"Yahweh told us about it."

"Don't you think that was just a figure of speech to scare you?" Lucifer responded. "Yahweh is a God of love. He loves you. How could a loving God do something so cruel? Did Yahweh really say he would throw you into a lake of fire? Forever? Surely that is inconsistent with Yahweh's character!"

Some angels saw through Lucifer's smooth talk. They knew that Yahweh's holiness and justice were just as central to his character as his love. His holiness could not tolerate disunity or disloyalty. His justice required action against rebellion. There was room for only one God and that was Yahweh himself.

Some of those angels who weren't quite sure what to make of Lucifer's arguments went back to Lady Wisdom for further counsel. Other angels and even a few cherubim were persuaded by Lucifer's silk tongue.

Gradually Heaven became divided into two camps—those who sided with Lucifer, and those who remained loyal to Yahweh. Those who sided with Lucifer avoided entering Yahweh's throne room in Heaven. They were repelled by Yahweh's glory and by the four living creatures who continually cried, "Holy, holy, holy is Yahweh God Almighty." They put their hands over their ears when angels sang in worship of the Holy One. They wanted nothing to do with Lady Wisdom and those angels who loved and worshiped Yahweh. Rebellion festered and grew in their hearts until it consumed them.

Similarly, the loyalist angels wanted nothing to do with Lucifer and his followers. They saw through the lies and seduction of Lucifer and Miss Folly. They were repelled by the thought of rebellion against Almighty God. They wished for Yahweh to act and to throw Lucifer and his followers into the lake of fire.

In the meantime, the flashes of lightning emanating from the throne in Heaven became more frequent. Yahweh's thunder rumbled ominously, then built to a crescendo and crashed with a force that made all who heard it jump.

The Holy One was angry!

Yahweh was aware of the defection of many of his angels to Lucifer's camp, but he deferred any action until every angel in Heaven had a chance to make a firm, final decision as to whose side he was on. As long as there was one angel who was still wavering in his loyalty, Yahweh would not give expression to his wrath.

Lucifer became bolder as Yahweh did nothing. He interpreted Yahweh's patience as indecisiveness and weakness. He began to tell himself that he was greater, stronger and wiser than the Holy One.

One day Lucifer made another attempt to ascend the holy mountain of God in Eden, determined this time to establish his own throne at the top. The fiery stones which were widely scattered at the mountain's base were closer and closer together on the ascent. Toward the top, the stones were not just closer together but piled deeper and hotter. Once again Lucifer was foiled in his attempt to reach the top.

Lucifer should have marvelled at the beauty of the fiery stones, which were designed to draw attention to Yahweh, his holiness and his dazzling glory. Instead, Lucifer focused on his own outstanding beauty. Pride distorted the wonderful wisdom Yahweh had given him. Rather than being thankful for the gifts Yahweh had bestowed on him and humbled by the fact that Yahweh had chosen him as guardian cherub of Eden, Lucifer wanted more. He shook his fist at the top of the mountain.

"I will ascend to the heavens," he said through clenched teeth. "I will raise my throne above the stars of God."

The First Rebellion

Turning on his heel, Lucifer strode quickly down the mountain of Eden looking for his followers. He went to Heaven and spread the word for all to attend a meeting in Eden. Miss Folly helped to round up any stragglers.

The rebels were buzzing with curiosity. What was about to happen? A hush fell over them as Lucifer took a few steps up the mountain so all could see him.

"Who is the most beautiful creature in the universe?" he called out in a loud voice.

"You are!" the crowd replied.

"Who?" Lucifer cried, cupping his hand to his ear as if he couldn't hear them.

"You are!" they shouted.

"Who is the wisest?"

"You are!" they responded louder yet.

"I am full of wisdom. I am perfect in beauty. I am perfection itself. I will be God!" Lucifer declared, his voice rising with each declaration.

The crowd cheered and whistled.

"Son of the dawn!" Miss Folly shouted.

"Morning star!" another voice called out.

"Lu-ci-fer! Lu-ci-fer! Lu-ci-fer!" the crowd chanted.

Lucifer basked in the glory for a while, then raised his hands for silence.

"I will climb to the highest heavens and set my throne above God's stars," Lucifer told them.

The rebels gasped at the audacity of the announcement. Then they broke out in cheers.

"I will run the assembly of angels that meets on the sacred heights. I will sit enthroned on the mountain!" Lucifer continued. His followers cheered each new declaration. "I will ascend above the tops of the clouds! I will make myself like the Most High! I'll take over as king of the universe! Are you with me?"[4]

"Yes!" the rebels shouted in unison.

"Then pledge your eternal loyalty to me!" Lucifer demanded. "Worship me!"

One by one the rebels filed past and kissed Lucifer's feet. Lucifer gradually became aware that with each new expression of worship he got a little less satisfaction than he did from the previous one. Lucifer had thought the opposite would be true. At the very least he expected to get equal satisfaction from each rebel's declaration of loyalty. Lucifer even began to doubt the sincerity of some of the declarations. He made a mental note to develop means of keeping these rebels fully under his authority. Maybe getting more angels to follow him and defect from Yahweh would satisfy his craving.

Dismissing his disappointment, Lucifer turned to the task at hand. "Follow me!" he shouted. "We are going to take Heaven by storm!"

---

[4] See Isaiah 14:13-14. Compare MSG, NLT, NIV.

5

Expelled

Lucifer and his followers arrived at the edges of Heaven to discover that they were expected. Yahweh's patience had run out. It was time for Yahweh to act.

Cherubim with their massive wings outspread held flaming swords in readiness for battle. Behind them were ranks and ranks of the rest of the angels loyal to Yahweh. Lucifer put his strongest angels, former cherubim now deserters, out front.

For a while the battle raged fiercely. For a while Yahweh stood in the background observing the fight. Then Yahweh stepped in and confronted Lucifer. Righteous anger was written across the face of the Almighty.

"I am Yahweh!" he thundered. "I am a jealous God. I will tolerate no other gods! I will not share my glory with another!"

Lucifer's bravado vanished in the presence of Almighty God.

His rebels cowered behind him.

"Lucifer," Yahweh continued, "you were my seal of perfection! I was the one who made you perfect in beauty and wisdom. You were blameless in your ways from the day you were created. But . . . ."

Yahweh paused for emphasis. Lucifer had to retreat as Yahweh moved closer to him.

"But you sinned! Wickedness was found in you. If there is anything I hate, it is pride! Never again will you be allowed anywhere near my throne room. From time to time you will report to me in the outer court of Heaven, but you and your rebel followers will come only at my

The Plan

bidding. Other than on those occasions, I limit your sphere of influence and activity to planet Earth and its atmosphere. No longer will you have the run of the universe."

Yahweh's voice thundered as heaven had never before heard it thunder.

"Woe! Woe! WOE! Woe to you and your followers! You all are banished! Expelled!"

Lightning flashed and thunder crashed as with one swing of his mighty arm Yahweh swept Lucifer and his followers out of the sky. Lucifer's strength was nothing in the face of infinite power.

The angels watched in awe as Lucifer fell like lightning from heaven.[1] For the blink of an eye he burned brightly, his rebel followers streaming behind like the tail of a comet. Then they all disappeared into the darkness.

There was silence in heaven as the angels tried to understand what had happened.

"Have Lucifer and his followers been totally destroyed?" one angel wondered.

"No," another responded, "I can see Lucifer down there, but he is no longer the beautiful angel Yahweh created. He is dark and ugly. So are they all."

"Why didn't Yahweh send them to the lake of fire?" one cherub asked. "Isn't that what Yahweh said was the punishment for rebellion?"

"We will have to ask Yahweh himself," another cherub advised.

Yahweh heard the angels' discussion and decided it was time to let them in on his long range plan.

"Our actions will have to withstand the scrutiny of the ages, not just the present," Yahweh explained. "Over time many things will happen which may not immediately make sense, but eternity will prove that we

---

[1] See Luke 10:18.

are perfectly holy, perfectly patient, perfectly merciful, perfectly loving and perfectly just.

"Some of you may not think that pride is such a terrible thing. By expelling my adversary—I will no longer call him Lucifer, I call him Satan, adversary—I am giving him enough rope to hang himself. I am giving Satan the opportunity to express his pride and I am giving all creation the opportunity to observe and understand what pride leads to. You will be horrified at some of the things that pride produces. When I have proved to all creation that Satan and his evil followers deserve their punishment, then and only then will I cast them into the lake of fire."

Again there was silence in heaven as the angels digested Yahweh's message. Then the four living creatures began to sing quietly,

> "Holy, holy, holy,
> is Yahweh God Almighty,
> who was, and is, and is to come."[2]

The cherubim took up the song, their voices swelling with praise:

> "You are worthy, our Lord and God,
> to receive glory and honor and power,
> for you created all things,
> and by your will they were created
> and have their being."[3]

Then heaven rang as every creature in heaven sang:

> "To him who sits on the throne
> be praise and honor and glory and power,
> for ever and ever!"

---

[2] Revelation 4:8
[3] Revelation 4:11

The Plan

Then one of the archangels spoke for them all. "You are just in your judgments, O Yahweh, God Almighty!"

The four living creatures shouted, "Amen!" and all the angels bowed and worshiped.

6

Chaos

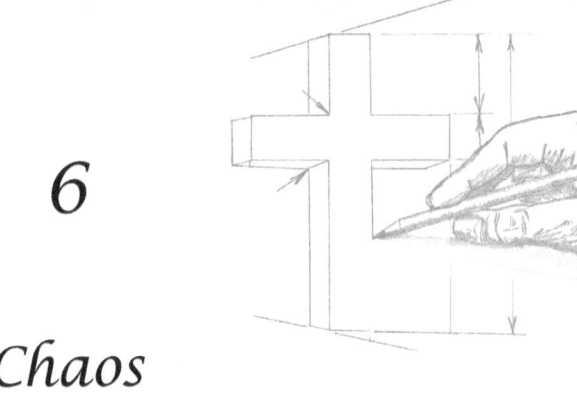

Satan heard all heaven praising Yahweh and gritted his teeth.

"They are happy in Heaven now, but that will soon change," Satan told his rebel followers. "What Yahweh loves I hate. We will destroy Earth, Yahweh's joy and delight, starting with Eden! Then we will see who is king around here! We will put a stop to their singing."

The demons went on a destructive spree as Satan gave them orders. The smaller ones uprooted shrubs and stomped on beautiful flowers while the more powerful ones worked together to pull down mighty oaks. They slashed and trashed fruit trees and vegetable gardens until all the fruitful places were wildernesses. What they could not cut down, they burned. What they could not burn, they defaced.

The birds of the air fled from the devastation. With no place to build their nests and no food to eat, they soon died. The demons chased down and killed every animal in sight, hooting and hollering as they did so, leaving bloody carcasses strewn everywhere. They poisoned the waters of the rivers and streams, killing all the fish.

When the rebels were exhausted from their rampage, they looked for a place to rest. Only then did they realize that they should have left some things for their own use. They could not return to Heaven, where they used to have a beautiful place to dwell.

Satan ordered his demons to build fortresses in case Yahweh should attack. Building was not nearly as easy as destroying, but Satan was a hard taskmaster, and no demon dared to openly defy his orders. Each demon thought of himself as a god and sought to exert control over lesser

The Plan

demons. Whenever they thought they could get away with it, they made weaker demons do the work that Satan had assigned to stronger ones.

The demons soon became aware of the contrast between their new reality and their former home in Heaven, but not one was willing to admit he had made the wrong choice. In Heaven the angels had frequently received a warm smile and a "well done" from their Supreme Commander. Here they received no word of appreciation for their efforts. In Heaven the angels frequently cooperated on major projects, working together in teams. Here there was stiff competition to gain the attention and approval of Satan, though he only commended them enough to get more work out of them. The demons formed gangs for strength and power rather than teams for unity and cooperation.

The rebels all operated under the delusion that Yahweh's sovereign rule was oppressive. They believed true freedom would be found in going their own way and in living independently of Yahweh. They preferred Satan's kingdom to Yahweh's, believing that Satan would give them that freedom.

While lesser demons were busy building fortresses, Satan and his most powerful cohorts advanced to the mountain of Eden to see what damage they could do. To their surprise there were no fiery stones, only piles of ash where the stones had been. Yahweh had withdrawn his presence from the holy mountain, so his throne required no protection.

Satan started climbing to the top of the mountain, planning to sit on the throne that had belonged to Yahweh. Though he was disappointed to be robbed of the challenge of dethroning Yahweh, he tried not to let his disappointment show.

When Satan reached the top of the mountain of Eden and saw the throne from which Yahweh had ruled, he was surprised at the contrast between it and the throne in Heaven. It was nothing more than an elaborate chair. No lightning emanating from it. No radiance. Not even a warm glow. Without the presence of Yahweh, it was merely ordinary.

Satan sat on the throne, hoping he would be able to produce some magical result. Nothing. It was hard and stone cold.

He turned to the powerful demons accompanying him, who quickly bowed and fawned before him with flattering words, knowing full well that Satan was more powerful, and not wanting to incur his wrath. Their words did not have the same ring of praise as the worship the angels in Heaven spontaneously offered to Yahweh.

"Sing!" Satan commanded them. "Sing praises to me!"

The fallen angels opened their mouths to discover that they could no longer sing. Their words came out in squawks and croaks.

"Oh, shut up!" Satan snapped. "You sound like a murder of crows."

Suddenly something hit the throne with an explosive crack, sending Satan, his followers, and debris from the throne flying through the air.

Almighty God was on the warpath!

Satan and his demons had done their utmost to ruin Earth out of spite. Now it was Yahweh's turn. He would not allow Satan to enjoy anything that was left. Yahweh's anger was fierce. One blast from his nostrils and the once holy mountain of Eden was gone! Another blast from his nostrils and the valleys of the sea were exposed. Yet another blast and the foundations of the earth were laid bare.[1] Any living creatures that escaped Satan's rampage were destroyed in this expression of Yahweh's anger.

With one final blast Almighty God created a deep pit and filled it with choking smoke. Then he swept Satan and his followers into the Abyss, withdrew his presence, and locked the entrance. He gave the key to one of his most powerful and trusted angels for safe keeping. He also covered the pit with thick darkness, a darkness that could be felt.

For a long time there was total silence. Very briefly were the foundations of the earth bared and the valleys of the seas exposed. Then the waters rushed in to cover the earth, wrapping it in an angry

---

[1] See Psalm 18:15

The Plan

wet blanket. Earth was empty and in disarray, and spiritual darkness covered the face of the demonic realm.[2]

For the first time Satan experienced what it was like to be in a world where Yahweh was totally absent. Inside the Abyss no one could see his hand in front of his face. The darkness was oppressive. The smoke was worse. Folly tried to put a positive spin on the situation.

"At least we are rid of Yahweh," she said. "Here we can do what we please. Here Satan is king. He understands our needs and our desires. He lets us do what we please."

The irony was that in the total darkness the rebels could do absolutely nothing. Nothing, that is, except complain and quarrel. When they complained about the darkness and the acrid smoke, Satan blamed Yahweh. In the face of lesser complaints, each demon pointed the blame at another. Often their quarreling rose to angry shouts. From time to time Satan told them all to shut up.

Not once did Satan or any of the fallen angels acknowledge that their own choices had put them into the Abyss. Each of them had rebelled against his Creator. Each had rejected the lordship of Almighty God. Each one wanted to be the center of his own universe, however small that universe might be.

Satan believed there was still a way to carve out a piece of the universe and rule there as king. If he could not be king of all of it, he determined to be king of at least some of it. He hoped more than anything else to be king of Earth because he knew how close Earth was to the heart of Yahweh.

But first he had to get out of the Abyss.

* * * *

In Heaven the angels wept as Satan trashed Yahweh's beautiful planet. They cried out in horror at each assault as the demons

---

[2] See Genesis 1:2.

systematically destroyed Earth and its inhabitants. They were awed by Yahweh's power when he vented his anger on his adversary, causing further collateral damage to the planet. They couldn't understand why the Creator would allow his masterpiece to be ruined. One angel voiced the questions all the angels were thinking.

"Why didn't Almighty God bind Satan and his followers so they couldn't harm the Earth? Why did Yahweh send Satan to Earth in the first place? Why not into outer space where it wouldn't matter as much?"

Lady Wisdom responded wisely and humbly.

"Even I don't know the answer to these questions, but I know who does. These events have not taken the All-Wise One by surprise. I will approach his throne and present your questions to him."

Lady Wisdom stood at the entrance to the Yahweh's court and respectfully waited for permission to approach his throne. Father was pleased to see her and held out to her the golden scepter that was in his hand. Son smiled warmly and Spirit glowed with a brighter radiance.

Lady Wisdom approached and touched the tip of the scepter.

"What is it, Lady Wisdom?" Father asked. "What can I do for you?"

"If it pleases you, Almighty King, please help us to understand what has happened on Earth. We know you could have protected Earth and Eden, your beloved masterpiece. Why didn't you?"

Father gently wiped away the tears falling down her face. The Holy One spoke in unison.

"Dear Lady Wisdom, in the ages to come both of us will shed tears of sorrow, but in the end joy will come, even greater joy than either of us has known in the past. Have patience. We have wonderful plans which no one can thwart—not even Satan, try as he might. We will re-create Earth and populate it with beings made in our own image. Satan will again do his worst to spite me, but as I said before, I am giving him enough rope to hang himself."

"But Satan is in the Abyss. How can he 'hang himself' there?" "I will let him out for a while," Yahweh replied, "and in the future Earth

The Plan

will again be severely damaged. But be assured that I am, and always will be, in control. I will put Satan and his followers away forever. Then I will make all things new. Never again will you see evil or shed tears of sorrow. Heaven and Earth will be places of indescribable joy. For all eternity!"

"How long will Satan be free to do damage?" asked Lady Wisdom.

"Not long. To created beings waiting for it to happen it may seem like forever. But I exist outside of time. To me it will be just a few days. Once the new Heaven and new Earth are in place, you too will look back and agree that it didn't take long."

The four living creatures overheard the conversation and began to sing quietly, "Holy, holy, holy is Yahweh God Almighty."

Soon all the angels heard Yahweh's answer to their questions and Heaven rang in praise to Yahweh.

"To him who sits on the throne be praise and honor and glory and power, for ever and ever!"

* * * *

Even though Yahweh knew he was about to re-create Earth, he was still grieved at the damage that had been done. It broke his heart to see Earth uninhabited, in chaos and darkness.

Spirit hovered over the face of the waters and could feel the mountains underneath them quaking and the hills swaying from the trauma they had experienced.[3] He fluttered here and there over the disturbed waters to quiet their fears.

"Shhh," he whispered soothingly. "It will not remain like this. We will make Earth beautiful again."

Even as he spoke, Spirit brooded over the fact that Yahweh's fix would be temporary. Earth would experience a series of traumas before all things were made new one last time and joy was restored forever.

---

[3] Jeremiah 4:23-24.

Taking a deep breath, Spirit returned to the throne room to plan the next move with Father and Son.

"Earth is a mess," he announced. "We can't leave it that way."

"The worst thing is the darkness," Father replied. "Earth needs light."

"The darkness is not just physical but spiritual," Son reminded them. "We withdrew our presence when we cast our adversary to Earth."

"But now that we have locked Satan in the Abyss, we can remove the cover of thick darkness," Spirit said.

"What about the long range plan?" asked Son. "We plan to let Satan out again, don't we, Father?"

"Yes, but only under our conditions," Father replied. "We will keep him locked up while we are re-creating Earth. Then we will let him out with strict limits on what he can and cannot do. He may think he is in control, but he is deluding himself. He will be accountable to us. He will report to us on a regular basis."

"Like an ex-prisoner reporting to his parole officer," suggested Son.

"Exactly!" responded Father. "And when he violates his parole, which we know he will do, we will send him to a place he will never be able to escape."

7

From Chaos to Order

The Holy One surveyed what was left of Earth.

"The foundations of Earth are unshaken," Spirit reported. "I inspected them. The cornerstone, of course, is more solid than rock." "That is testimony to the work of Yahweh's hands," Lady Wisdom whispered to the four living creatures who were listening in on the conversation in the throne room. "When Yahweh lays a foundation, nothing can move it!"

"Praise Yahweh God Almighty!" the four living creatures responded.

The conversation between Father, Son and Spirit continued.

"Not even your rebuke of our adversary, Father, could move those foundations. When you gave him a blast from your nostrils, you exposed the valleys of the sea and the foundations of the earth," said Son. "But we can and will rebuild on them."

The Holy One immediately began the rebuilding process, planning and strategizing while the planet rotated in darkness.

"We will set a strict time limit for this project," declared Father. "We will reshape, renew and create for six days. Then we will rest." "Not because we will be tired," continued Spirit, "but because this time we will also create humans, creatures in our image. We must set an example for them. They will get tired if they don't learn how to rest. Everything we do must point to The Plan so that the end result will be millions of creatures with whom we can have fellowship for all eternity. Those who try to please us by way of Plan A—by being good enough—will fail. So we have to build Plan B into everything we do—starting with this re-creation project."

"The pattern must show up everywhere," Son agreed, "so humans can't possibly miss it. Humans will start their lives in chaos and darkness just as Earth is now in darkness, but I will bring them light. I will give light to every one who comes into the world."

"Everything must point to you, Son," said Father. "You are the centerpiece, the cornerstone of The Plan."

"And I, Father, will point everyone to *you*."

"When Son arrives on Earth as a human, he will dispel the spiritual darkness created by Satan and his rebellion," said Spirit. "So that is where this renewal project must begin—with light."

There was no argument over that idea.

"Light!" the Holy One called out in unison. "Let there be light!"

And there was light. Light from Yahweh's holy presence shone in the darkness.

"The light is good," observed Yahweh approvingly. "Now let's separate the light from the darkness."

The thick spiritual darkness had to flee, dispelled by Yahweh's holy light. What remained was light and darkness separated by the planet itself. Yahweh called the light side of the planet "day" and he called the natural darkness on the other side of the planet "night."

"Day One!" said Yahweh as he surveyed his work with satisfaction. "Humans will look back on this day as the beginning of time. Today we brought light to Earth just as the Son will some day bring light to the world. That light will shine in the darkness so all people through the Son might believe. The light is a picture of his birth and his life on Earth when people will see his glory and through him get a glimpse of the glory of the Father."

"First evening, then morning," commented Father. "The day started with chaotic darkness and we brought order by introducing our light. Then we organized darkness and light into night and day." "The place where I buried the cornerstone will soon be in shadow marking the end of Day One," observed Son. "As the planet rotates and while the cornerstone is in darkness, we will plan our next day's work."

"The waters of Earth are chaotic," said Spirit. "I noticed that while I was inspecting the planet after Satan ruined it. Bringing order to the waters will be our next project."

"The waters are too toxic to support the forms of life we created the first time around," observed Son, "yet we can make whole anything Satan has tried to destroy."

The Holy One continued to discuss the problem and proposed possible solutions. They decided not to freshen all the waters. They would remove the toxins but leave the salts. Then they would make a huge dome-shaped expanse over the waters. Out of the salt water they would draw fresh water and suspend it in the dome. From there they could supply the earth with all the water it would need in the form of dew, which would condense out of the dome in the cool of the night.

When light dawned over the cornerstone, Yahweh spoke to the waters. At his word the waters parted into salt and fresh, with the salt water below, fresh water above and a huge expanse between.

"The expanse is beautiful!" declared Son. "Let's call it 'sky'."

"The life-giving waters come from above, not below," said Father. "Our creatures must remember that."

"The salt water reminds me of death," observed Spirit. "No living creatures can survive in it.[1] It is a picture of the Son's future death when he will come to implement The Plan. What do you think, Father? Is it good?"

---

[1] Author: It is my theory that the original creation of Gen. 1:1 did not have salt seas; salt water was the result of Satan's fall as described above. Genesis chapter 1 does not use the word "create" (*bara*: make from nothing) again until the fifth day (verse 21) when "God created the great sea creatures and every living creature that moves...." These new creatures, different from the original creation, could survive and thrive in salt water.

Father was slow and deliberate in his response.

"It is premature to call this good. I can't bring myself to declare my Son's death good, but it is necessary. Let's wait until this new creation pictures the resurrection before calling it good. But I do like the sky. It provides an atmosphere of hope."

"Darkness will soon fall on the cornerstone," observed Spirit.

"Evening and morning have come and gone," said Son. "Earth's second day. It's time to plan another day's work."

"I'm looking forward to the third day, Son," said Father. "It will give you a foretaste of your resurrection. The only thing new we are going to create today is the resurrection concept. Let's turn it into a rehearsal. Go into the ground, Son, under all that salt water. While you are there, touch the seeds buried in the ground. Watch what our power can do. It's irrepressible!"

"Exactly where on Earth should I go to start this rehearsal?" asked Son.

The Holy One thought for a moment.

"The cornerstone!"

"I'll go right now while it is still dark," said Son.

As light dawned over the water above the cornerstone, Yahweh called out with a loud voice to the waters under the sky, "Water! Be gathered into one place! Don't smother the Earth. Let dry ground appear!"

All the inhabitants of Heaven sang for joy as dry ground rose to the surface and the waters receded, collecting into large well-defined pockets throughout the planet. Yahweh named the dry ground "land" and the pockets of waters "seas."

"We have solved one problem but created another," Son noticed. "Up till now the land was drowned. Now it's dry! We can't let the land get too dry or it will not sustain life of any kind."

"We need a watering system that will deliver exactly the right amount of water," said Spirit. "Not too much, not too little."

The Plan

So Yahweh created streams to come up from the earth and mist to water the whole surface of the ground.[2] Spirit, laughing with joy, turned to Father.

"What do you say now, Father? Is it good?"

"It *is* good!"

"The timing is perfect!" exclaimed Son. "It's the third day! Resurrection day!"

"The day is not over," replied Father. "The resurrection has only begun to demonstrate its power. We have anticipated the needs of future life for water. Seeds from our past creation are still buried in the ground. Now the land can nourish them and make them grow." "Land!" Yahweh called out again, "produce vegetation! Make everything green!"

The land obeyed and Yahweh added his power to speed up the process. Soon the planet was filled with all kinds of seed-bearing plants—grasses, bushes, flowers and full-grown trees, many of them loaded with fruit or nuts.

As the light began to fade over the cornerstone, Yahweh surveyed his work with satisfaction.

"You realize what this day means," said Father. "It demonstrates the power of a seed. These seeds survived the worst that Satan could do. Our adversary tried to destroy what we had created. He was able to destroy the living vegetation, but he couldn't destroy the seeds which had fallen into the ground!"

"It will happen again," said Spirit. "The Son will be the seed of the woman. Satan will try to destroy him. The Son will fall into the ground and die, but he will bear much fruit through that process."

"Speaking of Satan, that reminds me," said Son. "Satan destroyed Eden. At least he tried to. Then we finished the job while expressing our anger against him. We will have to restore Eden."

The Holy One took great pleasure in planting a garden in Eden. They whistled while they worked, making all kinds of trees grow out

---

[2] See Genesis 2:4-6.

of the ground—trees that were pleasing to the eye and good for food. In the middle of the garden they planted two very special trees, the tree of life and the tree of the knowledge of good and evil. A river watering the garden flowed from Eden, then divided into four rivers flowing in four different directions.[3]

When they were finished, they looked at each other and smiled. "I can hardly wait until our first human sees this!" exclaimed Son. "Imagine the look on his face!"

"It is good!" the Holy One agreed. "Evening and morning. The third day."

As the fourth day began in darkness, the Holy One planned what they would do next.

"We don't need to remain here in order to provide light to the planet," said Son. "We have more important things to do. We must return to the throne room. We can put lights in the sky to do our job of separating day from night."

"The lights will serve more than one purpose," said Father. "Earth needs a sun to govern the day and provide light and warmth. Earth needs a moon to govern the night and also provide light. Together the sun and moon will mark days, months and years; and the stars will provide points of reference for navigation."

"Most importantly, the sun and moon will mark the seasons," said Spirit. "Time will not be an endless blur. The sun and moon will remind humans to worship us. We will establish appointed times, holy days marked by the sun and the moon to celebrate The Plan."

"Even the stars will give focus for worship," said Father. "We will arrange signs in Earth's sky—star-pictures to remind humans of The Redemption Plan. We will arrange those signs in a circle through which the sun will move each year. As Earth follows the sun's path through the stars, it will focus on a different sign each month, each having three

---

[3] See Genesis 2:8-14.

constellations assigned to it, each star-picture emphasizing one aspect of the redemption story beginning with the Son's first coming to Earth as a humble man and ending with his second coming as king."

Throughout the night the Holy One discussed the star-pictures and the stories they would tell. The stories would include people not yet created and nations not yet formed. The pictures would represent created beings grouped by their allegiance—some for Yahweh, some against him.

By morning the design was ready to be implemented. With his fingers Yahweh carefully fashioned the objects in space, adjusting their orbits to perfection, making sure the relevant ones were visible in Earth's sky.[4] Yahweh named each sign and constellation and star so the name would help tell the story of The Plan.

---

[4] See Psalm 8:3.

8

The Heavens Declare the Redeemer Promised

When their work in the heavens was finished, the Holy One called all the created beings in heaven together for the official unveiling of The Plan as told in the stars.

"In a few days we will be creating a very special kind of creature—human beings made in our own image," announced Father. "We know that doing so brings risks. Huge risks. You have witnessed what has already happened here in Heaven. We created angels and some of them rebelled and had to be expelled from our presence. We know that when we create humans, many of them will rebel. But there is a difference. Lucifer rebelled *after* experiencing the best that Heaven had to offer, so there is no point in offering him a second chance. His pride and jealousy would lead him to the same choice. He will never stop wanting to sit on the throne of God.

"But humans will be created on Earth, not in Heaven. They will not even *see* Heaven unless they choose to love us and be loyal to us. Some people may not even believe that Heaven exists. Our adversary will do his utmost to deceive humans and persuade them that we are not good. Yes, humans will rebel. They will choose either to follow Satan or to wander in a path of their own choosing. But many will learn how great is our love for them and will regret their initial rebellion. Those ones will be given a second chance. We have calculated that the pleasure of

The Plan

having even some humans in Heaven with us for eternity is worth the pain of having to banish others from our presence forever."

"We created the physical universe with the intent that it declare and display the majesty and glory of its Creator," Father continued. "People will not be able to look at the heavens without plainly getting the message that they were created by a wonderful God with eternal power. If they think about it, they will even understand some things about our divine nature. The heavens may not speak audibly, but they send out the message 24/7 nonetheless."

"Those who see no message in the heavens are clearly suppressing the truth," asserted Spirit. "They cannot plead ignorance. They have chosen to be blind."

"Those who examine the heavens closely will see even more than the simple yet wonderful message of God's glory and majesty," added Son.

"We have devised a plan which sets forth the conditions under which humans will be given a second chance," announced Father. "We will teach that Plan to humans in many ways—through feasts and rituals, through a Tent of Meeting modeled after our home in Heaven, through stories and events. In time we will put the entire Plan in writing. But right now, before man is even created, we have written The Plan in the sky."

A murmur of approval went throughout the angelic host, then silence fell. They listened intently for the explanation.

Father continued.

"The heavens declare the glory of God and the skies proclaim the work of his hands, do you agree?"

"Absolutely!" the angels chimed in unison.

"But who is the image and glory of God?"

The angels had no trouble answering that question.

"The Son!"

"Right!" replied Father. "Therefore . . . ?"

Lady Wisdom had the answer.

"Therefore the heavens must also declare something about the Son." She paused. "But exactly what do they say about him?"

Father turned to Son.

"You explain it to them."

"I'll show you," replied Son.

Father and Spirit and the angels watched as Son drew a giant circle in the sky.

"While Father, Spirit and I were rearranging the stars in the heavens, we paid special attention to those stars which were visible from Earth to the naked eye. First we mapped out the path that the sun appears to trace through the stars as Earth orbits the sun each year. This circle I have drawn is that path. Then we took note of the stars in the background as seen from the orbiting Earth. We formed those stars into constellations and pictures and gave names to both the constellations and the stars. The Plan is told by their names. The brightest star in each constellation is called its alpha star. Pay particular attention to its name."

"If nothing is written, how will people know the names of the stars?" asked one angel.

"We will tell them," said Spirit. "Then Lady Wisdom will keep retelling the story and the names to make sure the information doesn't get lost."

This was news to Lady Wisdom, but she was happy to take on the assignment. Son continued his explanation of the stars.

"Look at the constellations my circle runs through. I call them 'signs.' There are twelve of them on the circle and three more constellations within a few degrees of each of those twelve, some inside and some outside the circle. Each sign together with its accompanying three constellations has a story to tell."

"Signs are not significant in themselves," one angel ventured. "They always point to something. What do they point to?"

"If you think for a moment about what has just been said," Father responded, "I think you can answer you own question."

The Plan

"The Son!"

"Exactly!"

Another angel had a question.

"You mentioned pictures. Where are the pictures? I don't see any pictures. Just clusters of stars—mostly shapeless clusters."

"Keep watching," said Son.

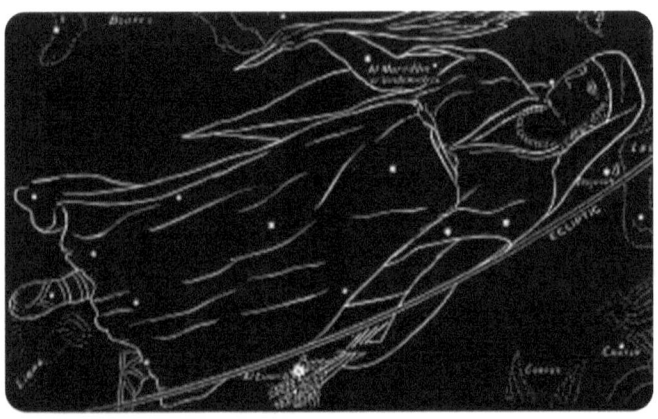

The Virgin

Son began to doodle around a group of stars on the great circle. It was more than a doodle. Soon a picture of a woman emerged. "I call her The Virgin. She has a branch in one hand and some ears of wheat in the other. I named the alpha star The Branch.[1] You know why, don't you?"

The angels weren't sure, so Father explained it to them. "When Son comes to earth, he will be born of a virgin. Prophets will call him The Branch because he will be a branch from the house of David. There are twenty Hebrew words meaning branch, but I used one of them, *Tsemech*, exclusively in reference to the Messiah."[2]

Son began to sketch again around a group of stars to the left of the Virgin's branch.

---

[1] Star name in Hebrew is *Tsemech*, in Arabic *Al Zimach*. Both names mean *the branch*. The star's name *Spica* means *seed*, indicating the Seed of the Woman.

[2] See Jeremiah 23:5-6; Zechariah 3:8; 6:12; Isaiah 4:2.

"It's a mother and child!" the angels exclaimed.

"I call this constellation *Coma*," said Son. "That means *the desired* or *the longed for.*"

Coma (the Desired)

"The child will be a branch of the house of David and will be the desire of all nations,"[3] Spirit told the heavenly host.[4]

Son began to sketch again around another constellation.

"It looks like a horse with a man's head and torso," said one of the angels.

"It's a Centaur," Son replied.

"I have never seen a centaur," one angel said. "Do you plan to create centaurs in this round of creation?"

"No," said Son. "A centaur will remain a fanciful figure to catch the imaginations of children and to make adults ponder the meaning of the stars. The centaur's dual form, man and horse, points to my future incarnation when I will have two natures, human and divine. I named him *the despised*,[5] but I also call him *a sin*

The Centaur

---

[3] See Haggai 2:7.

[4] This illustration of Coma was traced in 1820 from the Zodiac in the Temple of Denderah in Egypt, going back to at least 2000 BC, so this star picture is at least 4,000 years old! Shakespeare referred to this constellation in *Titus Andronicus*, Act IV, scene 3, when he spoke of the "Good boy in Virgo's lap."

[5] Star name: *Bezeh*

The Plan

offering.[6] I named the alpha star, which is in the horse's fore-foot, *the heretofore and hereafter*,"[7] indicating his eternal nature.

Father was slow to add his comment. There was deep sadness in his voice when he finally spoke.

"We have positioned the Centaur immediately over four stars in the shape of a cross, where he will be despised and rejected by men."

There was silence in Heaven as the angels tried to picture the unthinkable. How could people possibly despise the one who loves them so?

"But the story doesn't end there," said Son, breaking the silence as he started to sketch again. The picture which emerged showed a man walking rapidly, with a spear in his right hand and a sickle in his left.

"I have named this man *Boötes, the coming*," said Son. "He is both a shepherd—lovingly watching over the flock and protecting it with his spear—and a harvester of souls, as indicated by the sickle.

"His name[8] means *one who rules, subdues*, and *governs*. I called the alpha star, the star in his left knee, *Arcturus, he comes*."[9]

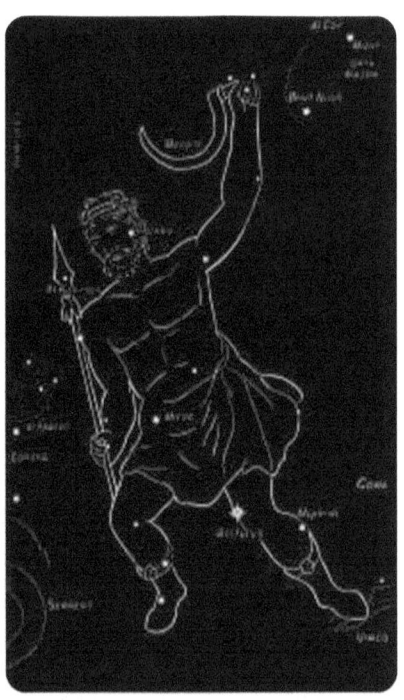

Boötes (the Coming One)

Son continued pointing out and naming individual stars.

---

[6] Star name: *Asmeath*
[7] Star name: *Toliman*
[8] Ancient Egyptian name: *Smat*
[9] Arcturus is named in Job 9:9, KJV, and his coming is described in Psalm 96:13.

"The bright star in the spear-head is *the branch, treading under foot*.[10] The bright star in his head is named *the pierced*, or *who bruises*. And that—the Virgin and these three constellations—constitutes the first sign."

The angels clapped their approval.

"This first sign contains the seed-plot of the entire story of Redemption," commented Lady Wisdom, summing up what she had learned. "A Virgin will give birth to the Coming One, who is both a Branch of the kingly line of David and the Seed of the woman. He will be longed for, will be rejected in his first coming, and will come again in triumphant power to rule the earth."

"That's The Plan in a nutshell," Son agreed.

"As we look at the Virgin from Earth, she appears to be lying down," one angel observed.

"She appears that way because she is fallen," Father responded. "Only the Son can lift her up to spiritual life. She knows that. That is why she is holding forth the good Seed in which she has put her hope and trust. The Branch is the only hope for fallen humanity."

"I see a few stars within these pictures that you haven't named for us yet," said one angel. "Are you going to tell us their names?" "I have named them all," Son answered, "but I have used only certain stars for the purpose of identifying the pictures. Those lesser stars aren't visible from Earth to the naked eye. I decided to keep it simple. Only the brightest stars have names relevant to the story which the stars tell. Besides, the rest of the twelve signs will develop the story in more detail."

Moving clockwise, Son began sketching around the next constellation on the great circle. The heavenly host were watching carefully and listening as the Son explained the story in the heavens.

"The story needs to take a step back and explain why redemption is even necessary," said Son as he sketched.

---

[10] Star name: *Al Katurops*

The Plan

"You have drawn a pair of scales!" exclaimed one of the little angels. "Who has measured the waters in the hollow of his hand, or with the breadth of his hand marked off the heavens?" Lady Wisdom whispered rhetorically to the angels nearest to her. "Who has held the dust of the earth in a basket, or weighed the mountains on the scales and the hills in a balance?"[11]

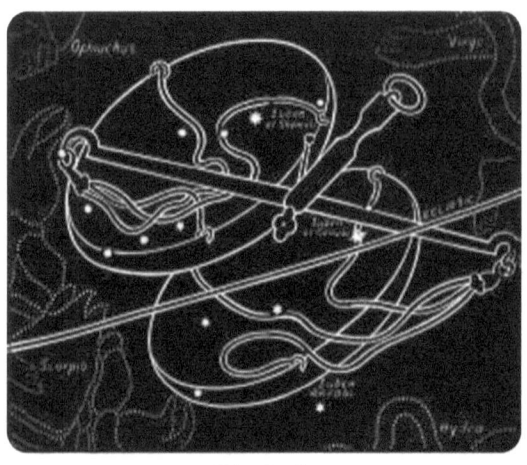

The Scales

Son overheard and replied, "These Scales[12] tell far more than the wisdom and power of Yahweh. These Scales are specific to the story of redemption. Scales suggest *weighing*," Son replied. "The name I gave the Scales means *purchase* or *redemption*."

"Humans will be weighed in the balances and found wanting,"[13] murmured Lady Wisdom, nodding her approval.

"Now look at the names in the scales," said Son. "I have named the brightest star in the lower scale *the price which is deficient*.[14] But ...."

He paused for effect, then pointed to the brightest star in the upper scale.

"This star is . . . *the price which covers!*"[15]

"Brilliant!" the angels exclaimed.

"Eternal justice weighs the actions of men with one hand, declares them deficient, then pays the price of redemption with the other!" Lady Wisdom added. "Amazing!"

---

[11] Isaiah 40:12
[12] Latin name: Libra. Hebrew name *Mozanaim* means *weighing*. Arabic name *Al Zubena*.
[13] See Daniel 5:27.
[14] Star name: *Zuben al Genubi*
[15] Star name: *Zuben al Chemali*

"I have named this bright star just below the Scales *the price of the conflict*,"[16] Son pointed out. "And again I have arranged three constellations to fill out the details of the story."

Son quickly sketched a Cross around the four stars immediately beneath the Centaur, stars the others had noticed earlier.

"I have given the Cross two names, *Adom* and *Tau*. *Adom* means *cutting off*,[17] indicating my death by crucifixion. *Tau*, which is the last letter of the Hebrew alphabet, will forever proclaim 'It is finished!'"[18]

Sketching again, Son drew a rather nondescript animal in the act of falling down dead.

"This is the Victim slain as a silent, willing sacrifice. Its name means *to be slain*.[19] But again the story ends in triumph."

Quickly Son drew around another cluster of stars and turned to his audience.

"Ta-dah!" he exclaimed triumphantly. "Behold the royal Crown! This is the glorious prize following my shameful death. The Scales

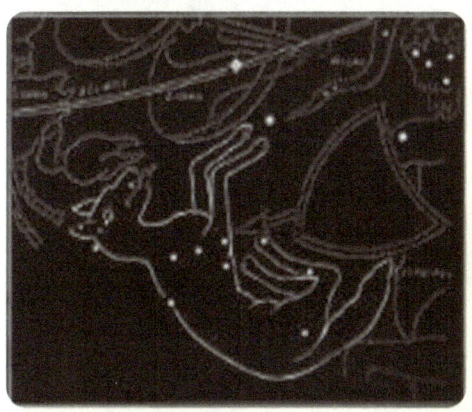

The Victim

---

[16] Star name: *Zuben al Akrab*

[17] Daniel 9:26 predicts, "After the sixty-two 'sevens,' the Anointed One will be cut off and will have nothing."

[18] Joseph A. Seiss asserts, "Formerly this constellation was visible in our latitudes; but in the gradual shifting of the heavens it has long since sunk away to the southward. It was last seen in the horizon of Jerusalem about the time that Christ was crucified." *The Gospel in the Stars*, p. 37. This constellation is now called the Southern Cross, as it is visible only to those near or south of the equator.

[19] Star name in Hebrew: *Asedah*

proclaim that the price which is deficient has been outweighed by the price which covers. That price was paid at the Cross and ended with the Crown!"

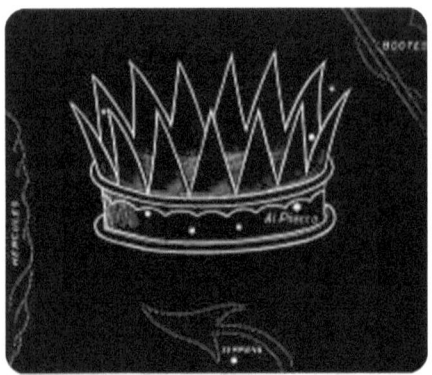

The Crown

Son continued clock-wise around the great circle and sketched a gigantic Scorpion.

"This sign gets to the heart of the conflict between me and my enemy," said Son. "The scorpion is a deadly enemy with poison in its sting. The scorpion's name *Akrab* can mean *the conflict* or *war* or *wounding him that comes*. Look what the scorpion is trying to do."

Above the Scorpion Son drew a picture of a mighty man struggling with a serpent. The Scorpion was endeavouring to sting the strong man's heel.

"The Serpent and the Serpent Holder are two constellations intertwined," explained Son. "They portray the conflict between Satan and the Redeemer. Notice that the serpent is struggling vainly in the powerful grasp of the man. The serpent is also trying to seize the Crown, which is

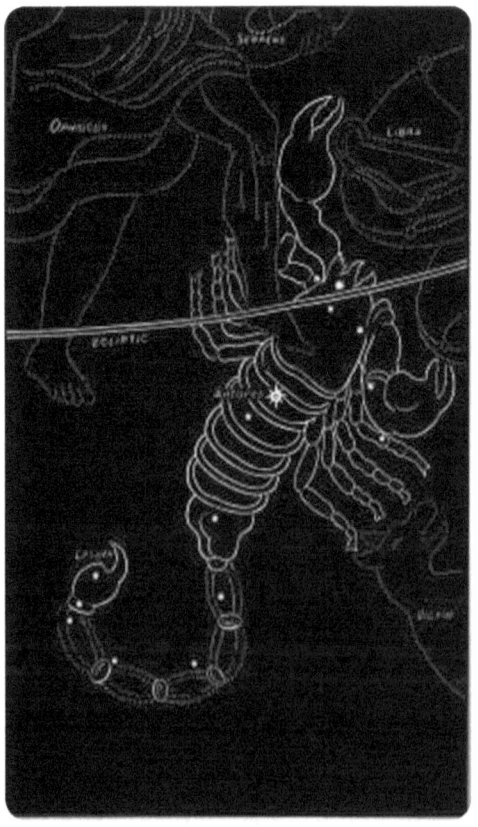

The Scorpion

situated immediately over the serpent's head. Now focus on the Serpent Holder. His foot is on the scorpion's heart, marked by the alpha star *Antares*."

"*Antares* shines ominously with a deep red light," observed one angel. "I assume that is significant."

"Yes," replied Son. "I hoped you would notice. *Antares* means *the wounding*. The Serpent Holder will trample all his enemies."

The Serpent and the Serpent Holder

"The Serpent is trying to seize the Crown, which is situated immediately over its head," Son continued. "The contest is for dominion! The Serpent robbed the first man of his crown, but he struggles in vain to wrest it from the Second Man. In that attempt the Serpent will be utterly defeated."

Son continued sketching above the Serpent Holder.

"This is another picture of the victorious Serpent Holder. Meet Hercules!"

Hercules was facing the center of the circle and thus was upside down in relation to the Serpent Holder, who was facing the circle itself, the path of the sun.

The Plan

The picture showed Hercules bending on one knee, with his right heel lifted up as if it had been wounded and his left foot firmly planted on the head of a great Dragon. He was wielding a great club in one hand, while grasping a triple-headed monster in the other. The skin of a lion which he had slain was thrown over his back. The Son pointed out stars within Hercules having names meaning *the head of him who bruises, the branch, kneeling, the wounding, the sin-offering* and *treading under foot*.[20]

Hercules

"Everything in the picture combines to depict just how mighty this Strong Man is!" said Lady Wisdom approvingly.

"Yes," agreed Father. "So mighty that he had to be pictured twice—as the Serpent Holder and as Hercules."

"So mighty that he conquered the Scorpion, the Serpent, the Dragon, a roaring lion and a triple-headed monster!" added Spirit.

Son summed up the meaning of the sign.

"The Scorpion tells the story of the contest for dominion. Satan, in the form of a serpent, struggles to rob the Redeemer of his crown. Not

---

[20] Star names: Ras alGethi, Kornephorus, Marsic, Ma'asyn, and Caaim or Guiam

only does he fail, but he is utterly defeated and trodden under foot in the attempt."

"Did you add an extra constellation, the Dragon, in order to underline the severity of the struggle?" asked one angel.

"No," replied Son. "The Dragon is actually part of the next sign, but I drew him now because you can't fully appreciate Hercules without seeing the Dragon under his foot."

Son turned his attention once more to the great circle and continued sketching.

The Archer

"Another centaur?" an angel asked.

"Yes, but with a difference," the Son said. "The last one carried a shield and spear. This one is holding a bow. I call him The Archer."[21]

"His bow is aimed directly at the heart of the Scorpion!" exclaimed another angel.

"That is not by accident," replied Father. "I am sending my Son to Earth not just to pierce and wound our adversary Satan but to disable him *completely*." His voice took on a fierce edge. "To destroy his works and his power *forever*!"

Son continued his explanation.

---

[21] In Latin, Sagittarius

The Plan

"The stories told by the signs flow together, one sign adding significance to another. The sign of The Archer concentrates on the triumph of the Coming One, who is represented as going forth conquering and to conquer. The names of the brightest stars are significant—they have meanings such as *the gracious one, the going* or *sending forth, the riding of the bowman,* and *Prince of the Earth.*[22] Representing the Archer as a centaur again points out my two natures—human and divine."

Between and below the Archer and the Scorpion, Son drew an Altar. "This represents . . . . "

"Let me guess," interrupted Lady Wisdom. "It represents the consuming fire prepared for the Archer's enemies."

Son nodded.

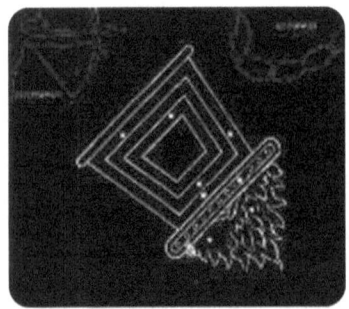

"And the altar is upside down," Father pointed out in case any angels had not noticed, "with its fires burning and pointing down below the Scorpion's tail towards the lower regions."

"Toward the abyss," added Spirit solemnly.

The Altar

Son raised his eyes to a cluster of stars near Hercules and drew a harp.

"The Harp represents praise to the Conqueror," he said. "That's why I drew it so close to Hercules. The alpha star is named *He shall be exalted.*[23]

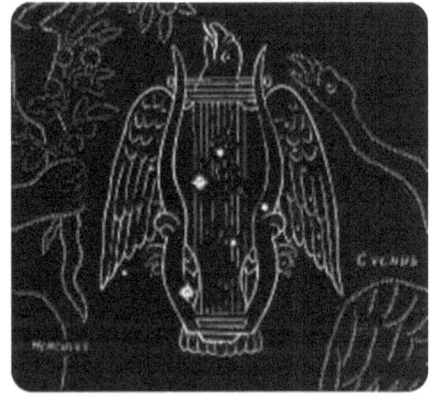

The Harp

---

[22] Star names: Hebrew *Naim, Nehushta,* Arabic *Ruchba or rami,* and Akkadian *Nun-ki*
[23] Star name: *Vega*

Son then drew a Dragon, positioning it strategically under Hercules' foot.

"Notice the position of the Dragon," Son said to the angels. "Hercules is treading on its head. The Dragon's name[24] means *the serpent accursed!* The Dragon's alpha star is *Thuban, the subtle*. Right now, as we are re-creating the heavens and the Earth, *Thuban* is in direct line with the Polar Star, making *Thuban* appear to be the star around which the universe revolves.

"As you can see, the old serpent appears to have the Polar star of the heavens wrapped in its coils. But it will not always be so. The Polar Star is moving ever so slowly in relation to the constellations in this great circle. By the time the story ends, thousands of years from now, it will be in a very different place. I will tell you about that later."

Son then pointed out stars within the Dragon having names meaning *the head of the subtle (serpent), who is to be destroyed, the long serpent* or *dragon, the punished enemy, the reptile* and *the bowed down*.[25]

"There is no mistaking who the Dragon is or what his destiny is!" exclaimed Lady Wisdom.

Son agreed.

The Dragon

---

[24] in Egyptian
[25] Star names: Hebrew *Rastaban*, Arabic *Al Waid, Ethanin*, Hebrew *Giansar*, Arabic *El Asieh*

"These first four signs focus primarily on me, the Redeemer, and my first coming to Earth —my suffering and humiliation, my conflict with the enemy, and my victory," said Son.

"The next four signs will focus on the redeemed ones and the blessings they receive as a result of my coming."

9

The Heavens Declare the Redeemer's People

Son turned to the sky and started drawing around the next cluster of stars on the great circle as the angels watched closely.

"It's a goat!" one angel whispered to another.

The Sea Goat

"Wait a minute!" interjected Lady Wisdom. "I have never seen a goat like this. The front half is a goat, but the back half looks more like a fish."

"You will discover that I use fish in my star pictures to represent the multitudes of the redeemed," explained Son turning to his audience. "One day I will call my disciples to be fishers of men."

The Plan

"The Goat[1] in this sign is bowing its head as though falling down in death," Son continued, pointing to his star picture. "His right leg is folded underneath his body, and he seems unable to rise. The tail of the fish, on the other hand, seems to be full of vigour and life."

"I get it!" exclaimed Lady Wisdom triumphantly. "The Goat is the atoning sacrifice, and living fish proceed from the dying goat. Humans will have life as a result of your death!"

"Exactly!" replied Son.

"This sign teaches that people must die with the Redeemer in order to rise with him," added Spirit. "There can be no resurrection where there has been no dying."

Son pointed out stars within the Goat with names meaning *the kid* or *goat, the sacrifice comes* and *the sacrifice slain*.[2]

Son started drawing inside the circle and above the Goat. He quickly sketched an Arrow alone in the heavens as if it had been shot forth by an invisible hand.

"This is the Arrow of God," Son explained, "the naked shaft of death. It shows that the Redeemer came to do the will of God, a work ordained in eternity past for the glory of God in eternity future. The Arrow is destined for the enemies of God, but it wounds the Redeemer in the process."

Next Son drew a falling Eagle, pierced and wounded by that Arrow.

"I chose to depict myself as an Eagle because it is the natural enemy of the Serpent," said Son. "The stars have names meaning *the wounding, wounded* or *torn, the piercing*, and *the scarlet-colored*,[3] indicating that the eagle is covered with blood."

"It was Yahweh's will to crush him and cause him to suffer,"[4] Spirit said quietly.

---

[1] Latin name, Capricornus, means *goat*.
[2] Star names: Al Gedi, Deneb Al Gedi, and Debih (Syriac) or Al Dabik (Arabic)
[3] Star names: Arabic *Al Tair, Tarared, Alcair, Al Shain*
[4] See Isaiah 53:10.

"Your arrows have pierced me," said Son, looking his Father in the eye, "and your hand has come down upon me."[5]

Son's tone was accepting, not accusing.

Turning again to the stars, Son drew a Dolphin, full of life and rising up, springing out of the sea.

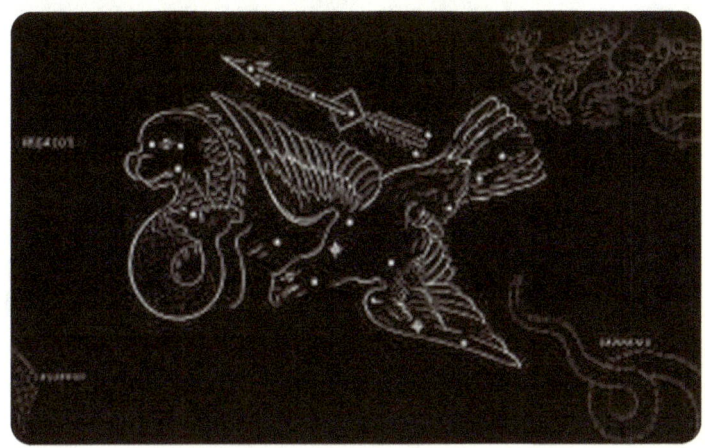

The Dolphin, the Arrow, and the Eagle

Son returned to the great circle and began sketching the next sign.

"It's a man pouring water from an urn," said Lady Wisdom. "The supply of water seems inexhaustible—like a river."

Son drew the water flowing down into the mouth of a large fish, which appeared to be drinking it all up.

---

[5] Psalm 38:2

The Plan

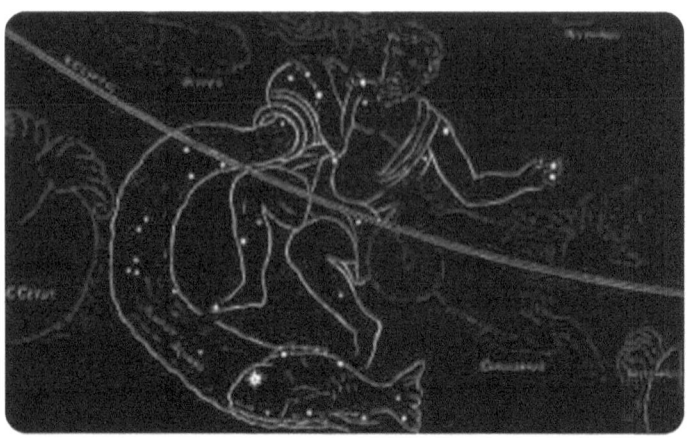

The Water Bearer and the Southern Fish

"The man is the Water Bearer," said Son. "His name Aquarius means the pourer forth of water. Living water is being poured out upon the redeemed. The redeemed ones, represented by the Southern Fish, are drinking in those heavenly waters."

Drawing inside the circle and oriented toward the centre, Son drew a Winged Horse.

Pegasus, the Winged Horse

"As you know, there is no winged horse in nature. This winged horse, Pegasus, is a picture of me, the Redeemer, coming quickly to bring the blessings from the Water Bearer and pour them forth upon a groaning creation," explained Son.

He pointed out stars with names meaning *who goes and returns, who carries, the waters* and *causes to overflow.*[6]

"I will leave my followers for their good," said Son, "and send Spirit in my place to pour out living water on all."

Sketching a swan in rapid flight circling and returning, Son spoke again.

"The principal stars which mark the Swan's wings and length of body form a large and beautiful cross, the most regular of all the crosses formed by the constellations.

The Swan

"The Swan emphasises the glorious truth that I will return speedily. Stars in the constellation of this mighty bird have names meaning *the judge, flying swiftly, flying quickly, who returns as in a circle, who goes and returns quickly* and *gloriously shining forth.*"[7]

"It's time to look more closely at the redeemed ones," said Son. Turning his attention to the great circle, he drew another sign— two large fishes bound together by a band fastened to their tails. One fish had its head pointing upwards towards the North Polar Star, the other was at right angles to the first fish, swimming along the line of the path of the sun.

---

6   Star names: Hebrew *Scheat*, Arabic *Al Genib, Enif, Matar*

7   Star names: *Deneb, Adige*, Arabic *Al Bireo*, Hebrew *Sadr, Azel, Fafage*

The Plan

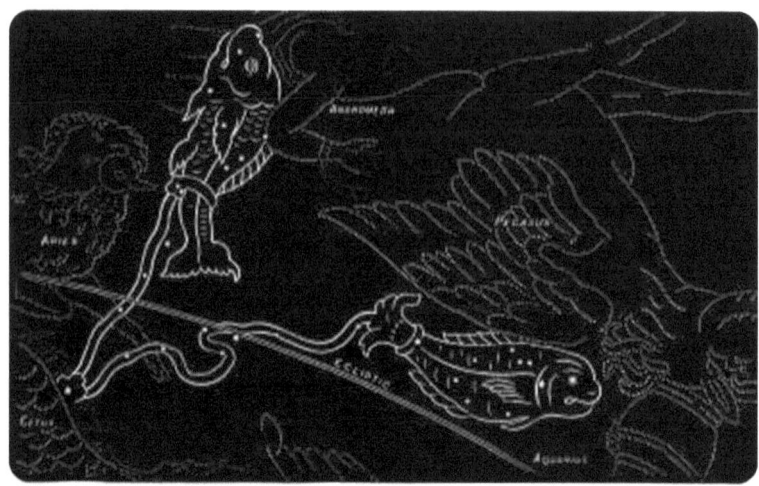

The Fishes and the Band

"I call these *The Fishes of Him that comes*,[8] said Son. "The two fishes express the idea of multitudes enclosed in the fisherman's net. Multitudes will come to me. The two fishes also represent two branches of the redeemed—the patriarchal church made up of those who believe in me before I appear on Earth in human form, and the Christian church made up of those who believe after my appearance. They are inseparably tied together by this Band,[9] which is a separate constellation."

"One fish is pointing upwards," ventured Lady Wisdom. "Does it represent those who believe in advance?"

"Yes."

"Then the other fish, the one swimming along the path, must represent those who come to faith later."

"Yes. But never lose sight of the fact that both are part of the one great universal church. To the one my coming is future, taught by types and shadows and symbols. To the other my coming is fact. But both come to me by the same faith."

---

[8] Ancient Egyptian name: *Pi-cot Orion* or *Pisces Hori*
[9] Arabic name *Al Risha*, meaning *the band* or *bridle*

"The stories told by the signs are interconnected," said Spirit, interrupting Son's narrative. "The next sign is *Aries*, the Ram or Lamb. Though the Son hasn't drawn the pictures for you yet, you will soon see that the Band is under the Ram's control. He guides and governs the Fishes by this Band. The Fishes don't move according to their own will. They are under the authority of the Lamb, empowered by him to fulfill his purposes."

"There is another connection to a future sign," Father pointed out. "One of the constellations in the sign of The Ram is a sea monster, the enemy of fish. The Band which is fastened securely round the tail of each fish, uniting them, is also fastened to the neck of the sea monster. The sea monster is attempting to drag the fishes in his direction."

"But the Ram intervenes," added Son significantly. "Let's finish this sign of the Fishes before getting too far into the next one."

Above the Fishes Son drew a beautiful woman with chains fastened to her feet and arms, unable to rise.

"This is Andromeda, the Chained Woman," said Son. He pointed out stars with names meaning *the chained, the broken down, the weak* and *the afflicted*.[10]

"Her story expands the story told by the bound Fishes. Just as the Fishes are bound to the sea monster who tries to drag them down with him, so Andromeda is bound by her fallen nature, though she longs to take her rightful place beside her King."

"Another way to interpret this picture is to see her as the persecuted Church," added Father.

---

[10] Star names: Hebrew *Sirra*, Arabic *Al Phiratz*, Hebrew *Mirach*, Arabic, *Al Mara*

The Plan

"She cannot enjoy her position as the royal bride because she is bound to this earthly life. Jealous rivals hate her. The powers of darkness war against her, exposing her to affliction, suffering and hardship. She is waiting for her King to rescue her and make her his bride."

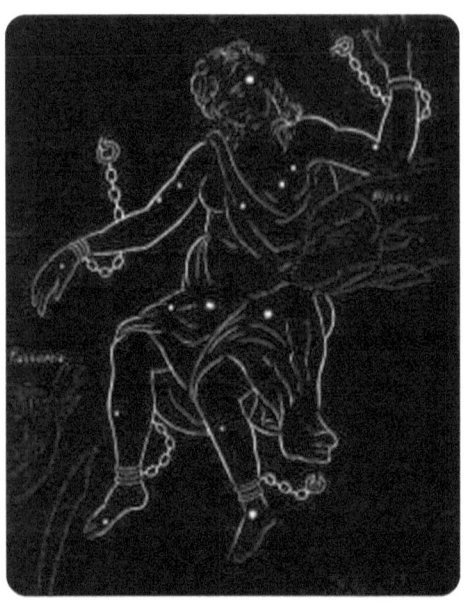

Andromeda, the Chained Woman

In the center of the circle Son drew a glorious king, crowned, and enthroned in the highest heaven, with a sceptre in his left hand, and his foot planted on the Polar Star.

"Meet Cepheus, the Crowned King," said Father. "I have invested him with dominion and all the royal rights due to him as my Son."

"We identified him by the names of the stars," added Spirit. "The bright star in his shoulder is *the Quickly-returning*. Other stars have names meaning

Cepheus, the Crowned King

the Redeemer, *the Shepherd*, *the Ruler that comes*, and *the royal Branch*."[11]

---

[11] Star names: Al Deramin, Al Phirk, Egyptian Pe-ku-hor

"The star-pictures never end in despair," observed Lady Wisdom. "Every sign ends in hope. The King will break every chain and bring deliverance to Andromeda."

"What is Cepheus holding in his right hand?" asked an angel. "It looks like ribbons."

Lady Wisdom immediately grasped their significance.

"It's the Band that we saw in the sign of the Fishes! It represents the King's authority, guidance and control over the redeemed ones. It's what binds the redeemed ones together in unity. It's what holds them to their King."

The Ram

"The last of the four signs concerning the redeemed ones will explain this hope more fully," said Son as he sketched a Ram around some stars on the great circle. "The Ram's full name means *the sacrifice of righteousness*.[12] Look at his foot! The Ram has his foot on the Band, as though he is about to loosen the bands, set the captives free, and bind their great oppressor. The brightest star, which is in the Ram's forehead,

---

12   Akkadian name *Bara-ziggar*

has a name which means *wounded* or *slain*. The next brightest star, in the horn, is named *the bruised, the wounded*."[13]

Between the Chained Woman and the Crowned King, Son drew a picture of a woman on a chair around five bright stars forming an irregular W.

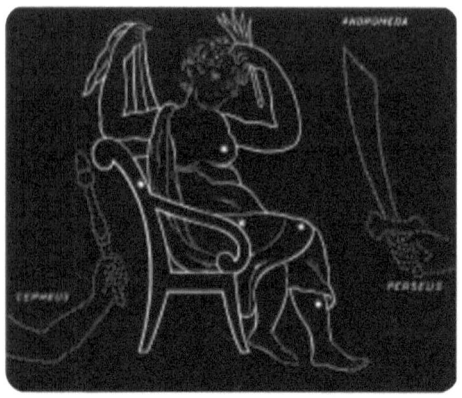

Cassiopeia, the Enthroned Woman

"This is *Cassiopeia*, the Enthroned Woman," said Son. "Her name means *the enthroned, the beautiful*. The name of her alpha star means *the freed*.

"This is the same woman who was chained in the previous sign, but now she is free."

---

[13] The ancient Egyptians considered that the sign Taurus marked the Spring Equinox. On the day that the sun moved from the sign of Aries into Taurus, the Egyptians held a festival in which they slew a Ram, placed branches over the doors, garlanded the Ram with wreaths of flowers and carried it in procession. Owing to the precession of the equinoxes, the sun, at the time of the Exodus, had receded into this sign of Aries, which then marked the Spring Equinox. But by the time that the Lamb of God was slain, the sun had still further receded, and on the 14th of Nisan, in the year of the Crucifixion, stood at the very spot marked by the brightest stars named *the pierced, the wounded* or *slain*, and *the bruised* or *wounded!* God so ordained "the times and seasons" that during that noon-day darkness the sun was seen near those stars which had spoken for so many centuries of this bruising of the woman's Seed--the Lamb of God! He who created the sun and the stars "for signs and for cycles," ordained also the times and the seasons. It is He who tells us that "when the fullness of time was come, God sent forth His Son" (Galatians 4:4, KJV) and that "at just the right time ... Christ died for the ungodly" (Romans 5:6, NIV).

"Her hands, no longer bound, are engaged in arranging her robes and adorning her hair. She is preparing herself for a great public manifestation.

"She is seated close by the side of Cepheus, the King, who is holding out his sceptre toward her."

Outside the great circle and below the Ram, Son drew a giant scaly beast with an enormous head, mouth and front paws, and having the body and tail of a whale. The Band under the control of the Ram was fastened to the neck of the monster, holding him firmly bound.

"The second constellation in the sign of the Ram is the Sea Monster, the natural enemy of fishes," explained Son. "The star in its neck is named *the Rebel*.[14] Its two brightest stars have names meaning *the chained enemy* and *the overthrown* or *the thrust down*.[15]

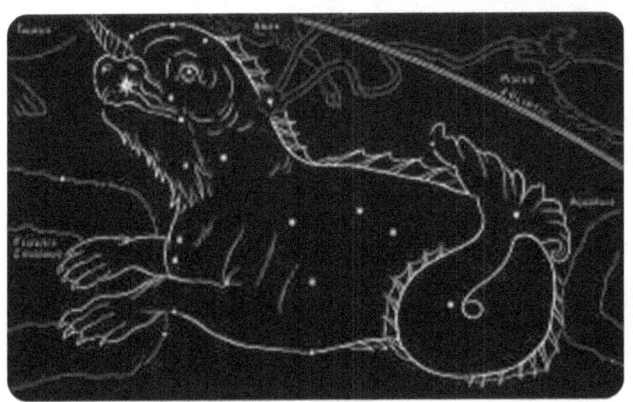

The Sea Monster

"The monster looks scary, but I have him firmly under my control. By the same power with which I uphold the Fishes I restrain the devouring enemy. With that same power I will bind the monster for his final destruction."

Inside the circular path of the sun, above and slightly to the left of the Ram, Son drew a man with wings on his feet, with a sword in his right hand and the head of the enemy, whom he had slain, in his left.

---

[14] Star name: *Mira*

[15] Star names: *Menkar, Deneb Kaitos*

"This is Perseus, The Breaker," explained Son. "With his sword he has defeated his enemy and broken the power of all his foes. He brings death and destruction to the monsters of evil, setting captives free.

Perseus, the Breaker

Perseus has wings on his feet to show us that he is coming swiftly.

"The enemy who has been decapitated is Medusa, which comes from a word meaning *the trodden under foot*. The head is also called *the head of the adversary*[16] or *the evil spirit*."[17]

"I notice that the bright star in Medusa's head is continually changing in brightness," observed Lady Wisdom.

"It is a fitting emblem of our great enemy who continually transforms himself in order to devour, deceive and destroy," commented Spirit. "Sometimes he appears as a roaring lion,[18] sometimes as a subtle serpent[19] and sometimes as an angel of light!"[20]

"So again the story ends in triumph," said Lady Wisdom. "The enemy has been decapitated. We have nothing to fear!"

---

[16] Star name: *Rosh Satan*
[17] Star name: *Al Ghoul*
[18] 1 Peter 5:8
[19] Genesis 3:8
[20] 2 Corinthians 11:14

10

The Heavens Declare the Redemption Completed

"The final four signs are star-pictures of my second coming and the consummation of The Plan," said Son to the angels, who were listening intently as he explained the story told by the stars. "This third set of signs shows the great judgment period and the completion of the whole mystery of God respecting man's world and the human race."

The Bull or Reem

He began drawing a powerful Bull, not a domestic animal but a Reem, a prehistoric wild ox[1]—formidable, fierce and untameable. Its great horns were outspread and sharp. The Bull, with its head down

---

[1] Similar to an *aurochs*, a European bison, once widely distributed, now nearly extinct.

The Plan

and horns forward, was charging with mighty energy and fierce wrath, ready to pierce his enemies through and destroy them.

"The Bull predicts a coming Judge and coming judgment. Its common name[2] means both *coming* and *ruling*. Its poetical name *Reem* conveys the idea of exaltation, power and pre-eminence. Stars within the constellation have names meaning *the leader* or *governor* and *wounded* or *slain*.[3] These stars," said Son pointing to a cluster of stars in the Bull's neck, "are called the *Pleiades*, which means *the congregation of the judge* or *ruler*. To underline my point, I called another group of stars on the face of the Bull *The Hyades*, meaning *the congregated*."

"The bodies of the Bull and the Ram overlap," Lady Wisdom pointed out, "and they are facing opposite directions."

"Yes," Spirit explained. "Toward the church Son is the Lamb, but toward those who reject him he becomes the terrible Reem."

Orion, the Bull, and the River of the Judge

Another angel noticed a different detail and spoke to Son.

---

[2] Common Hebrew name: Shur
[3] Star names: *Al Debaran, El Nath*

"I see that when you come the second time, when you come to rule, your saints... " he pointed to the Pleiades and the Hyades, "will be with you."

"Correct," replied Son.

Father wanted to make another point.

"Do you notice what sign is on the opposite side of the circle from the Bull?"

"The Scorpion."

"So what does that tell you?"

None of the angels had an answer.

"When the Bull rises to Earth's view, the Scorpion sets and disappears! The enemy cannot stand before the Bull's wrath."

A murmur of wonder and awe swept through the angelic throng.

Under the Bull Son drew a River running in a serpentine course towards the lower regions, down, down, past the Sea Monster and out of sight.

"This is *Eradanus*, the *river of the Judge*," explained Son. "The Sea Monster is trying to stop its flow, but he can't. Judgment is coming to the wicked."

Son then drew the picture of a man around some very bright stars just beneath the great circle of the sun.

"He looks like a great hunter who has just killed a lion," commented an angel.

"He is brandishing a mighty club high with his right hand while holding the token of his victory—the head and skin of the lion—in his left."

"He is the Coming Prince," said Son. "His name is Orion, which in various languages means *coming forth as light, this is he who triumphs*, and *the light of heaven*. His left foot is in the act of crushing the head of the enemy, represented by a giant Hare. From Orion's belt, studded with three brilliant stars, hangs a sharp sword."

The Plan

"Ooo, I like the detail you have put into your drawings," said an angel. "The hilt of Orion's sword is in the form of a lamb!"

"The River of Judgment is also under his foot," added another angel.

"What a brilliant constellation!" exclaimed still another angel.

"Orion is the most brilliant of all the constellations," said the Father with pride in his voice. "Only the brightest is good enough to represent my beloved Son. It is visible to all the habitable world. The name of the brightest star, *Betelgeuz*, in Orion's right shoulder means *the coming of the branch*.

Orion, the Coming Prince

"The bright star in Orion's foot, the foot lifted up over the head of the enemy in the act of crushing it, is named *the foot that crushes*.[4] The bright star in his left shoulder is *swiftly coming* or *suddenly destroying*."[5]

Son continued to point out star after bright star, naming them one by one.

"This is *the wounded One*.[6] This is *bruised*.[7] Other names describe him as *the branch, the mighty, the ruler, the prince, the strong, coming* and *coming forth*."

The angels clapped their hands in approval. One angel spoke for them all.

"He looks to me like the invincible Avenger! How beautifully Orion pictures the Light of the world!"

---

[4] Star name: *Rigel*
[5] Star name: *Bellatrix*
[6] Star name: *Al Nitak*
[7] Star name: *Saiph*

"There is a dark side to this bright picture," warned Son. "The Wicked, one whom Yahweh will destroy with the brightness of His coming,[8] will appear in the next sign. But first let me finish the last constellation in the sign of the Bull."

Above Orion and inside the circle, Son drew a Shepherd seated upon the Milky Way. He was holding up on his left shoulder a she goat,[9] who clung to his neck while looking down with fright at the terrible on-rushing Bull. In his left hand the Shepherd supported two little newborn kids, bleating and trembling with fear.

"This is Auriga, the Shepherd," said Son. "He gathers the lambs in his arm and carries them in his bosom."

"It's a beautiful picture of safety for the redeemed in the day of wrath!" exclaimed Spirit. "In the loving arms of the Shepherd they have nothing to fear."

"The Shepherd is holding a band in his right hand," observed an angel.

"We have seen that Band before," said Lady Wisdom. "It's the same band which ties the two Fishes to each other. The same band with which the Lamb lovingly guides and governs the redeemed. It is the Band of power by which the Shepherd on the one hand upholds and guides his people, and on the other hand binds the enemy."

Auriga, the Shepherd

"The goat in the picture represents an entire flock of goats,"[10] said Son, "and I have named the

---

[8] See 2 Thessalonians 2:8, KJV.

[9] Both names of the alpha star—Auriga (Latin) and Alioth (Hebrew) mean *a she goat*.

[10] Star name *Maaz* means *a flock of goats*

The Plan

bright star in the Shepherd's right arm[11] *the Band of the Goats.* Those who come to faith during the last terrible days will be protected. They will be safe in my arms."[12]

"In the midst of the scenes of judgment my Son still exercises his offices of mercy and salvation," commented Father approvingly. "In the midst of wrath he remembers mercy."[13]

"Now let's look at the completion of The Plan from another angle," said Son.

On the circle he drew two figures sitting close together with their feet resting on the Milky Way. One had his arm around the other. Their heads were leaning against each other in a loving attitude. The one with his arm around his companion held a club in his right hand. The second figure held a bow and arrow in one hand and a harp in the other.

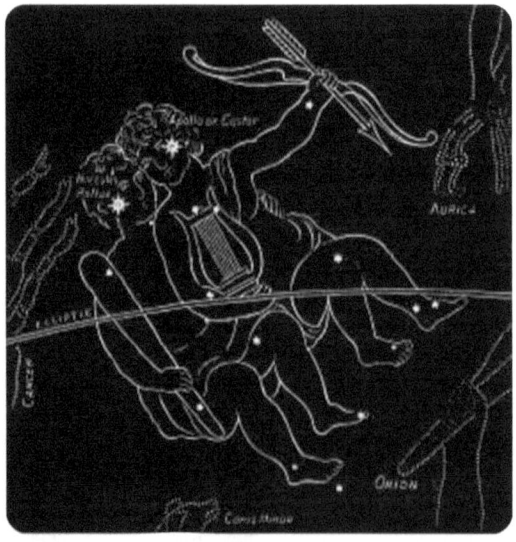

Gemini, the United

---

[11] Beta star: *Menkilinon*

[12] In the Zodiac of Denderah, a 4000-year-old temple in Egypt, the Shepherd is named Trun, which means *sceptre* or *power.* Instead of carrying a sheep or goat, he is holding a sceptre in his hand. At the top of the sceptre is the head of a goat, at the bottom is a cross!

[13] See Habakkuk 3:2.

"There's a strong resemblance between the two," observed one angel. "Are they twins?"

"No. Keep guessing."

"Is this another picture of your two-fold nature?"

"No." Son paused, giving the angel time to think. "I'll give you a hint. What is the second figure holding?"

"A bow and arrow."

"What else?"

"A harp."

"What does a harp signify?"

"Praise."

"Praise to whom?

"To Yahweh, of course."

"And who praises Yahweh?"

"His creation!"

"Do *all* created beings praise Yahweh?"

"No."

"Oh, I get it!" exclaimed Lady Wisdom, interrupting the dialogue between Son and the angel. "This is a picture of you and your bride, the Church!"

"Right," Son replied. "One of the names for this sign is *the United, the Completely Joined*.[14] Even the name Gemini, which some use for this sign, expresses the idea of something completed— not of twins, but of a long betrothal brought to its consummation."

"I see two very bright stars, one in the head of each," an angel said. "What are the stars' names?"

"Some call them Pollux and Castor, others call them Hercules and Apollo."

"Aren't those all male names? How can this be a picture of you and your Bride?"

"I'll answer that," said Father. "We don't need to quibble about gender in these star pictures. Consider it poetic license. My Son

---

[14] Sign name: *Pi Mahi*

The Plan

sometimes uses female imagery for himself. He compares his loving care for his people to a hen caring for her chicks.[15] We call the redeemed ones 'the Bride' but we also call them 'sons of God.'"

"What about the weapons the two are holding?" another angel asked. "Won't there be peace when you are united with your bride?"

"Absolutely! Both the Messiah-Prince and his bride are invincible warriors, but their weapons are at rest. Notice that the club is resting against the Prince's shoulder while the bow in the Bride's hand is unstrung."

Turning his attention to a cluster of stars well outside the circle, below Gemini and below Orion's foot, Son drew a gigantic Hare.

"This is the enemy trodden under foot," said Son. "The hare is one of the animals Orion most delights in hunting. Its alpha star is named *the enemy of Him that comes*.[16] Other stars are named *the mad*, *the bound*, and *the deceiver*."

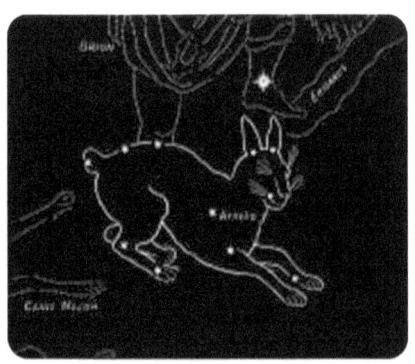

The Enemy

"This constellation shows that the enemy's end is near," added Spirit. "Once the heavenly marriage is celebrated, he will be utterly destroyed."

Immediately below Gemini, Son drew a little dog. Below it and beside the Hare, he drew a much larger dog. "The Big Dog looks as if he is chasing the Hare, ready to pounce on him and devour him," observed one of the angels. "Absolutely!" replied Son. "The Big Dog's alpha star is named *Sirius*, meaning *the Prince*, *Guardian*, the *Victorious*. It is one of the brightest in the whole heavens! The second brightest star is called *the Ruler*.[17] Other stars have names meaning *the Shining*, *the Glorious*, *the Mighty*, and *the Leader*."

---

[15] See Matthew 23:37 and Luke 13:34.
[16] Star name: *Arnebo*
[17] Star name: *Mirzam*

"The Little Dog, as you can see, is following after the Big Dog," added Father. "Its alpha star name means *redeemed*.[18] The Prince is going before, but his faithful people will share his sovereignty and reign with him forever."

"Now let's take a closer look at the future of the redeemed ones," said Son. "The truth taught by this next sign is difficult to put into a picture, so I will have to rely on the names of the stars within it to tell the story of believers gathered together in rest and safety."

Son drew a picture of a giant Crab.

"The Crab undergoes important changes as it grows and develops," he explained.

Little Dog and Big Dog

"Periodically it throws off it old shells and takes on new ones. This is a picture of the transformation that takes place in each of the redeemed.

Each saint puts off his old nature with his deeds and puts on a new nature which is renewed after the image of his Creator.[19] At the end of life he will trade in his dying body for an immortal one.[20]

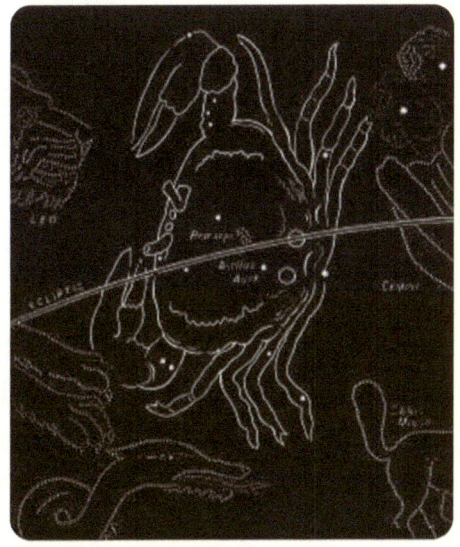

Khan Cer, the Crab

---

18   Star name: *Procyon*

19   See Colossians 3:9-10.

20   See Romans 7:24 and 2 Corinthians 5:2-4.

"Another way to look at the Crab is to consider its shape. The name of the crab is *Khan Cer*. *Khan* is the traveller's rest or inn, and *Cer* means *encircling*. The crab's front claws look as if they are encircling something.

"The sign represents *rest secured*. Stars within the sign have names meaning *holding, the sheltering* or *hiding-place, assembled thousands*, and *the kids* or *lambs*.

"I get it!" exclaimed Lady Wisdom. "It's a star-picture of the redeemed multitudes safely encircled in their heavenly home!"

"Right!" said Son. "The bright star in the centre is not a single star but a cluster of stars. It is made up of a great multitude of stars. Its name means *a multitude, offspring, the innumerable seed*."[21]

Above the Crab Son drew a Great Bear and at the centre of the circle he drew a Little Bear. At the tip of its tail was the Polar Star.

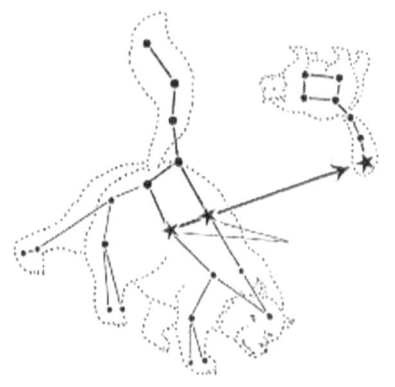

"You call those bears!" exclaimed an angel. "Bears don't have long tails! The constellations look like dippers."

"I arranged the stars in recognizable shapes—dippers—so that everyone, even children, would recognize them," said Son. "I call them bears because in several languages *bear* and *fold* have almost the same sound," said Son.

"The name of the alpha star of the Great Bear means *a fold*, and *rest* or *security*. The bears represent two sheepfolds which provide rest and security for the flocks within. The Little Bear or Little Dipper is the smaller of the two sheepfolds. It embraces those who put their faith in me prior to my first coming. Stars within this constellation have names

---

[21] Star name: *Praesepe*, commonly known as the Beehive

meaning *waiting Him who comes, the redeemed assembly, a travelling company*, and *the stronghold of the saved.*

"The Great Bear or Big Dipper represents the larger fold and flock—the great company of those who believe following my death and resurrection. Stars within the constellation have names meaning *the flock, guarded, umbered, the sheepfold, multitude, many assembled, separated, protected, covered, company of travellers,* and most descriptive of all, *the latter herd* or *flock.*"

The Little Bear

Outside the circle Son sketched a large sailing ship.

"This Ship is *Argo*," Son announced. "Argo means a *company of travellers*. The name of its alpha star, near the keel, means *the possession of Him who comes*. Picture in your mind the sailors in that ship coming back victorious to their own shores."

"What a picture of pilgrims brought safely home—all their toils and conflict over!" exclaimed Lady Wisdom.

"If you think that's cool, look at this! Keep your eye on the Polar Star."

Son speeded up the motion of the stars to show where they would be thousands of years into the future. At first the Polar Star was in line with the alpha star Thuban in the constellation of the Dragon, so that the Dragon's Thuban appeared to be the star around which all other stars revolved. Gradually the Polar Star moved across the sky until it merged with the alpha star at the tip of the Little Bear's tail!

"Right now, at the beginning of creation it appears as if the heavens revolve around the Dragon," explained Son. "Certainly our enemy believes he is the centre of the universe, but before the story is over, the Polar Star will be in *the Lesser Fold!*

Argo, the Ship

"The sheep which once were in the clutches of the Dragon will be safe in the sheepfold!"

Son reversed the motion of the stars and returned them to their original position.

"One day the universe will revolve around the Sheep and the Sheepfold," Son declared triumphantly. "I planned it all!"

Father and Spirit clapped their hands as a great cheer went up from all the angels in Heaven.

"Now for the final sign," said Son. "It tells the story of God's final conquest over Satan. This is how the great story ends for our enemy—with judgment!"

Son drew a picture of a mighty Lion with its feet over the head of a great serpent with a head like a dragon.

"The Lion's name is *Arieh*," said Son using the name for lion which means *an adult lion, having paired, hunting down his prey.*[22]

"This is the Lion of the tribe of Judah aroused to destroy his enemy. The alpha star, *Cor Leonis*,[23] marks the heart of the Lion. That heart controls its mighty paws which are about to crush the Serpent *Hydra*. She is a *female* serpent, the mother of all evil."

---

[22] The Hebrew language has six different words for *lion*. The choice of this Hebrew name, *Arieh*, is very specific and deliberate. The Syriac and Arabic names mean *the rending Lion*, and *a lion coming vehemently, leaping forth as a flame*!

[23] *Cor Leonis* means *heart of the lion*.

The Lion

Son then pointed out stars within the Serpent whose names predicted judgment coming to the Serpent—names such as *the Judge or Lord who comes with haste, the punishing or tearing of the Lion, the judge comes who seizes,* and *the putting down of the enemy.*

Son continued to draw the Serpent whose length stretched under three signs—the Lion, the Virgin and the Scales.

"The Serpent appears to be fleeing for his life!" exclaimed Lady Wisdom. "Fleeing from the Lion's fury!"

"He certainly is, and with good reason," said Son. "His end is near. Hydra means *the Abhorred*. The name of its alpha star means *the put out of the way*. Another star is named *the tearing to pieces of the Deceiver*."

Over the Serpent Son drew a Cup and a Raven.

"Not only is the Lion ready to tear him to shreds, but this Cup, as you can see, is being poured over the Serpent. It is the Cup of Divine wrath. The constellation has thirteen stars, the number of apostasy. The Raven is grasping the Serpent with his feet and tearing him with his beak. The star in the Raven's eye is named *the curse inflicted*. Another star is named *the Raven tearing to pieces*. There are nine stars, the number of judgment, in this constellation."

The Plan

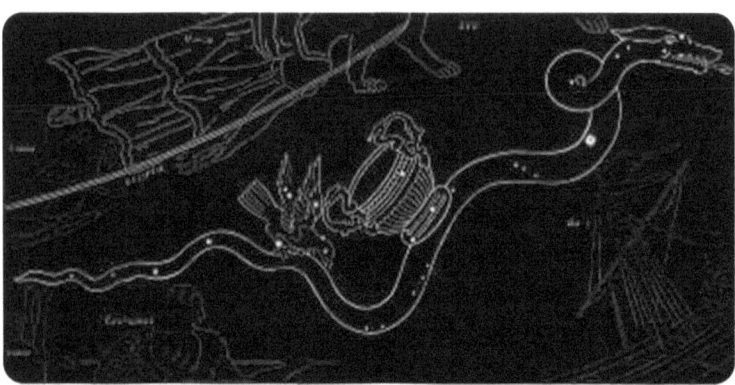

Hydra the Serpent, the Raven, and the Cup

"We have completed the circle and are now back to the first sign, the Virgin," said Lady Wisdom. "What a story the stars tell!"

"I had hoped to make that abundantly clear," replied Son.

The angels began talking amongst themselves about how perfectly the signs told the story of redemption, pointing out details that the Son had not mentioned.

"There is much more in the star pictures than I can explain now," announced Son. "The constellations are laid out like a poem. But that is a lesson for another day. We have work to do and more to create."[24]

The angels burst into song:

> The heavens proclaim the glory of God.
>> The skies display his craftsmanship.
> Day after day they continue to speak; night
>> after night they make him known.
> They speak without a sound or word;
>> their voice is never heard.
> Yet their message has gone throughout the earth,
>> and their words to all the world.[25]

---

[24] These three chapters draw heavily from two books – *The Gospel in the Stars*, by Joseph Seiss, 1882, and *The Witness of the Stars*, by E.W. Bullinger, 1893. Both books have now been reprinted.

[25] Psalm 19:1-4, NLT

Suddenly an angel called out, "The pictures are fading!"

All that remained in the dark sky were countless pinpoints of light, some brighter than others.

"Aren't you going to leave the pictures in the sky?" the angels asked Son.

"No, there is no material substance behind the pictures I have drawn for you. The names of the signs, the stars and the constellations will tell it all."

"But the stars themselves don't form any recognizable outline of the pictures you just drew," the angels objected. "How will people remember the names? How will people see the Virgin, for example, from a scattered handful of stars?"

"I agree that these signs bear no resemblance to the things they signify," said the Son. "Signs seldom do. But don't worry. I will describe the pictures carefully to the first few humans who follow The Plan. I will teach them the names of the stars and constellations. They will record what I show them and teach it to the generations following."

"What if future generations remember the meaning of the signs imperfectly, or forget the meaning altogether?" asked an angel. "Worse yet, what if they deliberately distort the meaning of the signs?"

Son smiled.

"Don't you think that the One who has the power to create the signs also has the power to sustain their meaning?"

"Our adversary, Satan, is the master of illusion and delusion," Father added. "He will do his best to captivate the gullible, side-track the unsuspecting and superstitious, replace the truth of God with the ideology of man, and pervert the message which Yahweh has declared in the heavens. But people who are trying to sort fact from fiction need remember only that the oldest names and pictures are the closest to the original."

"There will be those who distort the meaning of the signs," Spirit admitted, "but even that distortion will contain enough similarity to the original that the true meaning will shine through."

"I will see to it that even paganized distortions of these pictures and stories will preserve kernels of truth, thus pointing back to my original story," Son assured his audience of angels. "Those who are seeking truth rather than suppressing it will acknowledge that mine is the original."

11

New Creation

Having reviewed the stories told by the stars, Yahweh let out a sigh of deep satisfaction. The angels clapped in appreciation.

"Are you ready for the verdict on today's work?" Son asked.

"It is good!" the Holy One declared in unison.

"When we create man, we will be careful to share this story in the stars with those who can be trusted to pass it on to others," said Father to the angels who were watching the creation and re-creation process with interest.

"We know at some point in time people will fail to pass it on," Spirit added sadly. "But even if they lose some details, or even if the entire story in the stars gets lost, people have no excuse for not knowing about our eternal power and divine nature. If they know nothing more specific, they at least know that the heavens declare the glory of God; the skies show forth his handiwork. From the evidence of creation, people will praise God for his mighty power and be thankful that the One who can keep the stars in their orbits can surely supply their needs."

"You told us that the first three days of creation picture the Son's birth and life, his death, and his resurrection," said Lady Wisdom, addressing the Holy One. "What does your fourth day's work represent?"

"The focus of our work on the fourth day shifted from the land to the sky, from Earth to Heaven," answered Father. "It is a picture of Son's future ascension from his earthly ministry to his heavenly position."

The Plan

As evening fell once more, the Holy One began to plan the fifth day's work.

"Earth is once again a beautiful garden," said Spirit. "Now we need to fill it with creatures to enjoy it as we do."

"On the third day we made the sky and separated salt water from fresh," said Son. "Now let's fill those waters with living creatures and fill the sky with birds."

Lady Wisdom was aghast.

"Do you mean you will put creatures in the oceans and seas?" she asked. "That salt water is death to living creatures! They will die!"

"No problem!" said Spirit. "So far this week we have simply been renovating. Reworking things that were already there in some form. Now it's time to create totally new creatures. Creatures that can survive and thrive in salt water. It will be fun to create again!"

Yahweh spoke the sea creatures into existence. Immediately the water teemed with an infinite variety of creatures of all sizes and shapes, from gigantic whales down to krill and phytoplankton. Beautiful creatures. Colorful creatures. Comical creatures. Even a few ugly ones. All of them amazing. And they all thrived, whether in salt water or fresh.

"Let's fill the sky with birds," declared Son. "Though they are heavier than air, they will defy gravity and soar."

Yahweh spoke again and filled the sky with birds. Again the variety was infinite. Large and small. Drab and colorful. Birds with fancy tails—like peacocks and birds of paradise. Birds with fancy crowns—like crowned cranes, cassowaries, cardinals and secretary birds. Birds with fancy beaks—like toucans, sandpipers, spoonbills and pelicans. Just for fun the Holy One created a few birds that couldn't fly—like ostriches, kiwis and emus.

All the creatures were designed to reproduce after their kind. Before the sun set Yahweh added a final touch. He blessed what he had created.

"Be fruitful and increase in number," he told them. "Fill the water in the seas. Increase on the earth."

Turning to Father, Son declared, "I will return to Heaven after accomplishing my task on Earth in order to make way for the Spirit's more widespread work. My work in human form will be limited in time and space. My adult ministry will be limited to a radius of less than a hundred miles from my home town of Nazareth. I will teach only those people within sound of my voice. But my return to Heaven will enable Spirit to continue and expand on the work begun through my death and resurrection. Spirit is not limited by space. He is everywhere. He can work in the lives of everybody on the planet at the same time—convicting them of sin, teaching them, indwelling them, empowering them to live holy lives."

"Today's creation is a picture of Son indwelling his people through Spirit," the Father added. "Through the power of the indwelling Spirit redeemed ones can do the impossible. Like the fish, they can live and even thrive in 'death waters.' Like the birds, they can soar because their citizenship is in Heaven."

"The flightless birds show that Father, Spirit and I aren't always serious," said the Son. "We can be playful, we enjoy a good party, and we love to laugh. Yet these birds are more than a good joke. They also point out the sad fact that some people will fail to take advantage of the abundant resources available to them through the indwelling Spirit. I hope that when humans look at flightless birds they will reflect on whether they are soaring over their circumstances as they were created to do."

Yahweh surveyed the work of the fifth day and pronounced his satisfaction.

"It is good!"

With the setting of the sun, the sixth day began. The angels sensed the excitement with which the Holy One anticipated this day. This was the day they would create their masterpiece.

The Plan

But first they had land animals to create. Again the variety was infinite. Animals useful to man—like oxen for heavy labor, horses for transportation, sheep for wool, cows for milk. Animals wild and tame. Animals large and small. Prickly ones and cuddly ones. Swift animals—like cheetahs and horses. Slow ones—like sloths and turtles. Some beautiful, some graceful, some comical.

Some animals were a remake of animals which existed in the first creation. Some animals were entirely new. All of them reproduced according to their kind. And all of them were designed to inspire awe and wonder in their Creator.

Once more Yahweh surveyed his creation and declared it good.

"Now, at last," said the Holy One, "we can focus our attention on creating something never seen in Heaven or on Earth."

Knowing the angels were deeply interested in what Yahweh was about to do, Father addressed his divine council, the spirit beings of high rank.

"Let's make people in our image—intelligent, creative and with free will. Man's mandate will be to govern creation on behalf of the Holy One."[1]

"Wasn't that the mandate you gave all the angels and this divine council in particular?" asked one of the council members.

"Yes, but you failed," Father responded. "We gave all you spirit beings the run of Heaven and Earth and put Lucifer in charge of Eden, which was patterned after our heavenly home. Eden had a mountain with a throne on top much like our throne room in Heaven. But Lucifer did not follow my instructions. He aspired not to represent me but to replace me. He was disloyal. He became my adversary. He thought he

---

[1] In Genesis 1:26-27 a single person (God) is addressing a group (the members of his divine council) to make a grand announcement. For an in-depth defense of this, see Michael S. Heiser, *The Unseen Realm*, chapter 3. In verse 27 the verb "created" in Hebrew is singular, clearly indicating that God himself does the creating.

could sit on my throne, and he recruited a third of the spirit beings to his way of thinking."

"So we cast our adversary Satan and his rebels out of Heaven and out of Eden," continued Spirit. "Then we recreated Earth and Eden. We still want Eden to be governed as we would govern it, but this time we will put human beings in charge of Earth, first to care for Eden, then to bring Eden to the whole planet."

"We will start with one pair of humans instead of myriads of them," added Son, "and ask them to multiply and gradually bring our kingdom rule to all the Earth. We will let them rule over the fish of the sea, over the birds of the air, and over all the animals on the ground, wild and domestic."

"Now let's talk about this new man, this creature we are going to make in our image."

Father, Son and Spirit brainstormed as to how humans would be similar to his Creator yet different. The divine council added their suggestions. Finally, Yahweh was ready to act.

Even though people would be similar to Yahweh in many ways, there would still remain an infinite difference. Like the king's image impressed upon a coin, the likeness would be limited yet profound. Even the way humans were created would be different from the rest of creation. For six days Yahweh had been speaking things into existence. Now he would take a hands-on approach—literally!

The angels watched as the Holy One translated what had been created in concept into a physical reality. Son selected some dust from the earth, added water and mixed it carefully. He kneaded the clay through his finders, feeling for and discarding any imperfections. When he was satisfied that the consistency of the clay was perfect, he molded it into the perfect shape as Father and Spirit expressed their approval and added their ideas and input.

The Plan

As Yahweh worked his magic on the lump of clay, Lady Wisdom whispered to an angel beside her, "The Holy One reminds me of a potter practicing his skill. The ground he is working on could be a potter's wheel. Isn't it wonderful what he can do even without spinning the wheel?"

When Father and Spirit were satisfied with Son's workmanship, Spirit blew gently into the clay nostrils. The clay changed color from a pale grey to a deep healthy tan with a pink glow. Then it began to move, and Man stepped off the Potter's workplace!

Man's eyes widened with amazement as he took in his surroundings. He immediately knew that he was loved.

"Hello, Adam," said Yahweh, his voice full of love.

Adam turned in the direction of the voice, but saw nothing. "You can't see me because I am spirit, but I am real. More real than you are."

"Who are you?"

"I am your Creator and the Creator of Heaven and Earth. My name is Yahweh. I hope we will learn to know each other well. And I hope you will learn to love me. That's why I created you—so you would be able to fully comprehend the love that I have for you and return that love."

"You called me 'Adam.' I assume that's my name."

"Yes. I called you Adam for a variety of reasons. One is the material from which you were formed. I created you from the dust of the earth. Your name Adam even sounds like the word for 'ground.'[2] Another reason I called you Adam is your purpose in life. You were created to work, and the ground will be your source of employment for your entire life. Your name Adam also conveys the meaning 'red man' or 'blood man.' The red tinge in your face is from the blood running through your veins. Without that blood you would not be alive."

A big smile spread across Adam's face as he stretched out his arms and twirled around in delight, enjoying the sensation of being alive.

---

[2] *Adam* is both a name and the Hebrew word for *man*. The Hebrew word for *ground* is *adamah*.

New Creation

"Welcome, Adam. Man. Made in our image," said the Holy One.

" 'Made in *our* image?'" Adam asked. "Who are the others?"

"I hadn't planned to get into such a complicated question so soon," said Yahweh. "Let's just say that we—Father, Son and Spirit—are three in one. It is enough for you to know that you have only one God. Yahweh."

Having welcomed Adam into the world newly created and re-created, the Holy One spoke a blessing over him.

"I bless you, Adam, made in our image. Be fruitful and multiply. Prosper! Reproduce! Fill Earth and govern it. Take charge! Be Earth's master! Rule over the fish in the sea and the birds in the sky. Be responsible for every living thing that moves on the face of Earth."

As Lady Wisdom listened to Yahweh speak a blessing over Adam, she was concerned.

"Does Yahweh really know what he is doing?" she whispered to an angel beside her. "Does he know that he is making himself vulnerable by delegating authority? What if this new creature makes wrong choices?"

Spirit overheard Lady Wisdom's questions and stepped in to explain the Holy One's reasoning.

"Of course the Father knows what he is doing! The Father wants nothing but willing service from all of his created ones. Even in Heaven he gave the angels choice. Those who chose to rebel were banished from his presence. Here on Earth the Father is giving his new creation the freedom and the responsibility to choose just as he did in Heaven."

"I see," responded Lady Wisdom. "That fits with the blessing. The word 'blessed' has its roots in words which suggest bowing the knee. So if Yahweh truly blesses Man, he is not merely wishing him well, but also bowing to the choices he makes—good or bad."

"Exactly," replied Spirit. "Love does not force itself on anyone. The Father will not impose his will on anyone. He will wait for his creation to respond to the warmth of his love. Yahweh's will may not be accomplished on the first try, but it will be accomplished eventually."

The Plan

Adam was oblivious to the conversation going on in the background. All he could think was that the King of the Universe was stepping aside and yielding his authority on Earth to his newly created being.

In awe and gratitude he exclaimed, "I bless you, King of the Universe! I bless you for entrusting me with the Earth and its inhabitants. I want to be worthy of that trust."

Adam paused at the thought. He was beginning to be overwhelmed with the enormity of his responsibility when Yahweh eased his mind by adding what he had already done to make Adam's task easier.

"Look! I am giving you every seed-bearing plant on Earth and all the fruit trees for your food. To all animals and all birds, everything that moves and breathes, I give whatever grows out of the ground for food."

And that's what Yahweh did.

"Today we created Man to rule the Earth," declared Son. "Today's work is a picture of my rule over all things."

As the sun began to set on the sixth day, Yahweh surveyed his work with satisfaction. He saw all that he had made and declared, "This is more than good. It's very good!"

And all the heavenly host agreed heartily.

Darkness fell and the seventh day began.

Yahweh gently led Adam to a cozy place for him to sleep.

"Sleep, dear one. You will spend your first full day on Earth with me, getting to know me better. You need to rest up for the week to come, and I will rest with you. We—Father, Son and Spirit—have worked hard for six days. Now we too will rest, not because we need to, but to set an example for you and your descendants to follow for all eternity. Work six days. Rest. Work six days. Rest."

The rhythmic words lulled Adam to sleep.

"Rest. Work six days. Rest. Work six days. Rest. . . ."

Before he knew it, Adam felt a gentle touch on his shoulder.

"Good morning, Adam."

Light was dawning in the east. Adam sat up and looked around in wonder at the beautiful colors in the sky as the sun rose. When the brilliant colors faded and the sun broke over the horizon, Yahweh spoke again.

"Adam, the place where you slept last night is in a very special place we made especially for you to enjoy. It's a garden we call Eden. We planted it just for you. Do you want to see it?"

Did he!

Adam jumped to his feet and eagerly followed the sound of Yahweh's voice as he led him on a long walk around the perimeter of the garden. They stopped frequently as Adam examined beautiful flowers more closely. He was amazed to discover that most of them had a very pleasing scent. All day long Adam asked questions about the flowers and trees. When the sun began to set, Adam again marveled at the beautiful colors in the sky.

"Good night, Adam," Yahweh said. "You have work to do tomorrow. Sleep well."

While Adam slept on the edge of Eden, Lady Wisdom approached Yahweh with something that was puzzling her.

"O Holy One, Creator of Heaven and Earth, I have a question." She paused respectfully for permission to continue.

"Ask."

"You made all living creatures—the animals and birds and fish—in pairs, male and female, so they could reproduce, right?"

"Right."

"You told Adam to be fruitful and increase in number and fill Earth, right?"

"Right."

"But Adam is only one human being. How can he reproduce?" Yahweh smiled.

"I created Adam in my image—an intelligent immortal spirit capable of understanding, will and active power. Capable of knowledge, righteousness and true holiness. Capable of governing creation wisely. Capable of governing himself by the freedom of his will. Capable of expressing love while at the same time remaining holy. Capable of maintaining the perfect balance between justice and mercy. You know that, Lady Wisdom, because you listened in on our creative planning. What you did not see on the sixth day, as I created Adam in my image, was that I also made him male and female."

Now Lady Wisdom was really flabbergasted.

"Tomorrow, the eighth day, I will do a new thing," Yahweh continued. "Adam does not yet know that he needs a companion. But when I put him to work, he will see his need for a helper. I will satisfy that longing in him by bringing out the helper who already exists at his side. Adam and his female counterpart already are one. My plan is that their oneness not be lost when they are physically separated. It is another way in which Man is made in my image.

"We—Father, Son and Spirit—are three yet one. We are distinct enough that we can talk to each other. We perform different roles, yet we are always in total communication and agreement, always working toward the same goals.

"But more important than our distinctions is the fact that we are one in essence. We share the attributes that make us God. We—here the three-ness disappears—*I* am eternal, with no beginning and no end. I am everywhere, all-powerful and all-knowing. I am unchanging. I am sovereign. I rise above and beyond the limits of the universe. I am separate from creation and totally independent of it.

"Just as I am three in one, I designed Man to be two in one. That is another way in which Man is created in my image. When Adam and his female counterpart demonstrate a oneness that overrides their two-ness, they are displaying the truth that they are created in the image of Yahweh."

"Wow!" exclaimed Lady Wisdom. "What a privilege to be human!"

"I hope it doesn't go to Man's head," replied the Holy One. "We made him last to keep him humble. When he is tempted to be proud like Lucifer for being so special, we can ask him, 'Where were you when I laid the foundations of the earth?[3] Where were you when I set boundaries for the seas and wrapped the earth in clouds?'"

At the crack of dawn on the eighth day, Adam was awake to watch the sunrise. His heart overflowed with amazement at all that Yahweh had created for his enjoyment. Yahweh watched approvingly as Adam soaked in the beauty.

"Thank you, Yahweh," Adam said. "I can't thank you enough for this beautiful garden and this beautiful day."

"Come with me, Adam. I have work for you to do. It will be your job to work in this garden—to serve it, to till it, to keep it beautiful. It will also be your job to watch over it so that nothing and no one spoils it. But first I want to show you something."

Yahweh led Adam deep into the garden, pointing out the trees as they walked. Occasionally Adam plucked fruit from a nearby tree or bush and relished each new sensation of taste and texture. Toward the center of the garden, they stopped in front of two trees that were different from each other and unlike any of the others.

"This tree," said Yahweh, "is the most important tree in the whole garden of Eden—the tree of life. And that one is the tree of the knowledge of good and evil. You are free to eat from any tree in the garden except that one. Don't allow anyone to eat of it. When you eat of it you will surely die."

Adam shuddered. He couldn't conceive of such a thing as death.

Suddenly a pair of animals stepped out from behind some bushes and came scampering toward Adam. They barked excitedly and wagged their tails and licked Adam's hands as he held them out to touch them. Adam had never seen creatures that could move freely over the ground just like he could.

---

[3] See Job 38:4 and following.

The Plan

"What are they?" he asked Yahweh.

"You tell me," Yahweh said. "That is your job—to name the creatures that I bring to you."

"Dog," Adam replied, saying the first syllable that popped into his head.

"'Dog' it is," agreed Yahweh. Two more animals came into sight, barking and wagging their tails.

Adam looked back and forth from the first two animals to the second two.

"These ones are different, yet similar. I think they are all dogs."

Several more pairs of animals appeared, barking and wagging their tails. Each pair was distinctly different from every other pair.

"Okay, Adam, you will have to do better than call them all dogs. Think!"

Adam thought and came up with names such as terrier, hound, and husky. One rolly polly pair of fur balls he playfully called 'chow chows.'

Two of the dogs Adam had not yet named ran away and circled around a pair of woolly white creatures, skillfully directing them toward Adam. These new creatures obviously were not dogs.

"Sheep," Adam decided to call them. "And the dogs that so masterfully herded them in my direction I will call shepherd dogs because they herd sheep."

Next, Adam was amazed to see two creatures not walking along the ground but flying through the air. One landed on his outstretched hand and the other perched on his shoulder.

"What are these flying things?" Adam asked Yahweh.

"You tell me," Yahweh responded again, refusing to do Adam's work for him.

Again Adam voiced the first sound that came into his head. "Birds."

Again Yahweh brought Adam a wide variety of birds, forcing him to come up with more specific names.

Father, Son and Spirit observed the man carefully as he worked and sometimes struggled to come up with suitable names for the animals.

"It is not good for the man to be alone," commented Spirit.

"It would be so much easier for him to be able to talk things over with a companion," added Son.

"I am waiting for Adam himself to be aware of his need," said Father. "It shouldn't take long. Then we will introduce him to his helpmate."

The morning sped by as Yahweh brought animals and birds, some wild and some tame, to Adam to be named. About midday Yahweh noticed that Adam was getting tired and thirsty, so they stopped on a grassy knoll near a stream so Adam could drink and rest.

Adam lay down in the grass and closed his eyes, but he couldn't sleep. A question that had been hovering on the edge of his consciousness finally came to the fore.

"Yahweh, all the animals and birds I have seen today came in pairs, male and female, right?"

"Yes."

"Where is my female counterpart? I can't talk to the animals and they can't talk to me. I need someone to talk to besides you. No offence," Adam added hastily, "but it would be nice to talk to someone I can see. Someone like me."

"I am glad you asked that question, Adam. I have been waiting for you to ask. I will make a helper suitable for you. In fact, she already exists. She is inside you, at your side. When I created you, I anticipated your need for a companion and created you with a built-in helper. In many ways you are similar to other created beings, but in this aspect you are unique. You are created in our image."

"That is one of the first things you said to me: 'made in *our* image.' Tell me again what that means."

"I, Yahweh, am one God in three persons—Father, Son and Spirit. To the universe we are One. We never act without being in perfect agreement. But in private and to those who know us intimately, we are three persons. We can talk to each other. We can discuss things. We can love each other. Just as I, Yahweh, am three in one, you, Adam, are two in one. You are male and female."

Adam was too surprised to know what to say. More questions tumbled through his brain. Yahweh let him ponder for a while in silence.

"I made all the other creatures in twos. I began by making you one so that you would feel that longing for someone made in your own image. So you would feel that need for a helper. But more importantly, I began by making you one so that when I make you two, you will always strive for perfect oneness."

Adam began feeling around his ribs for something unusual.

"Where is she?"

Yahweh laughed.

"You can't feel her. I will start by taking some of your bone and your flesh and building her from that. Now go to sleep, and when you awake, I will introduce you to your companion."

Yahweh caused Adam to fall into a deep sleep and immediately began to operate on him. Yahweh removed some bone and flesh from Adam's side and closed up the wound, leaving only a faint scar. Next the Master Craftsman turned his attention to the bone and flesh he had taken out of the man. From it he built the most amazing creature the universe had ever seen. Yahweh did his most magnificent work while Adam was asleep.

"Hello, beautiful one," Yahweh said after breathing life into his newest workmanship.

Hearing Yahweh's voice for the first time, the woman looked around but saw no one.

"I am Yahweh, your Creator. Come with me. There is someone I would like you to meet."

Adam was yawning and rubbing the sleep out of his eyes when Yahweh brought his newest creation to the man. She had long flowing hair, flawless brown skin and the most stunning shape! Instantly Adam was wide awake. He inhaled sharply and his mouth dropped open.

"Wow!" he whistled softly.

For a while Adam was speechless. Finally he realized he needed to say something intelligent.

"At last!" he exclaimed, realizing this was the companion Yahweh had taken from his side. "This one is bone from my bone, and flesh from my flesh!"

Adam continued to stare at the gorgeous vision in front of him, hardly able to think. Then, remembering it was his job to name all creatures, Adam added, "I'll call her 'woman,' because she was taken from 'man.'"

Father took the woman by the arm, led her to Adam, and joined their hands together. As they gazed into each other's eyes, an angel choir began to sing.

> You are blessed, *Adonai* our God, king of the universe,
> > he who created all things for his glory!
>
> You are blessed, *Adonai* our God, king of the universe,
> > he who created humanity in his own image,
> > for creating them as mates so that they too may create life!
>
> You are blessed, *Adonai* our God, king of the universe,
> > he who makes the groom and the bride rejoice in each other.
> > May he give them gladness as he gave gladness
> > > to his creatures in the Garden of Eden!
>
> You are blessed, *Adonai* our God, king of the universe,
> > the Source of Joy and Gladness!
>
> You are blessed, *Adonai* our God, king of the universe,
> > he who causes the groom to rejoice in the bride! Amen.[4]

---

[4] *Sheva B'rakhot*, the Jewish wedding blessings, in *Prayers Jesus Prayed* by Timothy Paul Jones, (Ann Arbor, Michigan: Vine Books, Servant Publications, 2002), 48.

The Plan

After the music faded, Yahweh left the two to enjoy each other. Adam quickly took the woman's hand and led her on a tour of the Garden of Eden, proudly naming each tree and each new creature that came into sight. The woman was impressed with Adam's extensive knowledge.

"How did you learn all these names?" she asked him.

"Yahweh told me the names of a lot of the trees and plants," Adam replied. "I am still learning them. But naming the living creatures is *my* job. Yahweh brought me all the creatures living in the garden, and I named them. Sometimes I had a hard time coming up with new names. That's where you can help me. There are living creatures outside the Garden of Eden that haven't been named yet. Between the two of us, we should have no trouble naming them. Besides naming things, we also are responsible to take care of the garden and keep it pristine."

"Look at those two unusual trees!" the woman exclaimed as they approached the centre of the garden. "The fruit looks delicious."

Alarmed to see the woman reach for a piece of forbidden fruit, Adam grabbed her arm.

"Stop!" he almost shouted. "This is the tree of the knowledge of good and evil. Yahweh said we may eat from any tree in the garden except this one. He said, 'When you eat of it you will surely die!'"

The woman pulled back her hand as if from a hot fire. She didn't fully understand what death was, but she understood it was better not to know.

"That other tree is the tree of life," Adam told her as he drew her away a safe distance from the dangerous fruit. "It's okay to eat from it. But take a good look at the tree of the knowledge of good and evil so you don't eat from it by mistake."

* * * *

As Adam and his new companion wandered together happily in the garden, Yahweh reviewed the day.

New Creation

"It's been another busy day," commented Spirit. "Busy, but good."

"This eighth day has been full of new beginnings," added the Father. "It was the beginning of a new week. It was Adam's first day of work. He did a good job, don't you think? Naming all those creatures in the garden all by himself. I am pleased with how he threw himself into the task. He even formed some crude tools so he could work the garden and make some improvements. He will refine those tools over time."

"I think he enjoyed the challenge of work," agreed Spirit. "He would soon get bored simply wandering around the garden without a purpose in life."

"The most significant new beginning was the creation of the Woman," said Father. "She is a picture of the Bride I am preparing for my Son. She will be drawn from his wounded side. She will be another new creation."

Son nodded in full agreement.

"I watched you carefully, Father, as you put Adam to sleep and pierced his side. Father, did you know that when you lifted your scalpel and pierced Adam's side, I felt the pain? When I saw his blood flowing out, it felt to me like my blood. I had the same sensation before we began creating the Earth when we agreed on The Plan, when I agreed to die so humans can live."

"Brace yourself, Son. The pain you felt today will be multiplied many times over when The Plan is actually implemented."

"I know. But the joy that will follow will be worth it all! Joy for all eternity!"

12

Paradise Lost

While Adam and his companion enjoyed life in the Garden of Eden, Yahweh turned his attention to the Abyss. The fallen angels in the Abyss were complaining bitterly about the darkness. This place was such a stark contrast to their first home in Heaven where everything was light.

Yahweh handed the keys of the Abyss to one of his mighty angels. Satan heard a key turning in the lock and called to the demons to be quiet. For the first time in what felt like an eternity the inhabitants of the Abyss saw a crack of light and eagerly hoped for more. To them that faint beam of light was like a drop of water to someone dying of thirst.

"Satan!" the Holy One called down the shaft of the Abyss. "I am letting you and your rebellious crew out of the Abyss for a short time, not because you deserve it, but to demonstrate to all creatures who will ever be born that I am longsuffering and just. When you were first created, you had the run of the entire universe. But you rebelled against me when you lived in Heaven, so I banished you from my presence there. Now your territory will be limited to the Earth and its atmosphere. Occasionally I will call you to the outer courts of Heaven to report on your doings. When you are called to report to me, you must show up on pain of losing all your freedoms and returning directly to the Abyss. I will put strict limits on what you can and cannot do. Do I make myself clear?"

"Yes, sir."

Paradise Lost

Satan knew that outward rebellion would get him nowhere. He pretended to be submissive, but on the inside he was still rebelling. He did not fool the Holy One.

"As you overstep your bounds, I will limit your territory further. Eventually even the Abyss will be too good for you, and I will throw you into a lake of burning sulfur where you will be tormented day and night for ever and ever."[1]

"Yes, sir."

"Let them out for now," Yahweh instructed the angel with the keys. "We will lock them up again later."

Reluctantly, the angel obeyed. None of Heaven's inhabitants wanted to see Satan and his demons freed from the Abyss.

As soon as the gates of the Abyss were opened, smoke rose from it like the smoke from a gigantic furnace[2] while its inhabitants escaped. Satan and his followers flew as fast and as far away as they could to get away from their prison and from the Holy One. When they reached the outer edge of Earth's atmosphere, they hit an invisible ceiling.

Satan swore as he bumped his head. Miss Folly overheard Satan use the name of Yahweh and taunted him.

"So.... You admit that Yahweh is greater than you are!"

"I do not!" Satan replied. "*I* am the greatest in the universe."

"Why then did you swear using Yahweh's name? Why didn't you swear by your own name, if you are so much greater?"

"Huwawa!"[3] Satan muttered under his breath.

"You did it again," Folly needled him.

Satan turned away without answering. He tried several times to break through the ceiling but eventually gave up. He would not be able

---

[1] Revelation 20:1-10
[2] See Revelation 9:2.
[3] Huwawa is a derisive name for Yahweh used in stories of Nimrod's time. See *By Faith Isaac*, by Elsa Henderson, p. 291, © 2013.

to go higher unless summoned by Yahweh himself to the outer courts of Heaven.[4]

Frustrated by the limits put on his freedom to roam, Satan turned his attention to the Earth below. He was amazed to see that it was even more beautiful than when he had first visited it. For some strange reason its beauty grated on him.

In Heaven Satan had rebelled against the establishment and done it so effectively that he at least won his own kingdom. Now he hoped to become king not just over his corner of the spirit world, but over Yahweh's creation on Earth.

As Satan roamed the Earth, he noticed a number of new creatures not found in the original creation. In the Garden of Eden he was fascinated to see a couple of two-legged ones. Satan watched as Adam and the Woman strolled blissfully hand in hand, naked and unashamed. The Man bore a striking resemblance to the Son, but the Woman . . . ! Wow!

Satan was so wrapped up in his thoughts that he didn't notice Miss Folly was observing him and his reactions to the creatures created in Yahweh's image.

"She's beautiful, isn't she?" Miss Folly commented.

Satan was reluctant to admit that Yahweh had outdone himself in creating such a beautiful creature.

"Even without clothes she is more beautiful than you ever were. Without all those precious stones in settings of gold on your robes,[5] you wouldn't have caught anyone's attention. The angels noticed only the rubies and emeralds and sapphires, not you!"

Miss Folly's words stung, even if they were not altogether true.

"How does it feel to be out of a job?" Miss Folly asked.

"What do you mean?" Satan replied.

"Yahweh created these two to replace you and your gang of rebels. Adam and his wife have been given your job—to rule over Earth,

---

[4] See Job 1:6.
[5] See Ezekiel 28:13.

beginning in Eden. Their mandate is to make the whole Earth like Eden. Yahweh gave them dominion over everything. The fish in the sea. The birds in the air. All the animals. Everything!"

Miss Folly paused.

"And Yahweh gave them the same unspoken mandate as he gave you."

"What is that?" asked Satan.

"To be absolutely loyal to the Holy One."

"I'll spoil Yahweh's dream," Satan replied. "I'll ruin his new creation. The Holy One, being perfect love, is perfectly vulnerable to being deeply hurt. I'll break his heart."

"How?"

When Satan didn't reply, Miss Folly asked again, "How?"

"Shut up! I'm thinking!" Satan retorted. "As long as they are loyal to Yahweh, I know he won't let me touch those two who are made in his image, so I can't strangle them as I would like to do. I will have to find another way to destroy them. I will have to talk them into following me rather than Yahweh. Then I can count on Yahweh's own character—his justice—to destroy them for me and eliminate my rivals."

Satan lapsed into silence, then spoke again.

"I notice that Adam and the woman are inseparable. I will have a greater chance of success if I can get one of them alone— preferably the woman. Adam follows Yahweh around like a puppy dog and does exactly what he says. He is smarter than she is, but not as smart as I am. No one is as clever as I am. Not even Yahweh."

"You are exceptionally clever," admitted Folly, who walked a tight line between flattering Satan and antagonizing him. "You used to be wise. Isn't there something you are forgetting?"

"What is that?"

"You are forgetting what happened when Yahweh threw all of us out of Heaven. Look at you. You're ugly! Everything in Eden is beautiful. If you show yourself to either Adam or the woman, you will scare them away!"

The Plan

"Don't worry," Satan replied in a soothing tone. "I'll get back at Yahweh. I'll figure out something. I will make myself visible to her. She is used to Yahweh's luminescence. She will respond to mine. I will appear to the woman in a form she will like. I will attract her attention and lure her away from Adam."

* * * *

Adam and his wife were strolling along the river that waters the garden of Eden when they noticed a long skinny creature they had never seen before wrapped around the branch of a tree. When the humans approached, the creature wrapped itself around the trunk of the tree and slid down to investigate them.

"Look at its back," Adam said. "It looks like rows of leathery shields all tightly sealed together."

"What a beautiful creature!" the woman exclaimed. "Look at all the pretty colors in its skin as the light strikes it from different angles."

"Look at its eyes!" Adam remarked. "When it blinks, you can see all the colors of the rainbow in its eyelids. They remind me of the colors in the sky at dawn."

"Fascinating!" the woman agreed. "What shall we call it?"

She came up with the name 'dragon,' but Adam wanted to call it 'serpent.' They argued amicably about it for a while, but in the end Adam won. They called it a serpent.

The serpent blinked its eyes and opened its mouth as if smiling, showing lots of white teeth.

"Hello, serpent," Adam said.

The serpent waved its long forked tongue around as if replying. Then it sneezed, and sparkles of light flashed out of its mouth.[6] The humans laughed in delight.

* * * *

---

[6] Serpent details gleaned from Job 41:5, 15-19.

Adam and his wife were working happily in the garden when the woman caught sight of the serpent again. He winked at her and, with a turn of his head, beckoned her to follow. Not bothering to tell Adam where she was going, the woman followed. The serpent wiggled playfully and led her around several trees as she laughed and mimicked his movements. Before she realized it, they were in the centre of the garden. Quickly the serpent climbed the tree of the knowledge of good and evil, pointed to its fruit and spoke to the woman.

"Look at the beautiful fruit!"

"You can talk!" she replied in astonishment. "I didn't know you could talk. No one in the garden can talk except Adam and me."

"Yahweh talks to you. Why shouldn't I?"

The serpent quickly drew her attention away from himself and toward the fruit.

"I bet it's delicious. Have you ever tasted this fruit?"

"No. God told Adam we mustn't eat it."

The serpent replied in silky tones, twisting the truth. "Did God really say, 'You must not eat from any tree in the garden'?"

"Of course not! We may eat from any tree we want. Except one. We must not eat from the tree in the middle of the garden—this one!"

The woman babbled on, enjoying the experience of talking to someone new. She was also confident in her knowledge of what God had said. "God said we mustn't even touch the tree." She paused.

"Lest we die," she added quickly.

The serpent knew it was Adam who had told the woman not to touch the tree, but he didn't correct her. This was the opening he was hoping for. He drew her attention again to the fruit.

"Go ahead. Touch it."

The woman hesitated.

"Touch it. I'm touching it and I'm not dead."

The woman reached out, touched it gingerly, then quickly drew back her hand. Nothing happened. The serpent waited. She touched the fruit again, more confidently this time.

The Plan

"See," the serpent said soothingly. "You didn't die. And you won't die by eating it either. God knows that when you eat it your eyes will be opened, and you will be like a god, knowing good and evil."

"Do you know why God told you not to eat the fruit?" the serpent asked. The woman shook her head. "He didn't want you to become like him, knowing good and evil. He wanted you to be ignorant."

The woman swallowed.

"You want to be wise, don't you?" the serpent continued persuasively. "Don't you want to know the difference between good and evil? Isn't that important to know? Why should God be the only wise one in the universe?"

The woman thought it through. The fruit was good for food and pleasing to the eye. Best of all, it was able to impart wisdom. Wouldn't it be wonderful to be wise? What harm could there be in that?

She reached out, plucked the nearest fruit from the tree, and examined it admiringly.

The serpent watched patiently. He could see the wheels turning in her mind. He knew the temptations that were luring her—the desire to experience physical pleasure, the desire to have the things she saw, and pride in her own wisdom.

Only then did the woman notice that Adam had come looking for her. He had overheard the last part of the conversation.

Adam too was lured by the thought of wisdom, but he knew the consequences of disobedience. Before he could stop his wife, she took a bite. With a smile she offered some to her husband while still savoring the taste of the fruit.

Adam knew the ramifications of her action. She was going to die. If he ate the fruit, he too would die. Now he had to choose. It wasn't about the fruit. It was about the object of his allegiance. Who was more important to him? His wife or Yahweh? He had to choose between the Creator and the creature he had created. He had to choose between the Giver and the gift.

Adam could not imagine life without the beautiful wife he had learned to love so deeply. That was more real to him than the Voice that walked with him through the garden. So Adam took a bite.

It tasted good. He took another bite. So did his wife. But before the fruit was finished, Adam's eyes were opened. He looked at his wife and knew she was experiencing the same thing. They were full of fear and shame—emotions that were new to them. They were naked!

What could they do? Instinctively they tried to cover themselves with their hands. They hid behind a bush but soon realized they couldn't stay there all day. Then they spotted a fig tree with its big leaves. They pulled off some leaves to cover themselves but then realized they needed their hands to do things other than holding the leaves in place.

With clumsy fingers they sewed the leaves into loincloths for themselves. Adam was content with that, but the woman was still uncomfortable. She needed more fig leaves to cover her breasts. Finally, the humans were covered to their satisfaction.

By this time it was late afternoon. For the first time in their short lives Adam and his wife felt uncomfortably cool. When they sat down to rest and figure out how to stay warm, their fig leaf loincloths tore.

While they were trying to repair the damage, they heard the sound of Yahweh walking in the garden. The pair usually enjoyed this time of day. They usually looked forward to the time when Yahweh walked and talked with them in the garden. They usually ran toward the sound of his voice.

But today was different. They were afraid! Until now they had experienced only love from Yahweh. But they had disobeyed the one and only command the Holy One had given them. And they knew they would be punished.

"Adam, where are you?" The voice that called to him was both strongly compelling and filled with love.

Adam was surprised at the tone of Yahweh's voice—how warm it was. Not harsh. He was expecting to be punished, though he couldn't

The Plan

imagine what that punishment would look like or feel like. So Adam didn't answer the question. Instead he responded to the unspoken question, "Why are you hiding?"

"I heard you in the garden, and I was afraid because I was naked. So I hid."

"Who told you that you were naked? Have you eaten from the tree that I commanded you not to eat from?" The tone of Yahweh's voice was stern but not terrifying.

Trying to deflect blame from himself, Adam pointed to his wife. For the first time in his life they were not side by side. Their oneness was broken.

"That woman, the one you gave me—*she* gave me some fruit from the tree."

The silence which followed that statement made Adam realize that the Holy One was not satisfied with his reply. He needed to own his guilt.

"And I ate it," he admitted reluctantly, knowing that Yahweh already knew the truth.

Then Yahweh addressed the woman. "What is this you have done?"

She turned and pointed to the serpent, who was hoping to watch Yahweh strike the pair dead.

"The serpent deceived me."

Yahweh waited for her to own her guilt.

"And I ate," she finally admitted.

The Holy One knew this was the moment they had dreaded ever since they had conceived the idea of creating creatures with choice. This happened because innocence is not holiness. The angels were created innocent, but they had to choose to love and obey their Creator. A third of them made the wrong choice. So too these new creatures, made in the image of their Creator, were created innocent but not holy. Their innocence was lost before it could mature into holiness. Plan B would have to be put into effect.

Satan, wearing the costume of a serpent, turned and laughed at Yahweh. In his mind he had succeeded. He had forced Yahweh to destroy his own masterpiece.

But Satan did not know about Plan B. He and his demons had been locked in the Abyss when the Creator remade Earth and the heavens. The fallen angels were not there to watch when the Creator wrote Plan B in the stars and explained it all to the holy angels. The fallen angels were not part of the chorus that sang for joy at the end of Day Four.

Yahweh turned his attention to the serpent, seeing right through him to the evil one wearing the costume.

"Because you have done this, you are cursed. Cursed more than all animals, domestic and wild. Cursed to slink on your belly and eat dirt all your life."

Then the Holy One gave Satan a hint of what was to come, though he did not lay out Plan B in detail.

"I'm declaring war between you and the woman, between her Seed and yours. He will crush your head, and you will bruise his heel."

The serpent quickly slithered out of sight. Satan was left without a costume. Satan had no idea what Yahweh meant, but he realized he was losing the war. He hastily left the garden.

Turning to the woman, Yahweh said, "I will greatly increase your pain and your labor when you give birth to children. Your desire will be contrary to your husband. You will be torn between wanting to please him and wanting to control him, but he will lord it over you."

Yahweh saved the last rebuke for Adam.

"Because you listened to your wife and ate from the tree whose fruit I commanded you not to eat, the ground is cursed because of you. All your life you will struggle to scratch a living from it. The ground will sprout thorns and thistles and weeds. You'll get your food the hard way. By planting and tilling and harvesting. By the sweat of your face. You

The Plan

will work hard all your life, then you will return to the ground from which you were made. For you are dust, and to dust you will return."

Yahweh withdrew from the garden and left the pair to digest all that had happened that day. Just as Adam had had to work for a while in order to realize he needed a helpmate, so he and his wife needed time for the consequences of their choice to sink in.

They used to enjoy walking in the garden with Yahweh from late afternoon until sunset. Then they would thank their Creator for the beautiful colors in the sky. Now for the first time since creation they didn't even notice the sky. They were more concerned that the air was growing cooler. Their fig leaves were uncomfortable, kept tearing, and provided no warmth.

Even though the woman was angry at her husband for blaming her for his choice to eat the fruit, she wanted to be close to him, and they needed each other for warmth. They shivered—more from fear than from the night chill; but they were grateful for the covering of darkness. For the first time since creation they didn't sleep well. After a long, restless night, they awoke to the annoying crow of a rooster.

They welcomed the warmth of the rising sun, but the light made them painfully aware of their nakedness. Again they tried to sew leaves together to cover themselves. Each was irritated at the other when the leaves fell apart.

"What's the matter with you, Woman?" Adam blurted out. "Can't you do anything right?

13

Forgiven, But Expelled

"How about a name just for her," the Voice suggested.

Adam was startled at Yahweh's presence. He hadn't heard Him approach.

"You can't call her 'Woman' all her life, especially after you have daughters of your own."

Adam thought for a minute. He decided to call her Eve, meaning 'living.'

Being in Yahweh's presence made Adam and Eve more acutely aware of their nakedness. And they feared death, even though they didn't fully understand what death was.

"You two will die for your disobedience," Father told them, "but you won't die right away. Long before you were created we foresaw that you would disobey, so we came up with a Plan. The penalty for sin is death, but we have provided a remedy. You will produce a descendant who will ultimately restore my vision for Eden and destroy the serpent. There will always be war between your offspring, imagers of me, and the serpent's offspring, imagers of Satan. Some day one of your offspring will win that war. That's what I was referring to when I told the serpent that your Seed will crush his head but he will only strike the Seed's heel. In that statement I gave Satan a hint of what the future holds for him. But because of what your special Seed will do in the future, you can live today. Watch carefully while I show you."

Yahweh showed Adam and Eve what death was. He brought a couple of frolicking lambs over to them.

"These lambs are going to die in your place," Yahweh told them. "If you believe in my Plan, place your hand on the head of a lamb."

Adam lovingly scratched one lamb around its ears and neck then placed his hand solemnly on the lamb's head. His wife did the same.

Yahweh then killed the lambs right before their eyes. Adam and Eve had never seen blood before. They had never seen anything die. They were horrified to see the blood and gore! Their horror continued as God skinned the animals and cut them into pieces.

As Adam and Eve continued to watch, their horror turned into wonder. God turned the bloody hides into beautiful leather garments for them. They were relieved to have their nakedness covered, and happy to discard their inadequate fig leaves.

Then God built a fire. Adam and Eve watched from behind the bushes because they still were not comfortable in his presence. They saw God put pieces of meat on the fire. They had never smelled anything like it. When the meat was cooked, God called them over to join him. Hesitantly they sat down with him and together they ate the meat. Adam and Eve had never eaten meat before. It tasted wonderful, but with each bite they were reminded that a living creature had died so they could be fed and clothed.

As they ate, God talked with them and explained the significance of all he had done. The animals had died as a substitute for Adam and Eve. The death of the animals had satisfied Adam and Eve's felt need to be clothed. But more importantly, God was satisfied with the death penalty which an Anointed One, the Messiah, would pay for them at a future time.

Fellowship with God was restored. Adam and Eve no longer felt uncomfortable in his presence. God went on to explain that the sacrifice was temporary.

"When you sin again, you will need another sacrifice. But some day I will provide a permanent solution and no more sacrifices will be necessary."

"When will that be?" Adam asked.

"Not in your lifetime."

* * * *

Back in Heaven the Holy One discussed the events of the day.

"When we created Adam, we gave him only one command," Father said. "But today I gave him a whole list of new commands. I wrote them into his conscience."

"I saw you do that to Adam and to Eve," Spirit commented. "Now that they are sinners, they have opened the floodgates to countless ways of behaving that are counter to our holy nature."

"Do you think Adam and Eve fully understand what you did for them today, Son?" Father asked.

"They understand enough to experience peace in their souls," Son replied. "And they also know what to do in the future when they fail to obey the laws we have written on their hearts."

"But we have not explained The Plan fully," Spirit added. "We will disclose it in more detail throughout the centuries. We will always make sure that humans know enough to accept our Plan and receive eternal life by faith, but we want to keep Satan guessing so he won't know where to focus his malignant anger. The more he knows, the more dangerous he will be."

"True," Father replied. "But we can always count on our adversary overestimating his strength and being blinded by his pride. He likes to think he is stronger and wiser than we are."

"Speaking of eternal life, we have one more detail to take care of," Son added. "We don't have to worry any more about humans having access to the tree of the knowledge of good and evil. Writing our laws on men's conscience will ensure that they know right from wrong. But Adam must not eat of the tree of life. That would give him and his descendants access to the throne of God and our Holy City. Adam's descendants will be born with a sinful nature. We cannot have sinners

The Plan

in our presence in Heaven. Our Plan is that only holy ones will spend eternity with us."

"And thanks to our beloved Son, *many* humans will be made holy," said Father.

So Yahweh banished Adam from the Garden of Eden. Eve, not wanting to be separated from her husband, followed close behind.

Outside the garden the ground was cursed. Adam and Eve noticed the difference as soon as they exited the garden. They turned around, hoping to at least visit the garden from time to time, but the entrance was blocked. Two fearsome cherubim stood either side of the gate guarding the way to the tree of life. A flaming sword, with no visible hands holding it, flashed back and forth between the cherubim.

Eden would be off limits to human beings until the last detail of The Plan was fully implemented.

14

The Dragon

Satan's kingdom had been watching as their leader, Satan, masqueraded as a serpent. They cheered when Eve bit into the fruit of the tree of the knowledge of good and evil. They cheered even louder when Adam ate of the fruit. They sensed Adam was a greater victory for them than Eve.

The demons watched as the serpent fell to its belly on the ground and slithered out of sight. Moments later Satan appeared in their midst. But now he looked different. Yahweh's curse had affected his appearance.

Satan looked less like he did after he was cast out of Heaven and more like the serpent before it was cursed. But Satan was much bigger.[1]

"Look at his huge head and his glowering visage! He looks so fierce!" the demons remarked. They admired their leader for the qualities that made him formidable.

Many demons were awed by the texture of his skin. It appeared to be impenetrable.

"Who can strip off his outer garment?" one asked. "His back is made of rows of shields joined so closely to one another that no air can come between them."

"Javelins bounce harmlessly off his hide; harpoons ricochet wildly," another said.

"Could you shoot him full of arrows like a pin cushion, or drive harpoons into his huge head?" asked one demon.

---

[1] Details gleaned from Job 41, The Message and ESV translations.

The Plan

"No way!" answered another demon. "Lay your hands on him and you'll remember the battle. You won't do it again!"

"You won't even live to tell the story!" one added. "What hope would you have with such a creature? One look at him would do you in! He's so fierce no one dares to stir him up!"

"Nothing can get through that proud skin," another one said. "It's impenetrable! Even his belly is armor-plated!"

Other demons were fascinated by the serpent's mighty strength and formidable jaws.

"He is all muscle. Look at his neck—how strong it is! Sinewy and lithe, there's not a soft spot in his entire body. Terror dances before him!"

"Who would even dream of putting those jaws into bit and bridle? And who would dare knock at the door of his mouth filled with row upon row of fierce teeth?"

Another demon expressed the same sentiment more vividly, saying, "Who can open the doors of his face? Around his teeth is terror."

When the demons started talking about the serpent's mouth and teeth, Satan gave them a little demonstration. He blinked to show off his colorful eyelids. He sneezed, and light flashed from his nostrils. He exhaled, and smoke poured from his nostrils. He opened his mouth, and fire came out.

One poetic demon put it this way: "He snorts and the world lights up with fire; he blinks and the dawn breaks. Flames of fire stream from his mouth; his breath kindles coals. Smoke erupts from his nostrils like steam from a boiling pot."

The demons continued talking in glowing terms about the serpent.

"Sling stones are like stubble to him. Iron bars are so much straw; bronze weapons are beneath his notice. A battle ax is nothing but a splinter of kindling; clubs are counted as stubble. He laughs at the rattle of javelins; arrows don't even make him blink. To meet him is to dance with death."

Satan overheard his admiring minions and responded with bravado.

"How do you expect to stand up to *me*? Who could confront me and get away with it? Everything under heaven is mine. *I'm* in charge. *I* run this universe!"

The demons clapped in response and continued their praise.

"When he raises himself up, the mighty are afraid. Even angels run for cover. There's nothing on this earth quite like him, not an ounce of fear in *that* creature! He surveys all the high and mighty— and sneers!"

Satan acknowledged their praise, then said, "Serpent is too tame a name for me. I am the Dragon!"

The holy angels also were watching the historic moment when the first pair disobeyed and were expelled from the Garden. And they saw the transformation of the one they used to call Lucifer.

They gasped at Satan's audacity when he claimed to be in charge of the universe. Such a claim was blasphemy. They snorted in disdain when demons claimed angels would run for cover at the sight of the dragon.

And the angels had a few comments of their own.

"His heart is hard as a stone. His pride is invincible; nothing can make a dent in that pride. He thinks he is king of the universe, but he is not. He is king only over all the sons of pride."

15

The Plan Told and Retold

Centuries came and went. Though Yahweh had written the Plan in great detail in the stars, that wasn't enough. Most people couldn't read that story by themselves. It had to be read to them—the way Yahweh read it to the angels and later to Adam and Eve. Then each generation had to read it to the next.

So Yahweh wrote the Plan in history, telling it over and over again in different ways through people's stories. With every telling, the Plan was revealed in more detail and more clarity.

Adam's original task was to make the entire world like Eden, like God's home. When Yahweh commanded Adam to multiply, steward the creation and govern on God's behalf, his goal was that mankind harness Earth's gifts for the betterment of fellow human imagers, all the while enjoying the presence of God.[1]

The story of Adam and Eve revealed that to sin was not the end of the story. God was committed to preserving what he had begun. God still desired fellowship with man, and he was merciful. Adam and Eve sinned and had to hide from God, yet death could be avoided. Fellowship could be restored as it was when God killed a lamb to clothe their nakedness.

Meanwhile the dragon did his best to win the creatures made in Yahweh's image over to his team. Those who were most committed to following the dragon used violence to spread their influence. To many

---

[1] *The Unseen Realm*, op.cit., 59.

The Plan Told and Retold

people they seemed larger than life—giants. People who listened to Folly even considered them to be heroes.

The majority of mankind ended up in slavery to the dragon, but there were always some who were faithful to Yahweh.

The story of Noah and the ark showed that sin must be punished but there is a way of escape. Noah's family escaped God's judgment against sin by building an ark. By faith they entered it and lived.

Satan and his demons clapped when Yahweh covered the earth with floodwaters and destroyed all living creatures—humans and animals. But then they were disappointed to see an ark floating alone on the waters. Yahweh hadn't destroyed them all.

From the contents of that ark Yahweh started again. The first thing Noah did when he and his family came out of the ark was build an altar, sacrifice some of the animals, and worship Yahweh, saying, "God is good."

Yahweh smelled the sacrifice and was pleased with both the aroma and Noah's heart of worship.

"Noah has started well," Lady Wisdom said. "Let's pray that he succeeds in teaching his descendants to worship Yahweh as well."

The angels sang for joy when Yahweh made a covenant with Noah and promised never again to destroy the earth with a flood. They clapped when Yahweh put a rainbow in the sky to remind mankind of his promise.

The dragon gritted his teeth and went back to his work of sabotaging Yahweh's creation. He noticed the rainbow and determined to find a way to use it against Yahweh.

A few generations after the flood, people who rebelled against Yahweh invented other gods to worship. People in Babylon aspired to make a name for themselves and become famous by building a tower that reached to the heavens. Using brick instead of stone and tar instead of mortar, they constructed a massive ziggurat with a temple to their gods at the top. From the bottom it looked like a staircase climbing up into the clouds.

But Yahweh thwarted their plan. Before they were finished, Yahweh confused their language so the builders could not understand each other. Construction of the tower was stopped dead in its tracks. They called it Babel, meaning 'confused,' because Yahweh had confused their language.

To make sure people would not settle all in one place, Yahweh confused not just Babylon's language but the language of the whole world. In doing so, Yahweh slowed the progression of evil. With many languages as barriers to communication, it was harder for people to conspire together against the Holy One. They scattered over all the earth.

Even though many chose to go their own way rather than follow Yahweh, His eternal Plan was not thwarted. As Noah's family grew into many nations and spread out over the earth, Yahweh began anew the process of restoring Eden to Earth by choosing one man, Abraham, through whom to bless all peoples on earth. Yahweh's purpose was that Abraham's nation would be his imagers to represent him and carry out his wishes.

Yahweh blessed Abraham so mightily that he and his nephew Lot had to part company. Lot chose to move toward Sodom, where the pastures were lush. Though the inhabitants of Sodom were very wicked, Lot soon moved inside the city. While he was there, the Babylonians declared war against Sodom and Gomorrah, plundered the cities and took Lot and others as hostages. When Abraham heard about it, he sprang to Lot's rescue.[2]

The dragon took note when Abraham, with his personal army of 318 men, pursued the Babylonians, attacked them during the night and sent them running for home. Such a victory could not have been won by such a small army unless Yahweh was on Abraham's side fighting for him.

---

[2] Read the story in Genesis 14.

So the dragon chose bribery as his strategy to sidetrack Abraham from trusting in Yahweh. He used the king of Sodom as his agent.

As Abraham returned from rescuing Lot, he passed by Salem. There he was met by Melchizedek king of Salem, who blessed him and declared that God Most High had delivered Abraham's enemies into his hand. Melchizedek's voice rang with the authority of Yahweh himself.

Bera king of Sodom was in the background impatiently waiting to escort his people back to Sodom while Melchizedek was blessing Abraham and accepting his tithe.

"Give me the people," Bera said to Abraham, "and keep the goods for yourself."

Something about Bera irritated Abraham. He had just freely given his tithe to Melchizedek, and now the king of Sodom was offering him wealth—all the goods that had been retrieved from the Babylonians. The contrast bothered him. Abraham's thoughts flashed to the story of the serpent tempting Eve in the Garden of Eden. Bera was nothing more than a serpent wearing a robe and a crown. In Abraham's imagination Bera seemed to slither and hiss.

But Abraham had anticipated the lure of wealth. He knew where his wealth came from, and it was not from the king of Sodom. He was ready with an answer.

"I have raised my hand to Yahweh, God Most High, Creator of heaven and earth," Abraham told Bera. "I have taken an oath that I will accept nothing belonging to you, not even a thread or the thong of a sandal, so that you will never be able to say, 'I made Abram rich.' I will accept nothing but what my men have eaten and the share that belongs to Mamre and his brothers who went with me. Let them have their share."

Bera looked as if he had been slapped in the face. He turned without a word and distributed to Mamre and his brothers their fair share of the spoils. Then he ushered his people away without a backward glance.

The dragon lost that battle, but the city of Salem stuck in his mind. He would remember that place.

The Plan

Lady Wisdom also took note. "Watch that city," she whispered to a nearby angel. "That's where the Holy One buried the cornerstone.[3] That's where the foundation of The Plan was laid. Did you notice the name of that city's king? Melchizedek. King of Righteousness. When the Son sets up his kingdom, he will rule from there."

Abraham continued to put his faith in Yahweh, believing His promises against all odds. And Yahweh counted it to him as righteousness.

The story of Abraham and Isaac told how The Plan would work. Isaac was doomed to die when God told Abraham to sacrifice him, but God intervened and provided a lamb to die in Isaac's place. This foreshadowed the Son dying to save mankind from death.

Isaac and his wife Rebekah eventually had twin sons, Esau and Jacob. Yahweh told Rebekah, "The older will serve the younger." She understood that to mean that her younger son Jacob was Yahweh's choice for the firstborn, but she couldn't convince Isaac of that. Consequently, Jacob tried to figure out how to be recognized as the firstborn. He bought the firstborn rights from Esau in a moment of his brother's weakness, but he had to deceive his blind father in order to get the firstborn blessing.

Jacob's relationship with Yahweh was rocky for many decades, but eventually Jacob gained the mastery over his deceitful conniving tendencies. He wrestled with God—and prevailed! And God renamed him Israel. His walk with Yahweh after that was somewhat up and down, but in the important matters he shone.

When Jacob was in Egypt on his deathbed blessing his sons, Yahweh used him to drop another hint about The Plan.

> "The *scepter* will never depart from Judah,
> nor the ruler's staff from between his feet,
> until his *Seed* comes and the people obey him."[4]

---

[3] Isaiah 28:16
[4] See Genesis 49:10, NRSV, GW and YLT.

The Plan Told and Retold

The dragon was listening and took note. Yahweh was talking in riddles. Satan had been warned about the woman's Seed in the Garden. Now there was mention of him again. And it appeared that the Seed would be holding a Scepter. The dragon would keep an eye on Judah's descendants, especially any of them who became kings.

In Egypt Jacob's descendants grew to be a nation of more than two million, but they became slaves of Pharaoh. Then Yahweh delivered them in spectacular fashion.

First He had to get the attention of Moses and show him who He was. In the middle of the desert Moses saw a bush on fire that didn't burn up. Curious, Moses went for a closer look. Yahweh called to Moses from the bush and introduced himself.

"I am the God of your father, the God of Abraham, the God of Isaac and the God of Jacob. I have seen the misery of my people in Egypt and have come to rescue them. I'm sending you to Pharaoh to bring my people out of Egypt."

When Moses and his brother Aaron went to Pharaoh and announced, "Yahweh, the God of Israel, says, 'Let my people go,'" Pharaoh responded, "Who is Yahweh? We have lots of gods in Egypt but none by that name."

It would not be long until Pharaoh and the whole world took notice of the name of Yahweh. Pharaoh learned it the hard way. Yahweh sent ten plagues to persuade Pharaoh to let the Israelites go.

Before the final plague Moses instructed the Israelites to kill a lamb and paint their doorframes, top and sides, with its blood. That night the death angel went throughout the land and killed every firstborn male in every house that did not have the blood of a lamb on its doorframes. Yahweh said, "When I see the blood, I will pass over you."

Soon there was wailing in all the Egyptian households. When Pharaoh found his own firstborn son dead, he learned that Yahweh was greater than all other gods. Pharaoh couldn't get rid of the Israelites fast enough.

The Plan

A few days later Pharaoh changed his mind and sent his army to retrieve his former slaves. Yahweh responded by drowning all his horsemen and charioteers in the Red Sea.

That story, the story of Passover, revealed The Plan in more detail than previous stories of men of faith. It revealed the necessity of individuals putting their faith in the Plan by applying the blood to the doorposts of their hearts.

Yahweh's plan was that Israel develop into an army of messengers who would make The Plan known to the whole world. The dragon did his best to make sure that did not happen by attempting to destroy the young nation. He incited the Amalekites to attack the Israelites who, being fresh out of slavery, were untrained for battle.

But the dragon hadn't counted on Moses. Or Yahweh.

Moses climbed a hill to watch the battle being fought below and held the staff of God high in his hands as he prayed for victory for his fledgling nation. As long as Moses held up the staff of God, the Israelites were winning; but whenever he lowered his hands, the Amalekites were winning. When Moses' hands grew tired, Moses' brother Aaron and his assistant Hur brought a stone for him to sit on. Then they held up Moses' hands for the rest of the day.

By sunset the battle was over. Israel won; the Amalekites were defeated. With Yahweh fighting for them, the untrained former slaves overcame the Amalekites.

Not only was the dragon defeated, but Yahweh declared war on the Amalekites. Yahweh promised, "I will completely erase the memory of the Amalekites from under heaven."[5]

Yahweh continued to reveal the Plan in a variety of ways. Before the Israelites embarked on their long journey from Egypt to the promised land of Canaan, Yahweh spoke from Mount Sinai and gave

---

[5] Exodus 17:14, NIV

The Plan Told and Retold

his people instructions as to how to live to demonstrate that they were in relationship with the Holy One.

Yahweh laid out for the Israelites an entire system of worship. He instructed Moses in minute detail how to set up a Tabernacle, a Tent of Meeting, which was a place where Yahweh could meet with his people. Every detail of the worship system pointed to the Plan.

The tent was made of fine linen beautifully embroidered with cherubim in colorful yarns of blue, purple and scarlet. That was covered with a curtain made of goat's hair. And that was covered with a layer of ram's skins dyed red. For protection from the elements, the entire tent had an outer covering of durable leather. The layer of red ram's skins represented the blood of the Messiah, which would cover the sins of everyone who believed in the Plan.

The tent was subdivided into the Holy Place and the Most Holy Place, which was entered only once a year and only by the high priest. The only furniture in the Most Holy Place was the Ark of the Covenant. This was a chest made of acacia wood and overlaid with pure gold. The ark represented Yahweh's presence. Its lid was called the "mercy seat." There sinful people could acknowledge Yahweh as King and find mercy.

Though they didn't realize it at the time, acacia was the tree from which the crown of thorns would be made when the Son came to die on the cross. The acacia wood in the furniture signified that all human beings contribute to nailing the Son to the cross. Being overlaid with gold showed that all people are incredibly valuable in Yahweh's sight and that those who believe in the Plan will have their sins covered.

Inside the ark were the two stone tablets on which Yahweh had written the words he spoke to his people from Mount Sinai. These instructions were kept inside the ark to represent the fact that Yahweh wanted his people to live this way—with the Law written not just in stone but on their hearts.

The other pieces of furniture in the Tent of Meeting—the table on which bread was kept and the altar of incense—were also made of acacia wood and overlaid with gold. The only piece of furniture not made of acacia wood was the lampstand, which represented the Son himself. The Son was sinless. The lampstand was made of solid gold.

The altar of burnt offering outside the Tent of Meeting was also made of acacia wood, and it was overlaid with bronze. The sacrifices offered on the altar all pointed in some way to a future perfect Sacrifice who would die as a substitute for sinful man. The offerings enabled people to have a personal relationship with God.

The system of worship at the Tent of Meeting included an annual calendar of feasts which told the story of the Plan.

The first feast, called Passover, was held in the spring. It told two stories.

First, it rehearsed the story of Israel's deliverance from slavery in Egypt. Before the Israelites were delivered from slavery, they killed a lamb and sprinkled its blood on their doorposts. The Death Angel came during the night to kill every firstborn in Egypt, but he passed over the homes where he saw the blood on the doorposts.

Secondly, Passover foretold a future story—the story of the Plan. In the future a sinless Lamb of God would die to satisfy the death penalty which Adam brought on mankind because of his sin.

The Passover feast remembered and relived the Exodus. It also introduced the Feast of Unleavened Bread. This was a week in which no yeast was consumed. Leaven or yeast permeates the whole batch of dough just as surely and thoroughly as sin permeates the whole body, soul and spirit. The unleavened bread represented the holy life which is made possible by believing in the Plan.

During the Passover week on the day after the Sabbath, a sheaf of the first grain from the spring barley harvest was waved before Yahweh at the Tent of Meeting. This foreshadowed the resurrection of the Lamb of God on the first day of the week, the Lord's day.

The next feast, Pentecost, revealed that Yahweh's Plan was in essence a marriage relationship. Pentecost celebrated Yahweh's marriage as both a past and a future event.

The past event was the betrothal of Yahweh to the nation of Israel at Mount Sinai. On that day Yahweh spoke to Moses on Mount Sinai and made a betrothal contract with Israel. The terms of the contract were written in the Book of the Covenant, and a condensed version, the Ten Commandments spoken from Mount Sinai, were written on tablets of stone. When Moses read the contract to the people, they all responded, "I do. We will do everything Yahweh has said. We will obey."[6]

The future event celebrated by Pentecost was the betrothal of the Son to the Church, the Bride of Christ, though this would remain a mystery until it was fulfilled centuries later.

The spring feasts celebrated the first coming of the Messiah. The fall calendar contained three more feasts, which celebrated the second coming of the Messiah.

On the first day of the seventh month of the Jewish calendar, the Feast of Trumpets marked the beginning of the final feast season. The trumpets called the people to hold a sacred assembly and rest from their work. This feast represents the trumpet call which will summon the Bride to her marriage with the Son and which will usher in the events of the last days.

Next, on the tenth day of the seventh month, was the Day of Atonement. This was a day for people to mourn and fast for their sins. The day was instituted after two of Aaron's sons were struck dead by Yahweh for disregarding the instructions about the use of holy fire. The new Tent of Meeting had been inspected and Aaron's sons had just been ordained. Yahweh had accepted Aaron's offerings in spectacular fashion, by igniting the sacrifice with fire from his presence—from the pillar of cloud and fire.

---

[6] Exodus 24:3-4, 7

The Plan

But Aaron's sons wanted more fireworks. So they added to the ceremony by putting "strange fire" in their censers, fire not ignited by Yahweh. So Yahweh immediately struck them dead.

Aaron's sons were a reminder that everybody is guilty from time to time of not giving Yahweh his due respect. We forget that he is perfectly holy and we are perfectly sinful.

The Day of Atonement was another day and another way to remind us of the Plan. On that day two goats were presented to Yahweh for sacrifice. The high priest would cast lots for the goats— one lot for Yahweh and one lot for the scapegoat—choosing one goat to represent the death of the Sinless One and one goat to represent sin being taken far away, to be remembered no more.

The high priest would sacrifice the first goat in the usual way and sprinkle its blood on the mercy seat. He would then lay both hands on the scapegoat, and confess all the sins of the people over it. The scapegoat would then be led out into the desert and set free, carrying all the sins of the people with it.

The two goats are a picture of the Plan. Part of the Plan is that the Son pays for sin, satisfying the wrath of God. The Son also the scapegoat carries away our sins to be heard of no more. Our sins are lost in the desert! So far has he removed our transgressions from us! As far as the east is from the west! So that we can escape the death penalty.

The Plan was so important that it was told in the spring through the Passover story and retold in the fall on the Day of Atonement through the scapegoat story.

The final aspect of the Plan was represented in the final annual feast, the Feast of Booths or Tabernacles. Like Passover week, this was a seven-day feast, but it was not to be celebrated by the Israelites immediately. It was not to be celebrated until their days of wandering in the desert were over. When Israel reached the Promised Land, they could finally plant crops and reap a harvest. Then they would bring thank offerings from their harvests and rejoice before Yahweh for seven days. They would also live in booths or temporary shelters for seven days as a reminder of the days when they lived in tents.

But Yahweh didn't want the Israelites to think that living in the Promised Land was the end of the story. The Promised Land itself was a picture of a greater rest than they were experiencing after their desert wanderings. Yahweh wanted his people to look forward to eternal rest in a future place that he was preparing for them—a City with foundations, whose architect and builder is God.[7]

The worship system was designed to keep Yahweh's people in close relationship with him, but the dragon was determined to keep that from happening. The dragon knew he couldn't destroy Yahweh's people, but he also knew Yahweh was holy and would not tolerate evil. After all, it was precisely because people were so wicked that Yahweh had destroyed them all with a flood.

So the dragon incited Israelites to make a golden calf and worship it while Moses was away on the mountain. At Yahweh's command three thousand of those people were killed, and the rest of the idolaters were struck with a plague.[8]

The dragon incited two of Aaron's sons to offer unauthorized fire following the dedication of the Tabernacle, and Yahweh consumed them with fire.[9]

The dragon incited the people to complain about their hardships, and Yahweh consumed the complainers with fire.[10]

The dragon incited the people to complain about lack of variety in their food, and Yahweh consumed the complainers with a severe plague.[11]

---

[7] Hebrews 11:10
[8] Exodus 32:27-28, 35
[9] Leviticus 10:1-2
[10] Numbers 11:1-3
[11] Numbers 11:4-34

The Plan

When it came time to enter the Promised Land, the dragon incited ten of the twelve spies to convince the Israelites that the people of Canaan were unconquerable. So the people grumbled against Moses and Aaron and rebelled against entering the land. They feared the inhabitants of the land and doubted that Yahweh would help them defeat their enemies.

So Yahweh struck down the ten spies who had explored the land and brought back a bad report. He also promised, "All you grumbling Israelites will die in the desert—every one of you twenty years old or more who grumbled against Me. For forty years you will wander in the wilderness until all of you have died. Not one of you will enter the land."[12]

The dragon and his demons cheered at the pronouncement.

Just as the forty years were drawing to a close and the Israelites were about to enter the Promised Land, Yahweh dropped another hint about the Plan. The prophet Balaam uttered an oracle:

> "I see him, but not now;
> I behold him, but not near.
> A *star* shall come out of Jacob;
> And a *scepter* shall rise out of Israel."[13]

First, a Seed. Then a Scepter. Now a Star was added to the picture. But the Seed still could not be identified. All the dragon knew was that the time was future.

In the meantime he would do his best to undermine Yahweh's control of the city of Salem.

---

[12] Numbers 14:27-35, 37
[13] Numbers 24:16, 17.

16

The Battle for Jerusalem

Shortly after the Israelites crossed the river Jordan and destroyed Jericho, a confederation of five kings went to war against the Israelites. Yahweh fought for Israel in a famous battle in which the sun stood still for a whole day and Yahweh hurled down large hailstones on Israel's enemies. More of Israel's enemies were killed by the hailstones than by the sword.

As the Israelites obeyed Yahweh's command to possess the land, they went from city to city, putting everyone to the sword and leaving no survivors. During this campaign the Israelites conquered Salem, which by then was named Jerusalem.

They left no survivors, but Jerusalem did not stay empty for long. Its location was strategic and Jerusalem would rise from the ruins. The Jebusites moved in and renamed their city Jebus.

Jerusalem, which was on the border between Judah and Benjamin, was allotted first to Judah. When Judah failed to possess it, it was allotted to Benjamin.[1] But Benjamin did not succeed in conquering it.

After Joshua died, the men of Judah once again captured Jerusalem, killed its inhabitants with the sword and set the city on fire.[2] Yet Judah still did not possess the city. They just burned it and left, providing the Benjamites the opportunity to claim the city.

But Benjamin did not do so. They allowed Jerusalem to be re-occupied by the Jebusites.

---

[1] Joshua 18:21, 28
[2] Judges 1:3, 8

The Plan

The dragon was pleased to control a city right in the heart of Israel.

"What is the matter with Yahweh's people?" Lady Wisdom asked out loud to no one in particular. "Don't they see how strategic Jerusalem is? Especially the fortress of Zion. Its elevation, 2550 feet above sea level and 3800 feet above the Dead Sea, makes it a formidable natural fortress. The Jebusites boast that it can be defended by the blind and the lame."[3]

"Be patient," Father replied. "I have chosen Zion for my dwelling place on earth.[4] Jerusalem is waiting to be conquered by someone who loves it as much as I do. A man after my own heart. A man who understands that I have laid my cornerstone there."[5]

* * * *

Another generation grew up who knew neither Yahweh nor what he had done for Israel. For well over three hundred years Israel was ruled by judges. Israel had no king, and all the people did whatever seemed right in their own eyes, and Jerusalem was still Jebus, occupied by the Jebusites and avoided by the Israelites.[6]

Toward the end of this period a significant but tragic event occurred.

A Levite and his concubine were returning from Bethlehem to their home in the hill country of Ephraim. On the way home they debated whether to overnight in Jebus (later known as Jerusalem) or in Gibeah, which was a few miles further away.[7] Jebus was considered to be the more dangerous choice, being an "alien city" occupied by the Jebusites, so they stayed in Gibeah of Benjamin.

As it turns out, Gibeah was Israel's version of Sodom and Gomorrah. An old man, reminiscent of Lot, warned the Levite and his party not to

---

[3] 2 Samuel 5:6
[4] Psalm 132:13
[5] Isaiah 28:16
[6] Judges 2:10; 21:25; 19:10
[7] Judges 19:10-15

stay in the city square and invited them to stay at his house. During the night, wicked men pounded on the door asking the old man to turn the Levite over to them for their sport. Instead, the old man sent out the concubine. She ended up being brutally raped and killed.

All Israel was horrified and demanded that the Benjamites surrender the criminals to justice. The tribe of Benjamin refused, so Israel went to war against them. Benjamin lost, and the tribe was all but wiped out. Only six hundred men of fighting age survived, and only because they fled into the desert and hid for four months. Eventually wives were found for those 600 men so the tribe would not die out.

The angels in heaven wept at the wickedness in Gibeah. They wept again when the tribe of Benjamin protected the criminals rather than surrendering them to justice. Their sorrow knew no bounds when the rest of Israel, after defeating Benjamin in battle, went back to Benjamin, put all the towns to the sword—people and animals— and set the towns on fire. Then, slowly, sorrow mingled with praise as the angels acknowledged Yahweh was just.

"You are just, O Holy One," they sang, "who is and who always was, because you have brought these judgments."

"Yes, Lord God Almighty," Lady Wisdom echoed, "your judgments are true and just."[8]

Silence reigned for a while in heaven as the angels processed what they had witnessed. Then Lady Wisdom had a question.

"Why did Yahweh mention Jerusalem in his record? The Levite and his concubine chose not to go to Jebus, so why is Jerusalem even mentioned?"

The angels considered the facts, trying to understand Yahweh's motive. One angel had a further question.

"The Jebusites are Canaanites. God has those evil people targeted for destruction. Why did the Holy One not make the evil deed happen in Jebus and wipe the Jebusites out now?"

---

[8] Revelation 16:5, 7

The Plan

For a while there was silence as the angels struggled with their questions. Finally Lady Wisdom spoke.

"Yahweh does not make anyone do evil, nor does he decide where evil will happen. But there may be something deeper here. Father's name for Jebus is Jerusalem. Yahweh laid the cornerstone there in Zion. He has designs on Jerusalem. One day it will be his possession, his Holy City. Maybe he wants no such evil in Jerusalem's history. Maybe he just now protected Jerusalem from the stain of Sodom and Gomorrah."

17

The Battle for the Ark

The nation of Israel hit a spiritual low point when Eli was high priest. Corruption was rampant at the very top of the priesthood. Eli's sons were wicked men. They had no regard for Yahweh. They broke the rules that Yahweh had given regarding how to make a sacrifice, and they slept with the women who served at the entrance to the Tabernacle.

The Israelites picked a fight with the Philistines, expecting that Yahweh would give them the victory. When he didn't, the people decided that they needed the Ark of the Covenant with them in battle as a good luck charm.

This was no ordinary ark. It was called by the Name, the Name the dragon hated, the Name of Yahweh Almighty, who is enthroned between the cherubim on the lid of the Ark.[1] When the Israelites saw Eli's sons bring the Ark of Yahweh's Covenant into their war camp, they shouted so loud that the ground shook.

Hearing the uproar, the Philistines asked what the shouting was about. When they learned that the Ark of Yahweh had come into the camp, the Philistines were afraid. They had heard stories of what Yahweh had done to Israel's enemies.

"Woe to us!" they cried. "Who will deliver us from the hand of these mighty gods? They are the gods who struck the Egyptians with all kinds of plagues. Fight for your lives, or you will end up being slaves to the Hebrews."

---

[1] 2 Samuel 6:2

The Plan

But Yahweh refused to be used by people who did not honor him in their hearts. By the end of the day the Philistines had defeated the Israelites, Eli's sons were dead, and Yahweh's Ark was captured.

The dragon cheered.

The Philistines soon discovered that the Ark was too hot to handle. Every city where they took it, the idols fell on their faces before it and the people developed tumors.

The Philistines determined to send the Ark back to Israel. But how?

They put the Ark on a cart, but no one was willing to drive the cart. Nobody wanted to die!

After some discussion they wondered, "What would happen if we separated two cows from their calves and hitched them to the cart?"

They did so and sat back to watch. The cows didn't want to leave their calves, but they turned toward Beth Shemesh and pulled the cart, mooing all the way. Obviously Yahweh himself was driving them!

At Beth Shemesh the people were glad to see the Ark. But many still had not learned to treat Yahweh with respect. Seventy curious men looked into the Ark, which not even the high priest dared look into, and God struck them dead.

The people got the message: Yahweh is holy. He must be treated with respect.

"Who can stand in the presence of Yahweh, this holy God?" they asked. "And where will we take the Ark from here?"

Normally the Ark would have been returned to the Tabernacle in Shiloh. But the Philistines had trashed the town of Shiloh, and the whereabouts of the Tabernacle was unknown. Nobody in Beth Shemesh dared to keep the Ark. The town was reeling from the deaths of its seventy curiosity seekers. So messengers went to the nearest town, Kiriath Jearim. There they found a man—Abinadab, a non-Levite!—willing to house the Ark for safekeeping.

And there the Ark stayed in obscurity for most of a century.

The capture of the Ark jolted the Israelites into reality. They realized that the death of Eli and his wicked sons was Yahweh's judgment for the sin Eli knew about but did nothing to stop. With Eli and his sons all dead, who would be the next priest?

Samuel was not a descendant of Aaron, the family from which priests were drawn. He wasn't even a Levite. But he was from the tribe of Ephraim, where the Tabernacle had been located ever since the Israelites conquered Canaan. Samuel had grown up in the Tabernacle, ministered alongside Eli, and studied the Word of God. And Yahweh obviously was with Samuel. All Israel from Dan to Beersheba recognized Samuel as a prophet of Yahweh.

After the Ark was captured and returned to Israel, and after seventy men were struck dead for treating the Ark as a curiosity item rather than as the earthly throne of their holy God, the people of Israel realized that Eli and his sons were not the only ones who had sinned. They started to mourn for their own sins and seek after Yahweh. For spiritual leadership they turned to Samuel, and he helped them repent.

"If you are returning to Yahweh with all your hearts," he said, "then rid yourselves of your idols, commit yourselves to Yahweh, and serve him only."[2]

Samuel called them to assemble at Mizpah and fast and confess their sins. And he promised to pray for them.

The dragon decided it was time to intervene. He had to put a stop to people fasting and confessing their sins.

While Samuel was offering a sacrifice, the Philistines came to attack.

"Don't stop crying out to Yahweh for us," the people cried out to Samuel. "Don't just pray that we will repent and serve Yahweh only. Pray that he will rescue us from the hand of the Philistines."

So Samuel prayed to Yahweh on Israel's behalf, and Yahweh answered. He thundered against the Philistines, throwing them into a

---

[2] 1 Samuel 7:3

The Plan

panic. The men of Israel then chased their enemies, slaughtering them as they ran.

The Philistines learned not to mess with Samuel and his God. They didn't succeed against Israel while Samuel was in charge. The dragon would have to wait for a better opportunity.

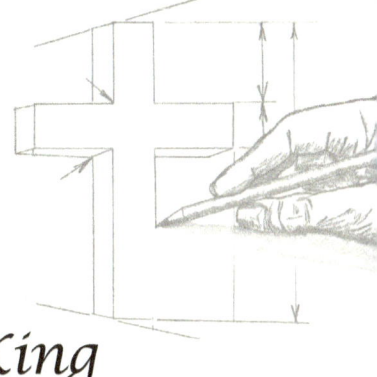

18

Israel's First King

The dragon's opportunity came when Samuel was old. He appointed his two sons as judges to replace himself, but his sons did not walk in his ways. They accepted bribes and perverted justice— not qualities you would want in a judge. At the same time Nahash king of the Ammonites was moving against Israel's eastern border and threatening to attack.[1]

So the elders of Israel asked Samuel to appoint a king.

Samuel was displeased. He thought the people were rejecting him. But Yahweh said otherwise.

"It is not you they have rejected as king, but me. Listen to them and give them a king."

* * * *

Yahweh could work this into his long range plan. At some point in history he wanted his people to possess Jerusalem. He also wanted the whole nation of Israel to be ruled by a king much like Salem's original king, the King of Righteousness. A king who would bring the Ark of the Covenant, Yahweh's earthly throne, to the nation's capital. A king who would lead his people to worship Him.

But first Yahweh had to warn them solemnly that a king might not make them happy.

---

[1] 1 Samuel 8:1-3 and 12:12

The Plan

"We must reclaim Jerusalem," Son said, "and put a righteous king on the throne there. And we must bring back our earthly throne, the Ark of the Covenant."

"But not immediately," Father cautioned. "We must show our people what happens if the wrong kind of king is on the throne."

* * * *

Father, Son and Spirit did some brainstorming in the throne room of Heaven.

"Whom shall we choose to be king?"

"Let's give Israel the king they think they want."

"He must be wealthy. That influences people."

"How about handsome?"

"Yes. And he must be tall."

"Do we have such a person in Israel?"

"I know just the one! Saul is the tallest man in Israel. He is head and shoulders taller than anyone else. He is also the best-looking man in Israel. And his father Kish is wealthy and influential."

"Sounds perfect! Does he have any faults?"

"He's rather timid."

"We can help him with that."

"What tribe is he from?"

"Benjamin."

"What town?"

"Gibeah."

"Uh oh. That sounds like bad news. In the time of the judges Gibeah was like Sodom and Gomorrah. And the Benjamites went to war to protect the men of Gibeah from justice. We almost wiped out that whole tribe because they were so wicked."

"But the survivors learned their lesson. Most of them are upright."

"How about Saul? Does he have a heart for God?"

"Well, that's where he falls short. Even though Saul lives in Gibeah only two or three miles from Samuel's home town of Ramah, Saul has never been to Ramah or met Samuel."

"Nor has he been to the worship center at Gibeah of God[2] just eight miles north of Gibeah of Saul. Prophets go through Saul's town all the time on their way to and from the Hill of God."

"Saul has never shown any curiosity about the prophets or about what goes on at the Hill of God. Is he really a good choice?"

"For our long range purposes, yes."

"So we agree that Saul is our choice for king?"

"Yes."

"A king will have to be anointed by Samuel to show the people that he is our choice. How will we introduce Saul to Samuel?"

"Saul's father Kish owns a lot of livestock," said Father. "I will send some of his donkeys astray. The donkeys know Me better than Saul does; they will go where I send them. Kish will send Saul and one of his servants to look for them, and the donkeys will lead them to Samuel in Ramah."

* * * *

Saul and the servant searched all throughout the hill of country of Ephraim without finding the donkeys. Finally they ended up in Ramah, which the servant recognized as being the home of a seer.

"Let's ask the man of God," he suggested. "Perhaps he will tell us where to find the donkeys."

Some girls in town pointed them in the right direction, and they found Samuel, who was expecting them.

"I am the seer," Samuel said. "Go up ahead of me to the high place where I will be sacrificing. Then stay and eat with me. As for the donkeys, don't worry about them; they have been found. By the way,

---

[2] Gibeath-Elohim, meaning Hill of God

The Plan

you know that Israel wants a king. Guess to whom the desire of Israel has turned."

Saul had no idea.

"To you!" Samuel said.

Saul was shocked that he—a Benjamite, from the smallest tribe of Israel and the smallest clan in his tribe—would be chosen as king.

Dinner was served in a large hall at the high place. There Saul was treated like royalty. He was seated at the head of a select gathering of thirty people who were there at Samuel's special invitation. With great fanfare the cook brought out the best piece of meat and set it before Saul—a whole leg of lamb.

Samuel invited Saul to stay at his place in town overnight. That evening he spent a long time talking with Saul on the roof. Samuel was especially careful to teach him what Moses had said about the time when Israel would have a king.[3]

"The first thing Moses commanded was that the king be the one Yahweh chooses," Samuel explained. "That person is you, Saul. Yahweh told me to anoint you leader over Israel. He said you will deliver His people from the hand of the Philistines."

Saul was amazed, but before he could say anything, Samuel continued.

"Moses left some very explicit instructions for you as the future king of Israel. First, you must not build up a large stable of horses for yourself or send people to Egypt to buy horses for you. For two reasons. First, Yahweh told you very clearly, 'You must never return to Egypt.' Secondly, Yahweh also implied that you must not depend on horses for success in battle. God is your defense. He will fight for you.

"You must not acquire many wives for yourself as the kings in the nations around you tend to do. They take the wives of the kings they vanquish. When they want to make a treaty with a king, they marry

---

[3] Deuteronomy 17:14-20

one of his daughters to make sure the treaty will not be broken. But those wives don't know Yahweh, and they will lead your heart astray.

"Don't accumulate large amounts of silver and gold. Being king is not about making yourself rich; it is about leading your people in the ways of righteousness.

"To do that—and this is the most important part of Moses' instruction—to be the king Yahweh wants you to be, to lead your people aright, you must copy for yourself the Law of Moses on a scroll. Copy it, all five books, in the presence of the Levitical priests. Have the priests check your copy to make sure it is accurate. Keep it with you at all times. Read it all the days of your life. That way you will learn to revere Yahweh your God and follow carefully all His words and decrees. This regular reading will keep you from being proud and thinking you are better than your fellow Israelites. It will also prevent you from turning away from these commands in the smallest way. And it will ensure that you and your descendants will reign for many generations in Israel."

In the morning, as Saul and the servant were leaving, Samuel sent the servant ahead so he could give Saul a message from God in private.

Taking out a flask of oil, Samuel poured it on Saul's head, saying, "Yahweh has anointed you leader over his inheritance.

"Now go to Gibeah of God. It is only a few miles from your home town, Gibeah of Benjamin. As you approach the town, you will meet a procession of prophets coming down from the high place preceded by people playing lyres, tambourines, flutes and harps. The Spirit of Yahweh will come upon you in power, and you will prophesy with them; and you will be changed into a different person. Once these signs are fulfilled, do whatever your hand finds to do, for God is with you.

"I'm going from here to Bethel to judge the cases the people bring to me and to make sacrifices and to teach the people. Then I'll go to Gilgal to do the same. You go ahead of me on my circuit. I will meet

The Plan

you in Gilgal and sacrifice offerings to Yahweh. But you will have to wait seven days until I get there. Then I will tell you what to do next."

Everything Samuel said came true. As Saul turned to leave Samuel, Yahweh changed his heart. When Saul and his servant arrived at Gibeah, they saw a procession of prophets coming toward them. Then the Spirit of God came powerfully upon Saul, and he, too, began to prophesy, proclaiming truths he had never studied.

When those who knew Saul heard him denouncing prevailing sins and calling people to repentance, they exclaimed, "What has come over the son of Kish? Is even Saul a prophet?"

When Saul stopped prophesying, he tried to understand what had happened to him. He could see the procession of prophets disappearing up the hill back to the high place at Gibeah of God, so he followed them there to the school of the prophets.

While Saul was standing outside, alone and looking a little bewildered, one of his uncles showed up. The donkeys had returned, so now he was looking for Saul. The chatter in town was all about Saul being a prophet, so he was easy to find—at the high place of Gibeah of God.

"Where have you been?" the uncle asked.

"Looking for the donkeys," Saul replied, somewhat embarrassed to be found at the school of the prophets.

"I heard that you talked to Samuel."

"Oh yes. When we couldn't find the donkeys, we went to Samuel."

"What did he say?" the uncle asked, curious for an explanation of Saul's behavior.

"Not much. He said not to worry. The donkeys had been found." The uncle was pretty sure there was more to the story, but Saul wasn't telling.

"Oh, by the way," the uncle said in parting, "every year Samuel makes a circuit from his home in Ramah to Bethel to Gilgal to Mizpah and back to Ramah. This year Samuel has summoned the elders from every tribe to meet with him the next time he arrives in Mizpah to make sacrifices there. What do you think that is about?"

Saul shrugged his shoulders as if he had no idea.

* * * *

The angels in heaven were watching Saul with interest. The anointing of the first king of Israel was a historic event.

"What I want to see," said Lady Wisdom, "is Saul copying the Law and beginning to read it. He could stay at Gibeah of God for a few days and copy it at the school of the prophets before going to Gilgal to meet Samuel, or he could go directly to Gilgal and copy it at the school of the prophets there. Saul has seven days before Samuel shows up. This would be the perfect time to do that."

"If he doesn't do it," another angel said, "he will lose the power that Yahweh gave him today. He will need that power when he is king."

"He will also lose the boldness that he had today when he was prophesying," added Lady Wisdom. "Saul is timid by nature. I'm not sure he is eager to lead Israel against the Philistines."

* * * *

Seven days later, Samuel showed up in Gilgal and Saul joined him as he made some sacrifices. After a week there the two of them headed for Mizpah, the next town on Samuel's circuit. Along the way Samuel talked more in depth about what it meant for Saul to be king.

Arriving in Mizpah, Samuel was pleased to see that every tribe and clan was represented. Samuel reminded them that they had rejected Yahweh as their king.

"You want to be like the other nations. You want an earthly king. So that is why we are here today."

When Samuel chose Saul by lot from the tribe of Benjamin, the people went looking for him, but they couldn't find him.

The Plan

"He must be here somewhere," Samuel said. "I told him to meet me here today."

Saul was hiding in a place where he thought no one would find him. But he hadn't counted on Yahweh. Samuel inquired of Yahweh, and He told them where to look.

"Yes, Saul is here," Yahweh said. "He has hidden himself among the baggage."

When Samuel presented Saul as "the man Yahweh has chosen," the people shouted, "Long live the king!"

Samuel then explained to the people the regulations of kingship. The king must be chosen by Yahweh. He must not accumulate horses or wives or great riches. And, most important of all, he must copy the Law for himself and read it all the days of his life. Then Samuel dismissed the people.

"I'm going home by way of the house of Abinadab," Samuel said to Saul in parting. "Just in case you haven't yet copied the whole law, I have written the regulations of kingship on this little scroll. I will deposit it there in front of the Ark of the Covenant so you can remind yourself how to conduct yourself as king. I hope you go to Abinadab's house frequently to worship Yahweh."

Not all of the people were impressed with Saul's height and good looks. The tallest man in Israel trying to hide himself among the baggage was a sight one would not soon forget.

"How can this fellow save us?" someone sniffed.

"This chicken-hearted beanpole is our king?!" another one exclaimed. "I'm not going to bring *him* any gifts."

"Nor I."

"Nor I," others said.

And so the troublemakers despised him.

Saul heard the criticism but said nothing. He went back home to Gibeah knowing he had behaved badly. Where was the boldness he had experienced two weeks ago when he was with the prophets?

But Saul did not return to his home in Gibeah alone. God had touched the hearts of some valiant men who had seen Saul cringing behind the baggage. They knew what it was to be fearful, but they had learned to take courage in Yahweh. They joined up with Saul and accompanied him home. Along the way they assured Saul of their support in the days ahead.

* * * *

The angels in heaven, noticing that Yahweh had prompted some valiant men to accompany the timid Saul, burst out in joyful songs of praise.

The dragon was surprised that Yahweh chose a man from Gibeah as king. The episode involving the Levite and his concubine had a profound impact on the psyche of the nation of Israel. Hebrews referred to the time up to and including that episode as "the days of Gibeah." For centuries Gibeah would be associated with corruption, wickedness and judgment.[4]

The dragon was pleased with Yahweh's choice of Saul. The dragon saw him as someone he could easily manipulate—provided Saul didn't make a copy of the Law for himself. Provided he didn't read it all the days of his life. Provided he didn't learn to revere Yahweh his God. And provided he didn't follow carefully all the words and decrees of the Law.

* * * *

Saul started his reign well. One month after Saul hid in the baggage, Nahash king of the Ammonites besieged Jabesh Gilead and threatened to gouge out the right eye of every man in town. When Saul heard about it, he did not react with fear. The Spirit of God came upon him in power, and he burned with righteous anger. He cut a pair of oxen into pieces and sent the pieces by messengers throughout Israel, calling

---

[4] Hosea 9:9; 10:9.

The Plan

them to battle. The men of Israel responded to his call and slaughtered the Ammonites. Those who survived were so scattered that no two of them were left together.

Two years later, Saul didn't do so well. He assembled a small army of three thousand men to attack a small Philistine outpost a few miles from Saul's home in Gibeah. Two thousand were under Saul's command; one thousand were under the command of Saul's son Jonathan. Jonathan and his men initiated the attack.

That stirred up a hornets' nest. The Philistines sent their entire army from their territory on the Mediterranean coast—3,000 chariots, 6,000 charioteers, and soldiers as numerous as the sand on the seashore.

Saul should have rallied more troops, but he could not inspire courage. He himself was afraid. Pretty soon Israelite men who should have joined Saul's army were hiding in any shelter they could find—in caves and thickets, among the rocks, and in pits and cisterns. Some even crossed the Jordan River for safety. Saul and his two thousand troops, who were at Gilgal on the west bank of the Jordan River, were quaking with fear.

Saul sent an emergency message to Samuel to make offerings to Yahweh and intercede for them, but Samuel was on his circuit. He said to wait seven days at Gilgal. Late on the seventh day Samuel still had not come and Saul's men were beginning to scatter, so Saul took things into his own hands and offered up the burnt offering without waiting for Samuel to come with the holy fire used for such offerings.

Just as he finished, Samuel arrived.

"What have you done?" Samuel exclaimed in horror.

Saul blamed Samuel.

"You didn't arrive on time, so I felt compelled to offer the burnt offering."

"You acted foolishly," Samuel replied. "You have not kept the command Yahweh gave you. If you had, he would have established your kingdom over Israel for all time. But now your kingdom will not endure. Yahweh has replaced you with a man after his own heart because you have not kept His command."

After Samuel left, Saul looked around to see how many men were still with him. Only six hundred remained of the original two thousand. Fourteen hundred had scattered.

Yahweh didn't immediately take the kingdom from Saul. He gave him a second chance, and for a while Saul did well. He secured his grasp on Israel's throne and fought against all his enemies on every side—against Moab, Ammon, Edom, the kings of Zobah, and the Philistines. Wherever he turned, he was victorious. He fought valiantly and conquered the Amalekites, saving Israel from all those who had plundered them.[5]

One day Samuel said to Saul, "Yahweh has a message for you: 'I have decided to settle accounts with the nation of Amalek for opposing Israel when they came from Egypt. Now go and completely destroy the entire nation—men, women, children, babies, cattle, sheep, goats, camels, and donkeys.'"[6]

Saul attacked the Amalekites and destroyed most of them, but he spared the king of Amalek and kept the best of the livestock. When Samuel came to meet Saul, Saul greeted him with, "Yahweh bless you! I have carried out Yahweh's instructions."

Samuel was not fooled. He could hear cattle mooing and sheep bleating.

"Oh yeah? What's this I hear?"

Saul tried to put a good spin on his actions, but Samuel interrupted him.

"Stop! Let me tell you what Yahweh said to me last night."

"Tell me."

---

[5] 1 Samuel 14:47-48
[6] 1 Samuel 15:1-3, NLT

"To obey is better than sacrifice. Rebellion is like the abominable sin of divination. Because you have rejected Yahweh's instructions, he has rejected you as king over Israel."

With that Samuel turned to leave. When Saul tried to stop him by grabbing the edge of his robe, it tore. Samuel saw that as a sign.

"Yahweh has torn the kingdom of Israel from you today. He has given it to one of your neighbors—to one better than you."

Then Samuel put the king of Amalek to death and went home.

Until the day Samuel died, he did not go to see Saul again, though Samuel mourned for him.

That was the end of Saul's successes as king. The Spirit of Yahweh departed from him, and Yahweh sent an evil spirit to torment him. Saul spent the rest of his reign trying to kill the one Yahweh anointed as his successor and eventually committed suicide after being mortally wounded in a battle against the Philistines.

19

The Giant Killer

When Samuel anointed David, an unknown shepherd boy, as Saul's successor, the dragon laughed out loud. When Yahweh assigned an evil spirit to torment Saul, the dragon was even more pleased.

But he stopped laughing when David was hired to play his harp and soothe Saul's torment. The dragon couldn't stand the songs David sang:

"Yahweh is my Shepherd; I will never be in need."

"I will sing of your love and justice. To you, O Yahweh, I will sing praise."[1]

The dragon made himself scarce when David played and sang such songs. What the dragon hated even worse was the effect David's music had on Saul. Whenever David played his harp, Saul started prophesying again just as he had done when he was with the prophets![2]

The dragon was increasingly alarmed the more he learned about the future king of Israel. From the dragon's perspective David was dangerous. He loved Yahweh with all his heart! From the day he was anointed, the Spirit of Yahweh came upon him with power.[3]

David demonstrated that power when the Philistines gathered for war against Israel.

For decades the Philistines had been an annoyance but not a real threat to Israel. They had not dared to come against Israel with their

---

[1] Psalm 101:1
[2] 1 Samuel 18:10
[3] 1 Samuel 16:13

entire army since the day Samuel called the Israelites to repentance and Yahweh thundered against the Philistines, throwing them into a panic.[4]

That was before Saul was anointed king. The next time the Philistines came against Israel again, Saul was king and David was a teenager. The Philistine army assembled on a mountainside as a show of force. It was a bluff. If Saul's god was as powerful as Samuel's God, they did not want to incur his wrath against them.

The Israelite army assembled opposite the Philistine army. Each side was afraid of the other. The Philistines sent out a giant named Goliath in a game of chicken, daring an Israelite to take him on. If Goliath killed him, the Philistines would declare victory without a further fight.

But the Philistines hadn't counted on a shepherd boy armed with a sling.

Three of David's brothers were fifteen miles away at the battlefront, when David's father Jesse asked him to deliver food to them. Early the next morning Jesse loaded David up with cheese and bread. David walked to Israel's camp, left the food with the keeper of supplies, and ran to the battle line to greet his brothers.

While David was talking with them, Goliath, the Philistines' champion, stepped out from the Philistine side and defied the ranks of Israel.

"Give me a man and let us fight each other," he challenged the Israelites.

If the man defeated Goliath, the Philistines would become subjects of Israel. If Goliath won, the Israelites would become subject to the Philistines.

Goliath was dressed from head to toe in bronze armor weighing 125 pounds. His weapons were equally impressive. The Israelites saw him as impervious to their puny weapons. They saw him as a formidable foe and quaked with fear.

---

[4] 1 Samuel 7:10-14

The Giant Killer

For forty days this Philistine had come forward every morning and evening and shouted defiance at the Israelites. David saw the giant as an uncircumcised Philistine who defied the armies of the living God. He couldn't believe this had been going on for forty days.

David exploded. "Someone must remove this disgrace from Israel!"

Since no one in the army dared to fight Goliath, David ended up being the one to remove that disgrace. To David the contest was a no-brainer.

"I've killed lions and bears while defending my father's sheep," he said. "This giant is no worse a foe. Yahweh, who rescued me from the claws of the lion and the bear, will rescue me from this Philistine!"

With those words David chose five smooth stones from the nearest stream and faced Goliath armed only with his sling. The giant cursed David by his gods.

"You come to me armed with sword, spear, and javelin," David told the giant, "but I come to you armed with the Name! I come in the name of Yahweh Almighty, the God of the armies of Israel, whom you have defied. Today Yahweh will conquer you, and I will kill you and cut off your head. And then I will give the dead bodies of your men to the birds and wild animals, and the whole world will know that there is a God in Israel!"

Sweeping his arms toward the two armies assembled on opposing hills, David continued.

"And everyone here will know that Yahweh rescues his people, but not with sword and spear. This is Yahweh's battle, and he will give you to us!"

With those words David put a stone into his sling and slung it at Goliath, striking the only place where he was vulnerable, the window in his helmet! The stone sank into his forehead, and the giant fell face down unconscious on the ground. Before the giant could move, David ran, stood over him, pulled the sword out of the Philistine's scabbard, and cut off his head.

The Plan

When the Philistines saw that their hero was dead, they couldn't believe their eyes. The death of that one giant demoralized them. They turned and ran.

David's victory inspired the Israelite army. Infused with new courage, they slaughtered their enemies, chasing them all the way back to their cities near the Mediterranean coast.

The dragon and his demons were stunned. This was the next king of Israel?! If a teenager could do this, what could he do as an adult? This must be the Scepter Jacob spoke of.

While the Israelite army was slaughtering the Philistines and plundering their cities near the Mediterranean coast, David went back to where Goliath had fallen and claimed his own plunder— Goliath's javelin, sword and spear. And further proof of his victory, Goliath's head!

Saul wanted to meet the victor. David couldn't let go of his trophy, so he came to Saul holding the giant's head by the hair.[5] Saul was surprised to learn this was the young man from Bethlehem who had been playing the harp for him whenever he was tormented by an evil spirit.

Saul immediately recruited David into his army and ordered him to report for duty at his stronghold in Gibeah. So David, still holding the Philistine's head, threw Goliath's weapons over his shoulder and headed for Gibeah, about twenty-five miles away. The road to Gibeah went past Bethlehem and Jerusalem.

David had been told not to go back to his father's house, so David couldn't take his plunder there. But he had a little tent pitched just outside Bethlehem in one of his father's sheep pastures. David could drop off his load there and rest for the night before continuing on to Gibeah.

---

[5] 1 Samuel 17:57

As he walked the fifteen miles to his tent, David began to think of Abraham. When the Babylonian army attacked Sodom and Gomorrah and carried off Lot and his possessions, Abraham chased after them with his own 'army' of 318 men. Abraham's strategy was to attack the Babylonians in the dead of night so they wouldn't know how small his army was. He took them by surprise and chased them for miles. With Yahweh on their side, 318 men defeated tens of thousands.

"That was just as unlikely as my hitting Goliath in his tiny vulnerable spot," David thought. *"Yet it happened. How? Yahweh fought for Abraham, and Yahweh fought for me. There is no other explanation."*

The further David walked, the heavier Goliath's head got. Part of David wanted to put it down, but another part of him couldn't let it go. This was his trophy, evidence that Yahweh was fighting for him.

David continued to think of Abraham.

After Abraham rescued Lot, he was met by the king of Salem, who blessed him by God Most High. Salem. Jerusalem. Currently it was occupied by Jebusites, who called it Jebus.

David had walked past Jerusalem a number of times in the past few months going back and forth between Bethlehem and Gibeah whenever an evil spirit tormented Saul. He had wondered what it would be like to live in a city with such a fantastic view of God's beautiful world. He remembered being told that neither the men of Judah nor of Benjamin had been able to occupy it in Joshua's time.

David recognized the strategic location of such an impregnable fortress. Right in the middle of Israel. At its heart. Surely Yahweh wanted his people to conquer Jerusalem. Surely Jerusalem was part of Yahweh's long range plan.

Then David remembered that Samuel had anointed him the next king of Israel. He resolved to conquer Jerusalem when he was king. But how? Even the blind and the lame could defend it.

David was dead tired when he reached his tent. Goliath's weapons were heavy! And his load was awkward to carry. He was glad to put

The Plan

Goliath's head down after carrying it so far. He put it just inside his tent door. If he left it outside, a wild animal might run off with it in the dead of night.

As David lay down to sleep, his mind was still buzzing. *The head. Abraham. Salem. Being anointed king.* Soon he was fast asleep.

In the middle of the night he was suddenly wide awake. Now his thoughts didn't seem so random. He began to connect the dots. *Jerusalem. Yahweh wanted him to conquer it some day. Yahweh would show him how.*

Then an idea popped into his head. *Water! The Gihon Spring.* One of the reasons Jerusalem had never been conquered was because it had an abundant supply of water. The enemy could not cut off their water upstream because their water came from under ground. That water ran out of the city from the southern end of the east ridge. The Jebusites accessed water without leaving the city.

They must have a shaft from the top of the hill of Ophel down to the spring, David thought. *If a few men could follow the stream from the water tunnel to the base of the water shaft, they could climb up the shaft right into the heart of the fortress!*

David needed to get a better look at the outflow to see if his idea was doable. He would look in the morning on his way to Gibeah. With that settled in his mind, he went back to sleep.

David woke up at dawn to the sounds of a dog sniffing at his tent door and flies buzzing around Goliath's head. After a quick breakfast, David picked up his own weapons and Goliath's head and turned toward Saul's fortress in Gibeah.

On the way he would pass Jerusalem. Passing on the south side would involve descending into a deep valley and then climbing a steep slope on the other side. Usually David bypassed Jerusalem on the north side to avoid those downs and ups. But this day David took the difficult route.

For a very good reason. He would plant Goliath's head in plain sight of the Jebusites![6]

David got as close as he dared to the Jebusite fortress without coming within range of their arrows. As he approached the base of the fortress, he looked for a small tree near the stream flowing from the city. While approaching the tree, David got a good look at the tunnel where the stream flowed out of the city. He was sure there was room to crawl in from outside.

People in the fortress above gathered to watch as David cut off the top of the little tree, stripped off its branches and sharpened it into a stake. Their curiosity turned to horror when David impaled a giant head on the stake.

"See this head?" David shouted to the people above. "Yesterday this head sat on the shoulders of Goliath, the Philistine giant. See what I did to Goliath? With Yahweh's help and my little sling I knocked him down and cut off his head with his own sword.

"And you are next!

"My name is David, and one day I will be king of Israel. Then I will conquer this fortress. Yahweh will help me conquer you just as he helped me conquer Goliath. Goliath couldn't protect the Philistines, and nobody—not your blind and lame, not even your best soldiers—will be able to protect you when Yahweh fights against you.

"The Philistines made the mistake of thinking Goliath was unconquerable. Don't you make the same mistake and think this fortress is unconquerable! The battle is Yahweh's, and he will give all of you into our hands. Jerusalem will be Yahweh's city!"

With that, David continued on his way to report for duty to Saul in Gibeah.

---

[6] 1 Samuel 17:54

20

Saul Fails, David Succeeds

The account of David's spectacular victory over Goliath spread like wild fire. When the Israelite army returned to their homes after defeating the Philistines, the women came out from all the towns of Israel to meet King Saul with singing and dancing and joyful songs. Saul was pleased—until he heard the words they were singing:

"Saul has slain his thousands, and David his tens of thousands." This refrain galled Saul and made him very angry. He saw David as a threat to his kingdom.

"They have credited David with tens of thousands," he thought, "but me with only thousands. David didn't kill tens of thousands; he killed just one man."

But that one man was the giant who struck fear into the entire Israelite army—including Saul—paralyzing them all.

The next day the dragon again tormented Saul, David again played his harp, and Saul again began prophesying. But this time the dragon didn't run. Instead an evil spirit came forcefully upon Saul, inspiring him with murderous hatred. Saul stopped prophesying and hurled his spear at David, attempting to pin him to the wall.

David dodged the spear and kept playing and singing, hoping to drive the evil spirit away. When Saul hurled his spear a second time, David dodged it again, but he knew it was time to leave.

After David escaped, Saul took a more sober view of the situation. Killing David would be a mistake if Saul did it, because David was so

Saul Fails, David Succeeds

popular. What Saul could do was set David up to be killed in battle. So Saul gave David command over an army of a thousand troops.

But that backfired. Yahweh was with him. David and his army had great success, and the people loved David all the more.

Next, Saul tried bribery—marriage to his eldest daughter.

"Who am I that I should become the king's son-in-law?" David objected. He could not afford the bride price.

Saul had a ready answer.

"Serve me bravely and fight the battles of Yahweh against the Philistines," Saul said to David. To himself he said, "I won't kill him. Let the Philistines do that!"

David agreed and went off to fight the Philistines.

Expecting that David would be killed, Saul wished him Godspeed and immediately gave his eldest daughter in marriage to the man she had been planning to marry.

Imagine Saul's surprise when David returned alive and victorious! Saul had egg on his face.

But he quickly recovered. He had just learned that his younger daughter was in love with David. How convenient! So Saul used her to lure David to his death. The bride price would be the foreskins of a hundred Philistines, to be produced within a fixed time frame. The greatest danger was not in killing the Philistines; it was in being exposed to the enemy while obtaining their foreskins.

This time David was pleased to become the king's son-in-law, perhaps because this daughter was not pledged to be married to another man, so he accepted the terms. Before the time had expired, David and his men went out and killed *two* hundred Philistines and presented their foreskins to Saul.

Saul couldn't back down this time, so he gave his daughter Michal to David in marriage. Now Saul was even more afraid of David. Not only was Yahweh with him, but his daughter loved David. If Saul harmed David now, he would lose his daughter.

The Plan

After David planted Goliath's head in plain view of their fortress, the Jebusites did not attack Israel. They thought of Goliath and shivered every time they heard the victory song, "Saul has killed his thousands, and David his tens of thousands."

The Philistines hadn't counted on a shepherd boy killing their champion with his sling, but they discounted the song about him. Unlike the Jebusites, the Philistine commanders continued to go out to battle against Israel. They didn't fear Israel's chicken-hearted king, but they hadn't anticipated the shepherd boy joining Israel's army.

Whenever the Philistines attacked, Saul made sure that David was in the fight. David and the men under his command had more success than the rest of Saul's officers, and David's name became well known. For many years David was a thorn in the collective Philistines' side.

Even as David racked up success after success in battle, Saul plotted to kill David. Soon Saul abandoned all pretense of fighting the Philistines and spent all his energy chasing David. For the rest of Saul's life he remained David's enemy.

After years of running from Saul, David figured out that the safest place for him to be was in the land of Israel's enemies, the Philistines! So David and six hundred fighting men and their families settled in Gath and lived peacefully there with the permission of Achish, son of the king of Gath. After convincing Achish that they were not dangerous, David asked permission to live in a country town rather than in the royal city of Gath.

Not suspecting any harm, Achish gave David the town of Ziklag. From that base David and his men went on daily raids against Israel's enemies. There were plenty of settlements scattered throughout southern Judah where Canaanites still lived unconquered. David even went east of the Jordan River to attack Geshurites and Amalekites. Whenever David attacked an area, he did not leave a man or woman alive, but he did return with their livestock and other plunder. This went on for a year and four months.

After each raid, Achish would ask David, "Where did you go raiding today?" David would answer with the name of some place in the deserts of Judah, so Achish thought David was working for him. As long as David lived in Philistine territory, he never left a soul alive after a raid so that no one could inform Achish of what was really going on.

Achish trusted David and said to himself, "David has become so odious to his own people that he will be my servant forever!"

About this time, Achish decided to gather the Philistine forces against Israel. King Saul was unwittingly helping the Philistines by spending most of his time chasing after David, the only one who was a real threat to the Philistines.

If Achish was to attack Israel, he knew exactly who he wanted fighting on his side—David! The giant killer! And David was already living in Philistine territory. Achish let David know he had a price to pay for the protection he had received from Achish.

"You must understand that you and your men will accompany me in the army."

David replied, "Then you will see for yourself what your servant can do."

Achish took that to mean the opposite of what David meant.

"Very well," Achish replied. "I will make you my bodyguard for life."

Fortunately for Achish, other Philistine rulers forced him to send David and his men back home before the battle began. Achish may have trusted David to fight on his side, but others didn't.

Saul's early disobedience in failing to completely destroy the Amalekites came back to haunt him. Had he joined forces with David rather than opposing him, the two of them together could have destroyed the Amalekites. That would have struck fear in the hearts of the Philistines.

The Plan

Instead, David's family was living quietly in Philistine territory while David went on raids throughout the countryside and the Philistines focused on Israel. The Philistine army assembled at Shunem in Israel while hundreds and thousands more troops were coming from Philistine territory in the far south to join them.[1] Saul and his men assembled on the mountain of Gilboa.

When Saul saw the vast Philistine army, he was terrified. Ironically, while Saul was quaking in fear, David was doing what Saul should have done long ago—destroying Amalekites.[2]

In desperation Saul finally inquired of Yahweh and asked him what to do, but Yahweh didn't answer. Not hearing from Yahweh, Saul resorted to witchcraft. He consulted a medium, who brought up the spirit of Samuel.

Samuel told Saul, "Yahweh has, as he predicted, torn the kingdom from your hands and given it to David. Because you did not obey Yahweh or carry out his fierce wrath against the Amalekites, you and your sons will die tomorrow. Yahweh will hand the army of Israel to the Philistines."

In battle the next day Saul was critically wounded by an arrow. Not wanting to die at the hand of an uncircumcised Philistine, Saul fell on his sword. Saul, three of his sons, his armor-bearer, and all the men who were fighting with him died together that same day. The rest of the army fled.

The initial news from the battle was that all four of Saul's sons had died, but that turned out to be not true. Esh-Baal, Saul's second son, knowing Yahweh had predicted the death of Saul's sons, fled from the heat of conflict—and survived.

Following Saul's death, the men of Judah anointed David as their king and the rest of Israel made Esh-Baal their king. The northern tribes

---

[1] 1 Samuel 28:4 and 29:2
[2] 1 Samuel ch.30

had always been loyal to Saul, and Samuel was not alive to insist that David be the next king of Israel.

For two years Esh-Baal he ruled in Israel. But rumor had it that he had deserted instead of fighting in the battle which took the lives of his father Saul and his three brothers. Soon everybody was calling him "Ish-Bosheth," man of shame.

Then Abner, Saul's cousin and the commander of Israel's army, took over. For five years he led the army in the war between the house of David and the house of Saul. But David's house grew stronger and stronger, while the house of Saul grew weaker and weaker.

Finally, knowing that Yahweh had anointed David as king, Abner went to Hebron to tell David that all of Israel wanted him as their king.

Saul's dynasty was ended.

21

David Conquers Jerusalem

The first thing on David's agenda after becoming king of both Israel and Judah was to conquer the fortress of Zion, one of the dragon's strongholds.

Zion was desirable partly because of its strategic location near international trade routes. The city, controlled by Jebusites and called Jebus, sat on a hill surrounded by steep valleys on the west, south and east. It jutted out over those valleys as an island of sorts, making it a natural stronghold, easy to defend.

The Jebusites boasted that their city was unconquerable. Even the blind and the lame could defend their fortress.

The city's greatest asset was water—the Gihon Spring, located on the southern end of the eastern ridge. The occupants of Jebus did not have to leave the city and expose themselves to danger in order to fetch water. Nor could their enemies access the spring and cut off the water from them.

It was true that a few lame men easily could have defended the fortress if the Jebusites suspected the enemy was coming up through the water shaft. But the Jebusites never imagined that an enemy would try that. Nor had any enemy of the Jebusites ever thought of using the water shaft.

Until David.

He came up with a bold plan. All he had to do was create a distraction. David's army surrounded the fortress and pretended to lay siege to the city.

Meanwhile David sent a few men led by Joab to go up through the water shaft to reach those 'blind and lame' who were David's enemies. Under cover of darkness Joab crossed the ravine to where the water flowed out at the base of the fortress.

The Jebusites, as David expected, yelled down to him from their fortress.

"You can't get in here. So don't bother even trying. The blind and the lame will ward you off!"

While the Jebusite troops were looking over the parapets and laughing at David's army, his special forces took the occupants by surprise and conquered the city.

* * * *

So David captured the fortress of Zion, made it his capital, and renamed it the City of David. And David became more and more powerful, because Yahweh, God of Heaven's Armies, was with him.[1]

* * * *

The angels in heaven gathered around to watch David conquering Zion. Heaven saw it not as an arbitrary decision, but as a public statement. Like planting a flag. They burst into songs of praise when he called it the City of David.

"Saul should have conquered Zion long ago," one angel said, "but Saul didn't have the courage to try. When the Jebusites said the lame and the blind could defend the fortress, Saul believed them."

"I'm not surprised that David chose Zion as his first conquest as king," said Lady Wisdom. "He has long known how strategic it is."

---

[1] 2 Samuel 5:9-10; 1 Chron. 11:8

22

David Brings Back the Ark

Jacob had prophesied that the scepter would not depart from Judah. Saul had the scepter for a while, but he was a Benjamite. David was from the tribe of Judah. The dragon figured that David just might be the Seed holding the Scepter.

When David conquered Jerusalem, he defeated not just the Jebusites but the dragon.

Score: Yahweh, one. Dragon, zero.

So the dragon recruited the Philistines to fight against David. The Philistines spread out in the valley around David, taking their idols with them to assure victory. But David inquired of Yahweh, and He promised to hand David's enemies over to him.

Yahweh kept his promise. David and his men defeated the Philistines, who abandoned their idols there. David's men carried them off and burned them.[1]

Score: Yahweh, two. Dragon, zero.

The Philistines tried again. Again David prayed and asked Yahweh what to do. Yahweh gave David the battle strategy. So David did what Yahweh commanded, and Yahweh fought the battle for him. The Philistines were again defeated.[2]

---

[1] 2 Samuel 5:21 and 1 Chron. 14:12
[2] See 2 Samuel 5:17-25.

Score: Yahweh, three. Dragon, zero.

* * * *

Inquiring of Yahweh entailed going to where the ark was and asking God for direction. Saul hadn't used the ark to inquire of Yahweh during his entire reign.[3]

David had a deep reverence for the Name. He had enquired of Yahweh and won his first two battles as king. But the ark was in Kiriath Jearim in the house of Abinadab, which was on a hill eight miles west of Jerusalem. It had been there ever since the Philistines returned the ark to Israel 'way back when Samuel was a boy. David wanted the ark nearby so that he could inquire of Yahweh regularly. He did not want to repeat Saul's mistakes.

So David made a grand proposal to his officers about bringing the Ark of the Covenant to Jerusalem.

"Let's bring the ark of our God back to us—the ark of God, which is called by the glorious Name, the name of Yahweh Almighty, who is enthroned between the cherubim on the ark."

David and all his men went to the house of Abinadab and put the ark on a new cart pulled by oxen with Uzzah and Ahio, sons of Abinadab, in charge. Uzzah walked behind the cart and Ahio walked in front of it while David and all Israel were celebrating with all their might before Yahweh with castanets, harps, lyres, cymbals and other instruments.

David's heart was in the right place, but his head was not. He had studied many things from the Scriptures, but he had not studied how to handle the ark of Yahweh's presence.

Uzzah and Ahio were too familiar with the ark. It had been in their house for decades. They had gotten used to its presence and were no longer in awe of it.

---

[3] 1 Chron. 13:3

The Plan

As a result of both David's failure and Abinadab's sons' lack of reverence, the ark was not being transported the right way—the safe way. The inevitable happened.

The dragon saw his opportunity. He tripped the oxen so that they stumbled.

Without thinking, Uzzah reached out his hand to steady the ark.

Yahweh immediately struck him dead right there beside the ark.

The celebration stopped dead in its tracks.

The dragon and his demons laughed and clapped with glee. The angels in heaven wept that David's good intentions had ended in such tragedy.

David was both angry at Yahweh and afraid of him for killing Uzzah.

"How can the ark of Yahweh ever come to me?" David wondered.

He still wanted the ark nearby. He saw it as representing the personal God Yahweh, not a distant God. He had already pitched a special tent to house the ark.[4] Yet he didn't dare take the ark into the City of David. He feared being struck dead.

So David found shelter for the ark in a house nearby, the home of a Levite named Obed-Edom. There it remained for three months, and Yahweh blessed his household and everything he had.

David returned home despondent. But then word trickled out that the house of Obed-Edom was experiencing unusual blessing. David wanted a share in that blessing. Maybe he wouldn't have to give up on the idea of bringing the ark to Jerusalem after all. He simply had to do it the right way.

The ark of God had been in obscurity for so long that nobody knew how to handle it. During the next three months, David studied the writings of Moses. The ark, David learned, should never have been

---

[4] 1 Chron. 15:1

carried in a cart. God had designed the ark with two poles attached to its base so it could be carried on the shoulders of four Levites.

When David made a second attempt to bring the ark to Jerusalem, he did it right. He called together the descendants of Aaron and the Levites and said, "No one but the Levites may carry the ark of God.[5] It must be carried with the poles on their shoulders, not on a cart."

When the time came to move the ark, the Levites consecrated themselves and carried the ark of God as Moses had commanded. David went above and beyond the rules Yahweh had laid out. He consecrated hundreds of priests and Levites in preparation for the move, and he organized singers and musicians for the procession.

Obed-Edom was rewarded for housing the ark for three months. Not only did he play his harp during the procession, but he was among those given the privilege and responsibility of being a doorkeeper for the ark. The doorkeeper screened people to prevent them from coming carelessly into God's presence and being struck dead.

The entire house of Israel followed the progress of the ark with shouts and the sound of trumpets. David had made sure that Yahweh would get all the glory. David even composed a psalm for the occasion and appointed Asaph and his associates to sing it. The angels joined in the praise.

> Give praise to Yahweh, proclaim his name;
> > make known among the nations what he has done....
> For great is Yahweh and most worthy of praise;
> > he is to be feared above all gods.
> For all the gods of the nations are idols,
> > but Yahweh made the heavens.
> Ascribe to Yahweh the glory due his name.
> Worship Yahweh in the splendor of his holiness.

---

[5] 1 Chron. 15:2

The Plan

> Tremble before him, all the earth!
> Let the heavens rejoice, let the earth be glad;
> > let them say among the nations, "Yahweh reigns!"[6]

The dragon clapped his claws over his ears when the music began. When he couldn't shut out the sound of the musicians singing praises to Yahweh, he fled the scene.

When the ark was safely in Jerusalem in the tent David had pitched for it, David blessed the people in the name of Yahweh Almighty and sent them home with gifts of bread, dates and raisins.[7]

David also appointed Levites to continue ministering before the Ark, to pray, to give thanks and to praise Yahweh. Some sang, some played musical instruments, and some blew the trumpets regularly before the Ark of the Covenant of God.[8]

But David did not neglect the original Tent of Meeting which Moses had made. It was at the high place in Gibeon, where worship continued even though the Tent did not contain the Ark.[9]

Immediately after David conquered Jerusalem, Hiram king of Tyre, who had long admired David and followed his career, sent messengers to say he wanted to build a cedar palace for David.[10] While the palace was under construction, David subdued the worst of his enemies. Then David put his feet up and enjoyed the rest that God had given him.

But he didn't rest for long. Having the ark in Jerusalem near the king's palace only underscored for David that the ark was not properly housed. The ark, the throne of God Almighty, was in a tent, while Israel's earthly king, David, lived in a palace of cedar.

How incongruous!

---

[6] From 1 Chronicles 16:8-36, partially quoted in Psalm 96
[7] 2 Samuel 6:8-19; 1 Chron. 15 & 16
[8] 1 Chronicles 16:4-6
[9] 1 Chronicle 16:39-42
[10] 2 Samuel 5:11

David resolved to build a temple as a dwelling place for Yahweh, but Yahweh turned down his offer.

"I didn't mind moving from place to place with a tent as my dwelling when Israel was wandering in the desert," Yahweh told David through the prophet Nathan. "I never said to any of your rulers—Moses, Joshua, Samuel or Saul— 'Why haven't you built me a house of cedar?' A fancy house isn't my priority. Providing a place where my people can live in peace is.

"As for a house. *You* want to build *me* a house. But I declare that *I* will establish a house for *you*.

"But not in your lifetime.

"I will make your name great, like the names of the greatest men on earth. I will raise up your Seed, one from your own body. He is the one who will build a house for my Name. And I will establish the throne of his kingdom forever. I will never take my love away from him as I took it away from Saul. Your house, your kingdom and your throne will be established forever."

23

Why Not David?

The angels in heaven saw the initial disappointment on David's face and were puzzled by Yahweh's decision not to let David build the temple.

"David has such a heart of worship," one angel said. "Surely that would qualify him for the task of building a temple."

"I agree," said another. "Samuel told Saul that Yahweh was looking for a man after his own heart to replace him.[1] Surely when Samuel anointed David, he was indicating that David was the man after Yahweh's own heart."

"Did David do something wrong?" another angel asked, "something that would disqualify him from building the temple?"

"He has killed a lot of people," one suggested. "He has blood on his hands."

"But Saul was rejected as king for not killing *enough* people," another one countered. "Saul's mission as king was to completely destroy the Amalekites. But he performed priestly duties, which kings were prohibited from doing, and he failed to kill *all* the Amalekites when Yahweh told him to. So Yahweh tore the kingdom from him."

"Yes," another angel agreed. "Yahweh told his people long ago to utterly destroy the nations that inhabited Canaan. The Israelites have been trying to do that ever since they crossed the Jordan River. David is trying to finish the job."

---

[1] 1 Samuel 13:14

"Yahweh can't penalize him for fighting many wars and shedding much blood in the process," said another angel. "Even Samuel in righteous indignation hacked the king of the Amalekites to pieces after Saul failed to do so. David does his killing on the battle field, but Samuel did it in Yahweh's presence—right in front of the altar where he regularly made burnt offerings and sacrifices!"[2]

Lady Wisdom had been listening in on the angels' discussion. Now she spoke up.

"I don't think Yahweh is penalizing David at all. David's primary function as king is to unite Israel and establish the kingdom. Saul was supposed to do that too, but he didn't do a very good job. He started not badly, but after young David killed Goliath and stole the spotlight from Saul, he became jealous of David. He spent the last half of his reign trying to kill David instead of his real enemies.

"Now that David is king, he is building a strong nation. A significant part of that is bringing Israel's enemies under control, and there are still more enemies to subdue. David's desire to build the temple is wonderful, but focusing on that will hinder him from accomplishing his primary task.

"As you have pointed out," Lady Wisdom continued, "David has a heart for worship. That is why he brought the Ark of the Covenant to Jerusalem. And that very act will unify the nation and make it strong. In unity is strength. Subduing his enemies is uniting the nation politically; worshiping Yahweh will unite the nation spiritually."

At this point Yahweh stepped into the conversation.

"You ministering spirits must remember something. Humans are limited in their powers. If they get distracted or try to do too much, they set themselves up for failure. They are most successful when they realize that one plants and another waters, but God gives the increase.

---

[2] 1 Samuel 15:33, ESV

The Plan

"To put it another way, one of the consequences or prices of obedience is that one assignment can disqualify someone from another assignment. In David's case, the task of destroying Israel's enemies requires that he stand down from what he considers the more glorious task—building a temple for Me.

"But just you watch! David will do *everything but* the actual building of the temple. He will destroy the Amalekites, but he will do so much more. For the rest of David's life, the temple will always be in his thoughts. He will find a location for the temple. He will contribute an enormous fortune from his personal possessions— tons of gold and silver—toward the construction. He will hire stonecutters to start cutting stone for the temple. He will provide tons of bronze, countless cedar logs, and iron to make nails.[3]

"I will show him my detailed plans for the temple and he will draw up the blueprints. He will organize the priests and Levites into divisions for worship at the temple. He will organize gatekeepers, singers and musicians, treasurers and other officials and assign them to various tasks. The system David will put in place will continue until a Better Plan is put in place.

"At some point in time I will gently point out to David that he has shed much blood and fought many wars.[4] This is not to say that he has displeased me by doing so. This is simply to point out that Jerusalem is the City of Peace, so I want his son, who will be a man of peace, to build a house for my Name there."

* * * *

For the rest of his life David dreamed about the temple. He even composed psalms as if he were in the temple. The temple was so real to David that when he was in the holy tent in the presence of the ark, he saw the temple as already built.

---

[3] 1 Chronicles 22:2-4
[4] 1 Chronicles 22:8

"Zeal for your *house* consumes me!" he wrote.[5]

"O LORD, I love the habitation of your *house* and the place where your glory dwells."[6]

"I was glad when they said to me, 'Let us go to the *house* of the LORD!'"[7]

"Blessed is the one you choose and bring near, to dwell in your *courts*! We shall be satisfied with the goodness of your *house*, the holiness of your *temple*!"[8]

"I bow down toward your *holy temple* and give thanks to your name."[9]

---

[5] Psalm 69:9, NIV
[6] Psalm 26:8
[7] Psalm 122:1
[8] Psalm 65:4
[9] Psalm 138:2

24

David's Flaw

After bringing the Ark to Jerusalem, David went back to his primary task of ridding the Promised Land of its pagan inhabitants who practiced idolatry and were an evil influence on the Israelites. Nation after nation was defeated, subdued and made to pay tribute.

In obedience to Yahweh's instructions for a king, David made a copy of the Torah[1] and read it regularly. He did not enrich himself from his battles. He dedicated to Yahweh the gold, silver and bronze from the tribute and plunder and put these precious metals in storage for the time when the temple would be built.

Nor did he acquire a great number of horses for himself, as per the Lord's instructions for kings.[2] He had the opportunity to do so when he captured a thousand chariots and their horses from King Hadadezer. The horses were the engines of the chariots. It took years to breed good war horses and train them for war. Rather than destroy them, David hamstrung all but a hundred of them so they could not be used against him in the future.[3]

David also established the good habit[4] of inquiring of Yahweh before engaging in battle.

---

[1] The five books of Moses: Genesis through Deuteronomy
[2] Deut. 17:16
[3] 2 Samuel 8:4.
[4] 1 Samuel 30:7-8; 2 Samuel 5:19, 23

David's Flaw

When David first joined the army, *Saul* directed him to go against the enemy in one place or another. When David was no longer taking orders from Saul, he turned to *Yahweh* for military direction.

When the Philistines attacked the town of Keilah, David did not assume that he should get into the fight. He asked Yahweh, "Shall I go and attack these Philistines?"

Yahweh answered, "Go."

David's men were too afraid to go, so David inquired of Yahweh again.

Again Yahweh answered, "Go. I'm going to give the Philistines into your hand."[5]

No wonder David was always victorious! No wonder his fighting men were so valiant! If they went to war at Yahweh's command, they could not lose!

Not only did David ask Yahweh where and when to fight, he even asked Yahweh, "Where should I make my home?"[6]

But he never inquired of Yahweh about taking a wife.

This led to David not obeying one of the rules for kings. Yahweh had instructed kings of Israel not to take many wives. And because David never asked Yahweh the question, *Whom should I marry?* he got into a lot of trouble.

Lust became his fatal flaw.

The topic of marriage was first brought up by Saul. He tried to lure David to his death by dangling his daughters one at a time before him as bait. David didn't inquire of Yahweh. He simply swallowed the bait. Yahweh saved David from marriage to Saul's first daughter when Saul gave her away to another man before David could claim his bride. But Yahweh did not interfere when David took Saul's bait the second time and David claimed his hard-earned prize—Michal.

---

[5] 1 Samuel 23:1-4
[6] 2 Samuel 2:1-3

The Plan

Though Michal loved David, there is no evidence that David loved her. He forever saw her as the trophy he had won for the price of a hundred Philistine foreskins.[7]

That marriage did not last long. While David was running from his father-in-law, Saul gave his daughter Michal to a man who truly loved her.

Yahweh was trying to send David a message: *I have a better woman for you.*

David found that woman in an obscure little town, Jezreel, a town we know nothing about other than that it was allotted to the tribe of Judah.[8] David and Ahinoam had a lot in common. Both were from insignificant small towns. Both were from humble, hard-working families. Neither was used to life in the spotlight. Ahinoam was the perfect wife to come home to after a hard-fought battle and after the excitement of victory parades with people dancing and singing, "Saul has slain his thousands, and David his tens of thousands."

A short time after David married Ahinoam, he was introduced to another wonderful woman. David was in his late twenties and not looking for another wife. He met Abigail by what seemed like an accident.

David and his army of six hundred men were down south in the Desert of Maon as far away from Saul as they could get. While there, they acted as self-appointed guardians of people's flocks, protecting them from thieves and wild animals. A very wealthy man by the name of Nabal was one who had benefited from David's protection.

Needing food to feed his personal army, David sent ten young men to politely greet Nabal in David's name, wish him long life and good health, and ask Nabal to give whatever he thought was appropriate.

---

[7] 1 Samuel 18:28; 2 Samuel 3:14
[8] The Jezreel that is frequently mentioned in the Bible was a different town—in the territory of Issachar but allotted to Manasseh. The whereabouts of Jezreel in Judah is unknown today. It is mentioned only in connection with Ahinoam.

Nabal responded rudely. "Who is this David? Who is this son of Jesse? Why should I take my bread and water, and the meat I have slaughtered for my shearers, and give it to men coming from who knows where?"

As if he had never heard of the lad who killed Goliath! As if he had never heard the song, "Saul has slain his thousands, but David his tens of thousands"!

When David heard of Nabal's response, he was angry enough to kill. He ordered his men, "Put on your swords!"

Fortunately for Nabal, his wife Abigail was intelligent and full of good sense. When she learned that her husband had insulted David and mistreated his servants, she knew immediately that her husband was in deep trouble. So she quickly loaded up donkeys with enough food for six hundred men and instructed her servants to take them and follow David's men.

Abigail and her entourage met David just as he and his men were returning to kill Nabal and all the men in his household. She immediately fell at David's feet and apologized for her husband's bad behavior.

"I wasn't there when the young men you sent arrived," Abigail explained quickly. "Here is a gift for you and your young men. When Yahweh has made you leader of Israel, don't let killing Nabal be a blemish on your record. And," she added, "when Yahweh has dealt with my husband, remember me, your servant."

David's expression changed immediately.

"Thank God for your good sense!" he responded. "Bless you for keeping me from murder and from carrying out vengeance with my own hands. For I swear by the God of Israel that if you had not hurried out to meet me, not one of Nabal's men would still be alive tomorrow morning."

Abigail returned home to find her husband presiding over a huge banquet, celebrating like a king, in high spirits, and very drunk. So

The Plan

she said nothing to him about what she had done. The next morning, when Nabal had sobered up, she told him the whole story. Right then and there he had a heart attack and died ten days later.

When David heard that Nabal was dead, his first reaction was to praise God.

"Praise be to Yahweh, who has kept me from doing wrong. If I had killed all the men in Nabal's household, I would have been as bad as Nabal. Yahweh has turned Nabal's wickedness back on his own head."

Then David remembered Abigail. He remembered being impressed by her. What a woman! How tactful and diplomatic she had been! She was intelligent. She was beautiful. And now she was a widow.

The shepherd heart of David wondered who would provide for her now that Nabal was dead. Then he remembered Abigail's parting words to him: "When Yahweh has dealt with my husband, remember me."

It was Yahweh, David realized, who had orchestrated his life to introduce him to this wonderful woman. David promptly sent his servants to ask Abigail to become his wife.

The dragon was not pleased to see David happily married to two wonderful women. He watched for the opportunity to trip David up.

During the final sixteen months of Saul's reign, David lived in Philistine territory. He went raiding from there. Some of his raids took him away up north on the other side of Jordan where Geshurites controlled sixty towns and villages. David and his men would attack a town, kill all the inhabitants, and take all the livestock and all the plunder they could carry. David's name struck fear into all the Geshurites who lived in the territory Joshua had allotted to the eastern tribe of Manasseh.

The dragon was watching. The dragon knew that David would eventually be king of all Israel, and when he became king, he would claim the land which Yahweh had promised to Israel—land which was now controlled by the king of Geshur.

And the dragon got an idea. In Joshua's time the Gibeonites had saved their skins by deceiving Joshua and making a peace treaty with Israel. Why not try the same tactic now? Would it be possible for the Geshurites to make a peace treaty with David? What would persuade David to agree to it?

David's first wife, Michal, was a princess whom he had won as a trophy for killing Philistines. Talmai king of Geshur had a beautiful daughter. Would David fall for her? Would he take a third wife?

The dragon whispered in Talmai's ear. Talmai went to Hebron, taking his daughter with him, and paid David a visit. Would David make peace with Talmai and take his daughter as a symbol of peace between them?

David made a fatal mistake. He rationalized that powerful men often took multiple wives, especially if their husbands had been killed in battle. Many nations considered multiple wives to be a status symbol indicating great wealth or great victories in battle.

But Yahweh didn't want Israel's kings to take pride in having many wives. He wanted Israel's kings to acknowledge the true source of their wealth and their victories. Yahweh had blessed them with riches. Yahweh had fought their battles and blessed them with victory. And Yahweh wanted to bless them with wives who were not just status symbols but soul mates.

Talmai's daughter was very beautiful. Even though David didn't know her, he couldn't resist such a beautiful woman.

And David did not inquire of Yahweh. Marrying his trophy wife Michal had set a precedent for him. If he had second thoughts, he ignored them.

David married Talmai's daughter, and Talmai returned to Geshur in peace, knowing that David would not attack him. David had another trophy.

After he married Talmai's daughter, the marriage floodgates were opened. David took three more wives in quick succession.

The Plan

Meanwhile Saul's cousin Abner was negotiating with David to transfer the loyalties of the house of Saul to David. David agreed on condition that the house of Saul return David's trophy wife, Michal, to him.

David didn't need another wife. He didn't even love Michal, but he wanted his trophy back. The order was given, and Michal was taken away from her loving husband, who followed her, weeping all the way.[9]

By the time David was king over a united Israel, he had six sons—one by each wife except Michal, who never bore him children.[10]

David threw off all restraint when he became king of both Judah and Israel and moved to Jerusalem. There he took more concubines and wives and fathered so many children that he could barely keep track.[11] When two of his sons by two different wives ended up with the same name, one of them had to revise his name.[12]

Nobody openly criticized David for this, but Yahweh was not pleased. He allowed David to fall flat on his face.

David was drifting away from his close relationship with the God he had once adored. For the first time in his reign David found that his presence was not needed in battle. He was surrounded by very capable warriors—his "Thirty" mighty men, "the Three," and Joab, his commander-in-chief. He could stay home and spend time with his growing family.

The dragon seized the opportunity.

"*You don't have to go to war, David,*" the dragon whispered. "*The nations nearby—the Ammonites and Philistines—will always give you trouble from time to time, but other nations won't join them. The last time the Arameans joined the Ammonites in battle, you defeated them in such spectacular fashion that they are afraid to help the Ammonites anymore.*"[13]

---

[9] 2 Samuel 3:12-16
[10] 2 Sam. 3:2-5; 6:23
[11] 2 Samuel 5:13-15; 1 Chronicles 3:4-9; 14:3-5
[12] Compare 1 Chronicles 3:6-8 and 14:4-5. One Eliphelet was changed to Elpelet.
[13] 2 Samuel 10:18-19

"Joab is plenty capable of commanding the Israelite army. Put him in charge and you can stay home and enjoy yourself and your women. You have killed your tens of thousands. That's enough. Let others go to war and risk their lives."

So in the spring, the time when kings usually go off to war, David stayed home. He sent Joab out with the king's men and the whole Israelite army. While the king's men were risking their lives in battle and destroying Ammonites, the king was lounging in his palace in Jerusalem. Instead of investing himself in his children, he spent most of his time in bed. He was more interested in pleasuring himself with his wives and concubines than in doing anything constructive.

But David was soon bored with going to bed whenever he pleased and making love with What's-Her-Name. One day as the sun was about to set, after being in bed most of the day,[14] instead of saying, "Who's next?" David got up out of bed and walked around on the roof of his palace on the hill for a breath of fresh air. From there he could see a woman bathing. She was very beautiful, even more beautiful than his wife Abigail. And David wanted her.

David made inquiries and discovered she was Bathsheba, the wife of one of his elite Thirty, Uriah the Hittite. Nevertheless David sent for her and slept with her, and then she went back home.

A couple of months later she sent David a message: "I am pregnant."

David knew he was the father. Uriah was away fighting. So David tried to cover up his adultery. He arranged for Uriah to be killed in battle and took Bathsheba as his wife.

The angels in heaven were increasingly distressed to see David accumulate more and more wives. But adultery! Then murder! Heaven wept.

---

[14] 2 Samuel 11:2

The Plan

Hell cheered. The demons all congratulated the dragon on the outcome.

But the thing David had done displeased Yahweh. David must not be allowed to continue on this path.

Yahweh sent the prophet Nathan to tell David a story that would prick his conscience and jolt him back to reality.

Nathan ended by telling him, "Yahweh, the God of Israel, says: 'I anointed you king over Israel, and I protected you from Saul. I gave you the house of Israel and Judah. And if this had been too little, I would have given you even more. But you despised me by killing Uriah with the sword of the Ammonites. You despised me by taking Uriah's wife to be your own. Why did you despise me?'"

"*You despised me.*"

The words burned into David's heart, and he cried out, "I have sinned against Yahweh."

Nathan assured David, "Yahweh has taken away your sin. You are not going to die." Nathan also told David that as a consequence of his sin he would suffer severe calamities and heartache for the rest of his life. And his little son, born of adultery, would die.

After Nathan left, Bathsheba's son became ill. David wept, refused to eat, and even slept on the ground. He pleaded with God to heal his child, but Yahweh didn't change his mind. The child died on the seventh day.

To his servants' surprise, David then got up from the ground, washed, changed his clothes, went into the tent which housed the Ark of the Covenant, and worshiped Yahweh. There David's relationship with his God was restored. He poured out his heart to God in confession and repentance. As he sat quietly in God's presence, he began to express himself as he so often had in the past—in song.

David's Flaw

He sang while weeping with contrition:

"Have mercy on me, O God, because of your unfailing love.
    Because of your great compassion, blot out the stain of my sins.
Wash me clean from my guilt. Purify me from my sin.
    For I recognize my rebellion; it haunts me day and night.
Against you, and you alone, have I sinned;
    I have done what is evil in your sight....

Purify me from my sins, and I will be clean;
    wash me, and I will be whiter than snow.
Oh, give me back my joy again;
    you have broken me—now let me rejoice....

Create in me a clean heart, O God.
    Renew a loyal spirit within me.
Do not banish me from your presence,
    and don't take your Holy Spirit from me.
Restore to me the joy of your salvation,
    and make me willing to obey you....

Forgive me for shedding blood, O God who saves;
    then I will joyfully sing of your forgiveness....

You do not desire a sacrifice, or I would offer one.
    You do not want a burnt offering.
The sacrifice you desire is a broken spirit.
    You will not reject a broken and repentant heart, O God."[15]

---

[15] From Psalm 51, NLT

The Plan

The angels in heaven wept for joy to see David once more become a man after God's own heart. Yahweh proved, as He had done so often in the past, to be merciful, compassionate, and always ready to forgive. And David felt that forgiveness.

As David sat in front of the Ark in the Tent he had pitched for it, he again looked around and compared the Tent to his palace. He again wished he could build a temple for his God. But Yahweh had said, "No. Not you. One of your sons will build a house for me."

While David was thinking of the temple and wondering which of his sons would build it, Yahweh spoke to him.

"You have killed many men in battle and fought in a lot of wars. You must not build a temple for my name because you have caused so much bloodshed in my presence. But you will have a son. His name will be Solomon, which means peace, and I will give peace and quiet to Israel during his reign. He will build a temple to honor my name. He will be my son, and I will be his father, and I will establish his royal throne in Israel forever."[16]

David realized that Yahweh was being very gracious to him, not rubbing his nose in the fact that he had murdered Uriah. When Yahweh had first told David he could not build the temple, he had said nothing about David having shed blood as a warrior. But now that David had murdered Uriah, Yahweh added that as a reason for denying David his dream of building the temple. The blood on David's hands was not the blood of his enemies; it was Uriah's blood.

When David returned home from the Tent of Yahweh's presence, he was a changed man. His servants noticed it, and his family noticed it. David was again the man they had always loved and admired.

The first one David wanted to talk to was Bathsheba. He hadn't really talked to her for a week. David found her in her room and shared with her all that Nathan had said, confessing that he had wronged

---

[16] 1 Chronicles 22:8-10

her terribly, first by luring her into adultery, then by murdering her husband.

David looked Bathsheba directly in the eye as he confessed, "Bathsheba, I am responsible for the death of our son. Your son. I don't blame you if you hate me."

But Bathsheba didn't hate David. In spite of everything she loved him. She held out her arms for his embrace.

David then told her about his wonderful experience in the presence of Yahweh. He knew without a doubt that God had forgiven him, and he assured Bathsheba that she could be forgiven too.

David comforted her with the assurance that they would see their son again in eternity. Then he told her what Yahweh had said— that a son yet unborn would be named Solomon. He would be a man of peace. Solomon would build the temple. Yahweh would love him.

Finally, David shared with her a conviction that had been growing in his heart.

"Bathsheba, God has forgiven me so thoroughly that I dare to believe Solomon will be not just my son but *yours*. I want you to believe it too."

What a comfort to experience God's forgiveness! Together they wept tears of joy. Then David drew her to bed and they made love.

David rejoiced when Bathsheba gave birth to a son, and they named him Solomon. Yahweh loved him as he had promised. So, to let David and Bathsheba know that He approved of their naming the baby Solomon, He sent word through Nathan the prophet, "I have a pet name for him. Jedidiah. Loved by Yahweh."

* * * *

The angels in heaven rejoiced to see Yahweh's abundant compassion and forgiveness of David and Bathsheba. Lady Wisdom expressed what they were all thinking.

The Plan

"Yahweh is righteous and holy. But he is also compassionate and gracious. He doesn't constantly accuse people, nor does he remain angry forever. He knows how weak humans are; he remembers they are only dust.

"We have just watched Yahweh crown David with love and compassion. He didn't treat David as his sins deserved.

"But Yahweh is still just. Sin must be punished even if it has been forgiven. Yahweh will visit the sins of the father on David's children."

* * * *

David never again gave in to lust. He had learned the hard way where that road ended. He married no more wives, but he had to live with the consequences of his sin for the rest of his life.

25

David's Impact on Solomon

When David spied Bathsheba, Joab and all the army of Israel were fighting against the Ammonites. They ravaged the Ammonites and besieged the royal city of Rabbah.

During David's fall into adultery and his subsequent restoration to fellowship with God, Joab continued the siege of Rabbah. Shortly after Solomon was born, Joab took control of the city's water supply and knew it was only a matter of days until the victory was complete.

When Joab was on the verge of taking the city, he sent a message to David.

"I have fought against Rabbah and taken its water supply. Now you come, encamp against the city, and finish the job. If you don't, I will take the city and name it after myself."

So David fought with his men and took the city of Rabbah.

While gathering the spoil, David found the king's crown. It was very heavy. The crown weighed 75 pounds! Too heavy to wear. The crown was made of solid gold and was set with a gigantic precious stone. The crown sat on the head of the true king of Ammon, the idol Molech.[1] Its single stone was like an eye that made it seem alive.

In jest some of David's men set it on David's head and held it while he sat under it and felt its weight.

Lady Wisdom, watching from heaven, shouted, "No! No! David! Don't wear that crown!" But David did not hear her.

---

[1] 2 Samuel 12:30 and 1 Chron 20:2, LEB and ESV, footnote

The Plan

As far as Lady Wisdom was concerned, David did not get out from under that crown fast enough. That crown represented the entire history of Ammon, a man who had been born of incest, a man who had created an abominable system of worship which included child sacrifice.

David and all the people returned to Jerusalem with the spoils from Rabbah. David put the crown of Molech on display in his palace.[2]

Lady Wisdom wept.

"O David, you don't know what you are doing," she cried. "Yahweh said he would raise up evil against you out of your own house, but you have made it worse. He said he would take your wives before your eyes and give them to your neighbor, who would lie with your wives in broad daylight. But now it will be worse than that. You, David, have opened the door for Molech to add incest to your family's sins. You have also opened the door to other aspects of Molech worship in your family."

* * * *

Solomon was born in the royal residence built for his father David compliments of Hiram king of Tyre, who had admired David and followed his career ever since he killed Goliath. There was plenty of beautiful stone in Jerusalem, so no stone was imported. But Hiram supplied the cedar logs needed for the construction as well as skilled carpenters and stonemasons. The end result was beautiful but not extravagant. It was a grand house, and David was grateful to consider it his palace.

Solomon was fascinated by some of the treasures in his home. Of special interest was a giant crown of solid gold set with one large precious stone. His father had won the crown by defeating the Ammonite king who owned it.

---

[2] The Bible does not say this specifically, but the very next chapter, 2 Samuel 13, shows the result of playing with items controlled by the spirit world. Even 1 Chronicles 20 records the incident, showing that it had spiritual significance.

As a child Solomon was fascinated by the single stone in it. Sometimes he imagined that it was an eye watching him. Sometimes it gave him the creeps. Solomon tried to lift it, but he could barely move it. Once David indulged his son by holding it over his son's head for a few moments while Solomon dreamed of what it would be like to be king.

Little did either of them realize the dangers of doing so. The power behind that crown was real, and it was evil.

* * * *

For more than twenty-five years, from the time David killed Goliath till he committed adultery and murder, David had been loved, respected and adored by all Israel. Then, immediately after his sin with Bathsheba came to light, his life fell apart. For the next twenty-five years David experienced heartache after heartache as his children followed in his footsteps of murder and sexual sins.

The dragon made sure that incest was among those sins. David's eldest son Amnon lusted after his half sister Tamar and raped her.

Then the dragon whispered in David's ear: "The Law says: 'You must never have sexual relations with a close relative. Do not have sexual relations with your sister or half sister.' You know the Law, David. The Law says: 'Whoever commits any of these detestable sins must be cut off from the community of Israel.'[3] Your son Amnon has raped his sister. Now you must put him to death. Follow the Law!"

"No!" David replied out loud. Startled to hear his own voice, David looked around. Seeing no one, he whimpered, "I can't! He's my firstborn son!"

* * * *

A chorus of angels gathered in heaven to watch what David would do. They were horrified by Amnon's treatment of his sister, but they

---

[3] Lev. 18:6, 9, 27-29, NLT, slightly twisted by Satan

understood David's turmoil. David needed to administer justice, but he couldn't bring himself to judge Amnon. David saw himself as partly to blame.

"Yahweh is visiting the sin of the father on the son," observed one angel. "Incest and adultery are both sexual sins."

"David has never challenged inappropriate behavior in his children by asking them, 'Why do you behave as you do?'"[4] added another angel. "David loves his children, but not enough to discipline them. Now he is reaping the consequences."

The conversation continued as various angels added their thoughts.

"The law says those who commit incest must be cut off from their people."

"David is between a rock and a hard place. If he judges Amnon, people will call him a hypocrite. If he doesn't, they will say he turned a blind eye to evil."

Lady Wisdom made the connection between Amnon's sin and David's brief wearing of the crown of Molech, the spiritual king of Rabbah. In doing so, David had inadvertently given authority to Molech to interfere with him and his family.

"There is a way David can obey the law and not put Amnon to death," Lady Wisdom said. "Yes, Amnon committed incest, a crime which usually brings the death penalty. But look at it from another angle. The gods Molech and Chemosh were invented by Ammon and Moab, sons of Lot by incest. Those gods demand child sacrifice. If David puts his own son to death, the dragon will cheer that he sacrificed his son to Molech. The dragon considers it a bonus that Amnon is David's firstborn.

"If David had been thinking clearly, he would have answered the dragon from the same passage the dragon quoted. He should have

---

[4] See 1 Kings 1:6.

replied, 'The Law also says: Do not permit any of your children to be offered as a sacrifice to Molech.'[5]

"The penalty for those who commit incest is 'such persons must be cut off from their people.' 'Cut off' usually means death, but it could also mean exile. David could send Amnon into exile and still fulfill the law. But David must not be seen as sacrificing his son to Molech."

In the end, David did neither. He did not put Amnon to death, nor did he send him into exile. David could not explain his inaction regarding Amnon.

* * * *

One of Solomon's earliest memories was hearing the loud wailing of his older brothers. Everyone rushed to find out what had happened.

Absalom had killed his oldest brother Amnon. But why? Four-year-old Solomon didn't understand much except that Amnon had done something terrible to Absalom's sister, and Absalom had given the order for him to be killed.

Solomon overheard his father and Absalom shouting back and forth at each other.

"What have you done?" David demanded.

"I did what you should have done two years ago," Absalom shouted in reply. "Why didn't you punish Amnon for what he did to my sister?"

"I – I – I … couldn't!" David's voice petered out to a whisper. Then he shouted again at Absalom. "You're banished! Get out of my sight!"

Absalom fled to Geshur in Syria near the northern border of Israel. There he stayed with his maternal grandfather, the king of Geshur, for three years.

---

[5] Lev. 18:21

The Plan

Later Solomon remembered hearing whispers around the palace. "David couldn't bring himself to execute his son Amnon because he was guilty of a similar sin—violating a woman."

As time passed, Solomon would occasionally ask his father about Absalom, but the subject was taboo. So Solomon almost forgot that he had a brother named Absalom.

Meanwhile Solomon basked in his parents' love. He grew up knowing that his parents loved him and that the Lord loved him. When his parents wanted to remind Solomon that the Lord loved him, they called him Jedidiah, which means 'loved by Yahweh.' Solomon felt special.

Solomon's parents were aware that Yahweh had a very special plan for his life, and they groomed him for it. Before Solomon was born, David had made his older brothers chief officials in the palace.[6] Knowing that Solomon would be his successor, David introduced him to royal activities at a very early age. Solomon's brothers, some of them almost twenty years his senior, had no idea that this little brother was the crown prince.

David in his later years had learned from his mistakes, so he pounded into Solomon's head the importance of wisdom. Very early in life, while Solomon was still the only child of his mother, his father continually urged him to gain wisdom and understanding.

"Take my words to heart," David said. "Follow my commands, and you will live. Get wisdom; develop good judgment. Don't forget my words or turn away from them."

David spoke of wisdom as if it were a woman to be loved.

"Don't turn your back on wisdom, for she will protect you. Love her, and she will guard you. Getting wisdom is the wisest thing you can do! And whatever else you do, develop good judgment. If you prize wisdom, she will make you great. Embrace her, and she will honor you.

---

[6]   1 Chronicles 18:17

She will place a lovely wreath on your head; she will present you with a beautiful crown."[7]

David also taught his son to love the Lord, not only by words but by example.

Solomon would watch his father, when he seemed to be carrying the weight of the world on his shoulders, go into the nearby tent which housed the Ark of the Covenant of the Lord. Later he would emerge from the tent looking peaceful and serene. He would enter weary, and come out renewed. He would enter sad or depressed, and come out humming a tune.

Solomon knew there was something very special about that tent, but mostly about the Ark inside it. David said the Ark was Yahweh's throne on earth. The lid of the Ark was the seat of the throne—the mercy seat. Solomon wanted to see the Ark, but his father would not let him.

"The ark is not for curious onlookers," David said. "Yahweh is holy. He is powerful. He must be treated with reverential respect. If you don't treat Yahweh with respect, you could die."

Then David told the story of the time when the Philistines captured the Ark, hoping it would bring them good luck. When the Philistines took the Ark into their temples, the idols fell on their faces before it, breaking to pieces in their fall. The people of the cities where the Ark was taken developed tumors.

The Philistines didn't want the Ark in their territory, so they put it into a cart. But nobody dared to drive the cart back to Israel.

Finally, they hitched the cart to a couple of cows that had been separated from their calves—and watched. Many of the Philistines were surprised at what happened next, but some weren't. The God before whom their idols bowed was capable of anything!

The cows headed straight for Israel, mooing all the way. When the cows stopped just inside the border of Israel, people were curious to see inside the Ark. It had always been hidden away inside the Tent of

---

[7] Proverbs 4:3-9, NLT

The Plan

Meeting. This was their chance to see it up close. Seventy men looked inside the Ark, and Yahweh struck them all dead right then and there.

To reinforce this story, David told his own story.

"When I became king, the Ark was in Kiriath-jearim, but I wanted to bring it to Jerusalem. I was ignorant of how to transport it, so we put it on a cart again. This time, when the oxen stumbled, the man guiding the Ark put out his hand to steady it. Yahweh struck him dead right there on the spot for his irreverent act.

"It was three months before I had the courage to try again to bring the Ark to Jerusalem," David said. "This time I did it the right way. Priests carried the Ark by its poles, resting it on their shoulders."

Solomon was duly impressed with the power of Yahweh and the need to approach Him with reverential fear. That respect would last the rest of his life.

"The fear of Yahweh is the beginning of wisdom," he would later write.

His father urged him to study the Scriptures and make a copy for himself. David also gave him some of his own psalms to read. The psalms were songs of praise which David would often compose and sing while playing his harp.

From these psalms Solomon learned how much his father loved Yahweh, and Solomon was inspired to love Him just as much. Reading his father's poetry made Solomon thirsty to know God the way his father did.

One day something in one of his father's psalms caught Solomon's attention.

"Father, I read in one of your psalms, 'I, by your great mercy, will come into your *house*; in reverence will I bow down toward your holy *temple*.' I know you often enter God's house. I see you going into God's tent all the time. But where is His temple that you bow down towards?"

"It doesn't exist yet," David replied. "I don't even know where it will be built, but it *will* be built. One day the Ark of God's Covenant will be housed in a magnificent temple. I like to go inside God's tent, close my eyes, and imagine that I am in a beautiful temple with everything inside covered in gold. The inner sanctuary will contain nothing but the Ark. Soft light will be provided by narrow windows high up in the temple walls. It will be beautiful and pleasing to Yahweh."

"So why don't *you* build a temple, Father? You could do it."

"Yahweh knows my heart's desire, Son. He knows I would love to build such a temple, but he said, 'No. You're not the one to build me a house to dwell in.'"

David was careful not to say too much to his young son at this time. Later David would tell him the whole story. Solomon had brothers almost twenty years older than he. If word got out now that little Solomon was to be the next king, there could be trouble.

"What you need to do, Son, is apply yourself to your studies. Get understanding. And above all, get wisdom."

Solomon nodded solemnly.

"Come here, son," said David as he reached for his ever-present harp. "Let me teach you how to play the harp."

Solomon took his father's advice and set his heart on acquiring wisdom. He read psalms his father had written and composed many psalms of his own.[8] When he heard a wise saying or a proverb, he wrote it down. He also came up with many proverbs of his own. He studied nature and architecture and agriculture. He asked probing questions wherever he went. How? What? Why? When? Where? And he had an amazing ability to retain all he learned.

* * * *

---

[8] Solomon ended up writing over a thousand songs (1 Kings 4:32).

The Plan

David's failure to deal with Amnon's sin led to more heartbreak both for him and for Absalom.

After Absalom had spent three years with his uncle in Geshur, David allowed him to return to Jerusalem. There Absalom lived in his own house but was not allowed to see his father.

Another two years passed before David allowed Absalom to come and see him, but the damage was done. Absalom no longer loved his father.

Over the next four years Absalom worked diligently to steal the hearts of the people away from his father David. He spent a lot of time at the side of the road that led to the Jerusalem city gate where people came to bring their complaints to the king. There he quietly stole the hearts of the people who were looking for justice. When enough people sided with him, he went to Hebron and declared himself king.

When such a coup happens, the lives of the ousted king and all his sons are in danger. So David and his family were forced to flee from Jerusalem, leaving ten concubines to take care of the royal residence. Solomon was thirteen at the time.

Absalom moved into David's palace. There he disrespected his father by pitching a tent on the roof of the royal palace and sleeping with his father's concubines, committing incest in the sight of all Israel.

Yahweh had said a neighbor would sleep with David's wives; but instead, thanks to the influence of Molech, it was David's own son who did it.

Being forced to flee, David couldn't bear the thought of leaving the precious Ark of God's presence behind, so he contacted the high priest. Levites carrying the Ark on their shoulders went ahead of David and set the Ark down outside the city. There they offered sacrifices until David and his entire retinue—his household, his bodyguards, and six hundred soldiers who had spent years with David running from Saul— had finished leaving the city. All the people loyal to David—it seemed

David's Impact on Solomon

like the whole countryside—lined the road and wept out loud as David crossed the Kidron Valley and headed toward the desert.

When David passed the Ark, he stopped to talk to the high priest.

"Thank you for bringing the Ark out to me," he said, "but it belongs in Jerusalem. Take the Ark of God back into the city. If I find favor in Yahweh's eyes, he will bring me back and let me see it and his dwelling place again."[9]

Young Solomon knew how hard it was for his father not to have access to the Ark. He would never forget that day and his father's reaction.

David watched as the Ark disappeared back into the city. The thought of leaving the Ark behind was more than he could bear. David took off his shoes, covered his head, and wept as he walked barefoot all the way up the Mount of Olives. Soon everybody was weeping. Solomon and all the people with David covered their heads too as they tearfully climbed the hill.

David didn't dare stop until they had crossed the Jordan River, a fifteen-mile journey. The next day they continued on another thirty miles until they reached the southern tip of East Manasseh. There they finally felt safe in Mahanaim, on a ridge from which they would have a good view if any enemies should be following them. In Mahanaim an elderly friend of David brought bedding and food enough for the hungry, tired, thirsty refugees.

David wanted to march out with the army that assembled to fight Absalom, but Joab vetoed that idea. After all, David was now 65 years old.

"You must not go out," Joab insisted. "If we are forced to flee from Absalom, his army won't care about us. They want *you*. You are worth ten thousand of us. You can help most by giving us support from the city."

So David stayed in Mahanaim and waited anxiously between the inner and outer gates of the city for word about the conflict between

---

[9] 2 Samuel 15:25

The Plan

his troops and Absalom's. Later in the day a man came running with news from the battle.

David's only concern was for his son. "Is Absalom safe?" Though Solomon couldn't hear the answer, he knew what it was by watching his father. David left the gateway and went to the room above, weeping as he went.

"O my son Absalom! My son, my son Absalom! If only I had died instead of you. O Absalom, my son, my son!"[10] His wailing could be heard by anyone entering or exiting the city.

Thirteen-year-old Solomon didn't understand his father's reaction. Absalom had been in Jerusalem for years and his father had ignored him. Now that Absalom was dead, his father was weeping uncontrollably. It didn't make sense.

A few days later Solomon raised the issue with his father. David decided to be open with his son.

"Son," David said with tears in his eyes, "I weep not just with sorrow over the death of my son. I also weep with regret for the sins and failures of my past. This calamity has happened because of me."

David saw the shock on his son's face, but once he started, he had to continue.

"I brought this on my own head." David paused. "By my adultery. If you don't already know the circumstances around your birth, you might as well hear it from me."

David started talking more quickly.

"I met your mother because I was in the wrong place at the wrong time. I should have been out on the battlefield with my men. Instead, I was lounging around the palace. I went out on the roof, and from there I saw your mother on the roof of her house below. She was beautiful, and I wanted her. I made inquiries and discovered she was the wife of one of my mighty men. Against my better judgment and to my eternal shame I sent for her and slept with her. When I learned she was pregnant, I

---

[10] 2 Samuel 18:33

tried to cover my guilt. To make a long story short, I arranged for her husband to get killed in battle and I married her."

"So I am the product of adultery?" Solomon asked in horror.

"Oh, no," David replied. "We had a son, but he didn't live long. Yahweh took him as punishment for my sin. I had despised Yahweh by deliberately doing what I knew was wrong. As king I need to set the example for my people. If they are to love and obey Yahweh, I must love and obey Him first. Yahweh told me through Nathan the prophet that the sword would never depart from my house because I had despised Yahweh and broken his law."

Solomon was silent as he absorbed what his father was saying.

"So learn from me, son. Don't do as I did. Don't ever commit adultery. The consequences will follow you all your life. Your mother's first son died because of my adultery. Both Amnon and Absalom died too early in life because of my adultery. That's why I wept so uncontrollably when Absalom died. Not just from the grief of losing a son, but from regret. If I hadn't committed adultery, Absalom would still be alive."

26

Failures and Glory

Absalom's attempt to steal the throne from David exposed some long-existing cracks in the nation of Israel. Israel had a long history of disunity. Those cracks had appeared at the very beginning of Saul's reign when members of the army were identified as "men of Israel" and "men of Judah."[1] Both King Saul and Crown Prince Jonathan were aware that Samuel had anointed David as the next king. Yet after Saul's death the house of Saul fought to continue his dynasty. It took seven years for northern Israel to anoint David as their king.

During Absalom's temporary rule, Shimei, a Benjamite from the same clan as Saul's family, openly cursed David and declared that Yahweh had handed the kingdom over to his son Absalom.

Shortly after Absalom's death David was restored to his throne, supported by all the troops of Judah and half the troops of Israel.[2] The troops who weren't involved in restoring David to the throne felt left out because they hadn't been asked to help with bringing back their king. An argument broke out and soon harsh words were exchanged.

A troublemaker named Sheba, another Benjamite, seized the opportunity to again turn Israel against Yahweh's anointed. He sounded the trumpet and shouted, "Down with the dynasty of David! We have no interest in the son of Jesse. Come on, you men of Israel, go back to your homes!"[3]

---

[1] 1 Samuel 11:8
[2] 2 Samuel 19:40
[3] 2 Samuel 20:1, NLT

Failures and Glory

That rallying cry convinced all of Israel, the ten northern tribes, to abandon David and side with Sheba. David's loyalists were confined to the tribe of Judah. Eventually Joab besieged the city where Sheba was living, and Sheba was killed.

* * * *

While his father was busy fighting off troublemakers in his kingdom, Solomon was pursuing learning. But learning did not completely satisfy him. He wanted more than head knowledge. He wanted to use his hands. So he built houses. When that wasn't challenging enough, he looked for bigger projects. He designed and built entire communities—including houses, gardens, parks, vineyards and fruit trees. The gardens, vineyards and fruit trees needed water, so he made reservoirs to water them and keep them flourishing. And he accumulated flocks and herds.

All these projects needed to be built and maintained, so he bought male and female slaves to do the work. With the profits from his labors Solomon amassed silver and gold. He became a rich man while he was still in his teens.

The dragon watched Solomon acquiring wisdom and being successful at everything to which he turned his hand. It was time to twist things.

When he was sixteen, Solomon met a lovely girl and fell in love. Her name was Naamah, meaning 'sweet and pleasant.' She was just as sweet and pleasant as her name suggested, but she was an Ammonite. She worshiped the god Molech.

No form of idolatry was more abhorrent to Yahweh than Molech worship. Honoring Molech involved sacrificing children by making them walk through fire. When Solomon raised the issue, Naamah denied vehemently that she would ever make any of their children walk to a fiery death.

The Plan

Naamah was beautiful and Solomon desired her. The dragon whispered, *"Marry her!"*

Solomon wanted to consult with his father, but the Philistines were stirring up trouble again, and David had gone down with his men to fight against the Philistines.[4] Solomon had to make his own decision.

The dragon whispered in Solomon's ear.

"Don't commit fornication or adultery! You know how strongly your father warned against that. Do what is right. Marry her!"

So he did, and they moved into one of the new houses Solomon had built.

By now Solomon had learned that he would be the next king of Israel. His parents had told him the whole story surrounding his birth—that before he was born Yahweh had named him and commissioned him to build the temple that his father had wanted to build.

David showed Solomon all the materials he had amassed over the years to build the temple. Then he showed Solomon the stonecutters in the quarry cutting blocks of stone.

"I told all these workers that you were going to build a temple, Son. I told them it would not be built in my lifetime; I was just making advance preparations. I asked them to help you build it. I told them you were young and inexperienced. I stressed that the Temple must be exceedingly magnificent because it is being built for Yahweh. I want it to be glorious—praised and honored not just in Israel, but famous throughout the whole world, the talk of all the nations.

"That's why I'm starting preparations now. I have even started to import cedar logs from Tyre and Sidon. But I don't yet know where the temple will be built. Yahweh hasn't shown me."

Solomon soon found himself struggling in the tension between loving Yahweh and loving his wife. A year after their marriage Solomon and Naamah welcomed a son whom they named Rehoboam.

---

[4] 2 Samuel 21:15

Failures and Glory

With all his learning, Solomon was aware of the meaning of the name Rehoboam. The name suggested 'being or becoming wide'— in territory, fame, abilities or courage.

On the surface the name was good, but it had sinister connotations. The name had roots in common with 'Rahab' and 'Ammon'. By naming his son Rehoboam, Solomon was suggesting that his marriage to Naamah the Ammonite was broadening his territory to include other peoples, even those that Yahweh had condemned to destruction.

"*Rahab the Canaanite was my great-great-great grandmother,*" Solomon reasoned. "*She converted from paganism to Judaism, right? Surely I can influence my wife to follow Yahweh!*"

Naamah saw naming her son Rehoboam as evidence she was accepted in Israel even though she was an Ammonite and her people were idolaters. The 'mm' in 'Ammonite' expressed the idea of making secrets or information available to an in-crowd. She would start by teaching her son about her god Molech, and in time Solomon would be swayed to her way of worship as well.

* * * *

The angels in heaven wept to see Solomon taking a wrong turn so early in life. By marrying an Ammonite he had planted seeds for the destruction of Israel as a nation. It would take decades for that seed to mature, but the rot was setting in.

* * * *

The dragon had long been trying to destroy David—if not through lust, then through physical harm—through Saul, Absalom and Sheba. The decades of opposition had finally succeeded in wearing down David's confidence in Yahweh. David could no longer relax in the knowledge that all the people of Israel loved him. When would the next conspiracy arise? Would one of his enemies succeed in killing him?

The Plan

The dragon saw how vulnerable David was and knew it would be easy to further undermine his confidence in Yahweh.

"Are you sure Yahweh is protecting you?" the dragon whispered into David's ear.[5] *"Why don't you check the size of your army? How many of them will fight on your side if another conspiracy arises?"* So David ordered a census of the fighting men of Israel as if it were *his army* and not God who gave the victory. David asked for an inflated count which included under-aged men and Levites (whose job was to serve in matters pertaining to God, not war). For most of his life David had recognized that Yahweh was the source of his victory. He had even written a song about it.

> "For **you** equipped me with strength for the battle;
> > **you** made those who rise against me sink under me.
> **You** have delivered me from the attacks of my people;
> > **you** have preserved me as the head of nations.
> [**You**] brought me out from my enemies,
> > **you** delivered me from men of violence.
> **For this I will praise you, O LORD,**
> > **and sing praises to your name."**[6]

Yahweh had never ordered a census simply to measure military strength. Yahweh was Israel's protection. He could win battles with or without Israel's army. And he was David's protection.

But now David was no longer saying, "In God I trust. I will not be afraid."[7] He didn't pour out his fears to Yahweh and say as he had said earlier, "But as for me, I trust in you."[8]

Joab recognized that David's census was a denial that Yahweh could and would protect him. Joab was so disgusted that he quit counting.

---

[5] 1 Chronicles 21:1
[6] 2 Samuel 22:40, 44, 49-50
[7] Psalm 56:4, 11
[8] Psalm 55:23

Yahweh was angry at Israel for the way they had treated David. He was Yahweh's choice for king. He was Yahweh's anointed. David once composed a song in which he quoted Yahweh as saying, "Touch not mine anointed, and do my prophets no harm."[9]

So Yahweh's anger burned against Israel. It also burned against David for his lack of trust. Yahweh used David's sin as an opportunity to punish both David and Israel.

God gave David a choice of punishments: three years of famine, three months of destruction by enemy swords, or three days of plague—the sword of Yahweh. David chose the sword of Yahweh.

For three days David and the elders of Israel watched the death angel going throughout the land. The angel was standing at the threshing floor of Ornan with his sword drawn over Jerusalem when Yahweh stayed his hand in mid swing.

A prophet told David to build an altar on the threshing floor where Yahweh had stayed the angel's hand. David couldn't build an altar on property that didn't belong to him, so he bought the site. All the while that David was negotiating with Ornan, then building the altar, then preparing the sacrifice on it, the death angel had his sword up in the air.

When it came time to light the fire, David didn't have any holy fire—fire from the tabernacle several miles away. David didn't dare leave the threshing floor to get the fire—the angel would swing his sword. So David did the only thing he could think of.

He called on Yahweh.

And Yahweh answered with fire from heaven!

Only then did Yahweh order the death angel to put his sword back into its sheath. Later that day David reviewed what had happened. And the light dawned!

This was where the temple was to be built!

Yahweh had lit the fire on the altar for the tabernacle in the wilderness long ago. Today Yahweh had also lit the fire for *his* sacrifice.

---

[9] 1 Chronicles 16:22

The Plan

Yahweh was showing him where to build the temple. Right on Mount Moriah! Where Abraham had sacrificed his son Isaac! On the threshing floor he had just purchased!

God had turned David's disastrous decision to count his fighting men into something beautiful. The glorious temple—the replacement for the worn out tent—would be built there. When people gazed at the temple, they would not think of David's lack of trust in God. They would think of God's glory!

* * * *

The Plan shone brightly in spite of the dark stains on David's past. Yahweh used David's failures to demonstrate the magnitude of The Plan. Yahweh did not treat David as his sins deserved. Instead, He crowned him with love and compassion. He removed David's transgressions as far as the east is from the west. He displayed his amazing forgiveness by choosing Bathsheba to be the mother of the next king and allowing her son Solomon to build the temple.

In spite of personal failure of the worst kind—adultery and murder—David was still a man after God's own heart. Why?

Because he never worshiped another. His belief in who Yahweh was among all gods never faltered. He always came back to God in repentance.

And God used David's sin of counting his fighting men to show him where to build the Temple. Such is the grace and mercy that all who truly repent and believe in The Plan will receive!

27

Preparations for the Temple

David came home from Mount Moriah bursting with excitement, called for Solomon, and formally charged him to build a house for Yahweh, the God of Israel.

"Son," David said, "Building the temple was my personal dream, but God said, 'No, you aren't the one. But you will have a son who will be a man of peace. I will give him rest from all his enemies. His name will be Solomon and he will build a house for my Name. He will be my son, and I will be his father. And I will establish the throne of his kingdom over Israel forever.'[1]

"For decades I have wondered where the temple should be built," David said, "and today he showed me! Yahweh sent fire from heaven to consume my sacrifice today just like he did for the dedication of the Tabernacle in the wilderness. On Ornan's threshing floor! On top of Mount Moriah! Where Abraham sacrificed Isaac! That's where you, my son, will build the temple, a house for Yahweh, the God of Israel."

Solomon would always remember how excited his father was that day. He had never seen his father so energized.

David had paid fifty shekels of silver to purchase Ornan's threshing floor so that he could immediately erect an altar and offer a sacrifice to stop the plague.[2] But a threshing floor was not big enough for a

---

[1] See 1 Chronicles 22:7-10.
[2] About 1¼ lbs. 2 Samuel 24:21-24

The Plan

magnificent temple, so David bought Ornan's entire property on the top of Mount Moriah, paying six hundred shekels of *gold* for the site.[3]

David had been amassing materials for the temple ever since he got the idea of building it. He had stockpiled gold, silver, bronze, iron, wood, onyx, turquoise, stones of various colors, all kinds of fine stones, and marble—all in large quantities. Much of this was plunder which he had dedicated to Yahweh.[4] But he also gave generously from his personal wealth—over and above all the plunder—110 tons of gold and 260 tons of silver.[5]

Now he began to prepare in earnest for the construction of the future Temple. He turned over his supply of iron to make nails. He stockpiled cedar logs. He began the search for workmen—not just stonecutters, but masons, carpenters, and craftsmen skilled in working with gold, silver, bronze and iron.

David organized those who were to supervise the work of building so that everything would go smoothly. He told the stonecutters and those who were bringing cedar logs, "My son Solomon is young and inexperienced, and the house to be built for Yahweh should be of great magnificence and fame and splendor in the sight of all the nations."[6] So the foremen freely gave expertise where Solomon did not yet have it.

By the time David turned seventy, all the battles he had fought caught up with him. He was in such poor health that he couldn't keep warm even when people put covers over him. Expecting that his father would soon die, Adonijah, David's fourth son, with the cooperation of Joab and Abiathar the priest, seized the opportunity to make himself king.

David had never announced who would be his successor. He wanted to give Solomon time to grow up without being hassled about

---

[3] About 15 lbs. 1 Chronicles 21:25. See NIV marginal note.
[4] 2 Samuel 8:6-12
[5] 1 Chronicles 29:3-5
[6] 1 Chronicles 22:5

Preparations for the Temple

why he was chosen over many of his older brothers. Many knew that Solomon had been put in charge of building the temple, but nothing had been said publicly about who would be the next king. Only David, Bathsheba, Solomon and Nathan the prophet knew that Yahweh had chosen Solomon before he was born.

When David heard that Adonijah had been made king, he had to act quickly. He called Zadok the high priest, Nathan the prophet and Benaiah his chief bodyguard, and ordered them to put Solomon on King David's mule, escort him to Gihon at the bottom of the hill below the palace, and anoint him king immediately.

Adonijah's coup was stopped dead in its tracks. His celebration didn't even last a day.

Shortly thereafter David gave Solomon some fatherly advice. He knew there were a few people who could cause trouble for Solomon, so he pointed them out and charged Solomon to have them executed, which he did.

With Solomon on the throne, David seemed to gain a new lease on life. No longer burdened down with the affairs of state, with Solomon ably handling the daily tasks of ruling the kingdom, David concentrated on the Temple.

Though Solomon was tasked with building the Temple, it was not up to Solomon to come up with the blueprints. That was information that David himself had to provide as Yahweh put ideas into his mind.[7] The dimensions and the layout and all the details had to come directly from God himself. To discover these details, David needed to spend hours in the presence of Yahweh, listening to His voice.

But David was in poor health. Some days he could barely get out of bed. He could not freely go back and forth between the palace and the tent which housed the Ark of Yahweh's presence. So David consulted

---

[7] 1 Chronicles 28:12

The Plan

with Zadok the priest, who agreed that David could have the Ark brought into a special place in the palace. Zadok arranged for Levites to carry the Ark so it would not be touched by irreverent hands. David spread out his writing materials on a table nearby. Then he worshiped Yahweh and listened for his voice.

During this time Yahweh reaffirmed what he had said to David about Solomon. "Solomon your son is the one who will build my house and my courts. I have chosen him to be my son, and I will be his father. But he will have to keep walking in obedience to Me. I will establish his kingdom forever if he is unswerving in carrying out my commands and laws as he is doing at this time."[8]

Little by little, the ideas about the Temple came to David from God. The Holy Place and its dimensions. The Most Holy Place for the Ark with its mercy seat. Upper rooms, treasuries, inner chambers. Various courts. As the Holy Spirit put into David's mind all the plans for the Temple, David wrote them down.

Those plans included detailed instructions for the Temple furnishings—lamps, tables and altars. For the vessels—plates, forks, cups and basins. What materials to be used for each—cedar, gold, silver or bronze. The dimensions or weight of each vessel for service, whether silver or gold. Last of all was the plan for the golden chariot of the cherubim that spread their wings and covered the Ark of the Covenant of Yahweh. David sketched the decorative details as God revealed them to him.

As David thought about the Temple, he began to think also of the worship that would happen there. Here again the Holy Spirit instructed him and put into his mind all the plans for worship in the Temple.[9] And David wrote them down. Since Levites were no longer needed to carry the Ark and the Tabernacle from place to place, they needed

---

[8] 1 Chronicles 28:6-7, paraphrase
[9] 1 Chronicles 29:12-13

Preparations for the Temple

new duties.[10] David took a census of them and organized them for the services the Spirit required.

The prime movers of worship were a special section of Levites, the sons of Aaron, whom David separated into twenty-four divisions. These divisions served in rotation throughout the calendar year, each division serving at the Temple one week at a time twice a year, with all hands on deck during Passover week, Pentecost, and the Feast of Tabernacles. When not serving at the Temple as "officials of the sanctuary," they returned to their home towns where they served the spiritual needs of the people as "officials of God."[11]

For the musical portion of worship, David refined the procedures he had organized for moving the Ark from Kiriath-jearim to Jerusalem. He again assigned singers and musicians from three families of Levites. Their work was to prophesy in song accompanied by harps, lyres and cymbals.[12] Certain priests had the duty of blowing trumpets before the Ark of God.

The remaining Levites also needed to be organized. Gatekeepers were stationed at the entryways as guards "so that no one who was in any way unclean might enter."[13]

Some Levites were put in charge of the treasuries of the house of God, taking care of the things dedicated to God. Others were assigned throughout the country as officials and judges, to guide the people in their responsibilities towards God.

When all the plans were complete, David summoned all the officials of Israel to assemble at Jerusalem for the grand announcement about the coming Temple. During the ceremony he presented all the plans for the Temple to Solomon.

---

[10] 1 Chronicles 23:2-5, 25-32
[11] 1 Chronicles 24:5
[12] 1 Chronicles 25:1
[13] 2 Chronicles 23:19

The Plan

"I have all this in writing as a result of Yahweh's hand on me," David told him. "He enabled me to understand all the details of the plan.

"And you, my son Solomon, Yahweh has chosen you to build this sanctuary. Acknowledge the God of your father, and serve him with wholehearted devotion. If you seek him, he will be found by you. If you forsake him, he will reject you.

"Be strong and courageous. Do the work. Don't be afraid or discouraged, for Yahweh my God is with you. He won't fail you or forsake you until all the work of the temple is finished. I have already instructed the priests and Levites. They are ready for the work of the Temple according to their divisions. All the craftsmen are skilled and willing to help you with the work. The officials and all the people will obey your every command."[14]

The temple would require massive amounts of materials, including gold and silver, for its construction. David had contributed a lot, but much more was needed. So David used his own generosity to inspire others to give. He told of his own contribution to the work– more than 300 tons in gold and silver![15]

"Now then," David challenged the people, "who will follow my example, make an offering and dedicate himself to Yahweh today?"

Then all the leaders—leaders of families, leaders of tribes, the generals and captains of the army, and the king's administrative officers—all gave willingly. Their gifts totaled 188 tons of gold, 10,000 gold coins, 375 tons of silver, 675 tons of bronze, and 3,750 tons of iron. They also contributed numerous precious stones, which were deposited in the Temple treasury.

David then turned his materials and plans over to Solomon. All he had to do was to carry on from there!

---

[14] 1 Chronicles 28:9-10, 19-21
[15] 1 Chronicles 29:2-4; see NIV footnotes.

The people rejoiced over the offerings, given so freely and enthusiastically. And King David was filled with joy.

The next day was spent feasting as thousands of animals were sacrificed in thanksgiving for the future Temple. To top it all off, Solomon was anointed king a second time. David had carefully planned the timing of this coronation. It was the Feast of Trumpets, the day when most future kings of Judah would be crowned. The first anointing had been done in a hurry with very few in attendance. This anointing was well planned and joyfully celebrated. All the officers and mighty men, as well as all of King David's sons, pledged their submission to King Solomon.

Solomon's grand coronation was David's last public appearance. He stepped out of the picture and let Solomon shine. Eventually he died at a good old age, having enjoyed long life, wealth and honor.[16] He rested in peace, content that he had served God's purpose in his own generation.[17]

---

[16] 1 Chronicles 29:28
[17] Acts 13:36

28

Solomon Starts Well

With the grand coronation, the kingdom of Israel was firmly in Solomon's hands.

One of the first things Solomon did was form an alliance with Pharaoh king of Egypt. Solomon had become aware that a city in Israel, Gezer, still contained Canaanites who were a threat. The clan of Rapha still lived there. Goliath had been a member of that clan. But God had declared that Solomon would be a man of peace. So how could he make war on Gezer?

Idea: Get someone to do it for him.

Egypt didn't want war with Israel. They had feared Israel's God Yahweh ever since he had killed all their firstborn sons and drowned their army in the Red Sea. Egypt would gladly do a favor for Israel in order to assure peace.

So Solomon sent a proposal to Pharaoh: "Let's make a treaty. If you destroy Gezer for me, I won't ever attack you."

Pharaoh was happy to oblige. He agreed to destroy Gezer and kill the Canaanites in the city. In keeping with customs between kings of that time, Pharaoh suggested that the treaty be sealed with marriage to his daughter. Gezer would be her dowry.[1]

Solomon reminded Pharaoh of his priorities—building the Temple and the royal palace. Gezer would not be rebuilt until the Temple was built. Pharaoh had no problem with the conditions, and the treaty

---

[1] 1 Kings 9:16

was made. The last of the Canaanites in Israel were destroyed, and Solomon's throne was firmly established.

Pharaoh's daughter arrived in Jerusalem expecting to live in the palace, but Solomon said, "No." He had deep respect for the Ark. He knew that others in the past had died for not giving it due reverence. How could he bring an Egyptian wife into a place where the Ark had been? Egyptians worshiped many gods and goddesses—gods made in the image of falcons and hawks, jackals and cows, cats and rams.

So Solomon said, "My wife must not live in the palace of David king of Israel, because the places the Ark of Yahweh has entered are holy."[2]

Before his new wife could raise a fuss, Solomon promised to build her a palace that was much more luxurious than David's simple cedar palace. But she would have to wait. The temple must be built first.

Apart from marrying two foreign wives, Solomon started out well in his reign as king. Shortly after his second coronation, Solomon made a grand display of his love for Yahweh. He called all the leaders of Israel together, went to Gibeon where the original bronze altar made by Bezalel was located, and offered a thousand burnt offerings.

The aroma of the offerings was pleasing to Yahweh. That night he appeared to Solomon in a dream and said, "Ask for whatever you want me to give you."

"I'm only a little child," Solomon replied. "I don't know how to carry out my duties. Give me wisdom, knowledge and discernment to administer justice and govern your people. For who is able to govern this great people of yours?"[3]

Yahweh was pleased with Solomon's request.

"Since this is your heart's desire and you haven't asked for wealth, riches or honor, I will give you wisdom and knowledge. I will also give you what you didn't ask for—wealth, riches and honor—such as no

---

[2] 2 Chronicles 8:11
[3] See 1 Kings 3:6-9 and 2 Chronicles 1:8-10.

The Plan

king before you ever had and none after you will have. And if you walk in obedience to me and keep my decrees and commands as David your father did, I will also give you a long life."

When Solomon awoke, he returned to Jerusalem, stood before the Ark of the Yahweh's covenant and sacrificed more offerings. Then he gave a feast for all his court.

The next court case after Solomon received supernatural wisdom from God was a dispute between two prostitutes who lived in the same house and had babies three days apart. During the night one woman rolled over onto her son and killed him, so she switched the babies. Each woman declared that the living baby was her own. Solomon called for a sword and ordered that the living baby be cut in half. Each woman would get half. The true mother said, "Please! Give her the living baby. Don't kill him!"

Solomon declared her the mother of the living baby.

When all Israel heard about Solomon's verdict, they held the king in awe. They saw that he had wisdom from God to administer justice.[4]

Solomon's wisdom in court soon became legendary.

The first executive action Solomon took after receiving wisdom from God was to give orders to build a temple for the Name of Yahweh and to build a royal palace. Preparations began immediately, and in the second month of the fourth year of his reign, the actual construction began.

The temple was extravagantly beautiful. It was liberally adorned with precious stones. The whole interior was overlaid with pure gold—23 tons of it! All the furniture was overlaid with gold.

Outside the temple everything was made of bronze. Two giant bronze pillars 52 feet tall stood at the front of the temple. The altar, a giant washbasin called the Sea, and ten moveable stands with their ten basins were all made of bronze.

---

[4] 1 Kings 3:28

Seven years later the Temple was completed and dedicated to the glory of God. When the Ark was brought into the inner sanctuary, the cloud of God's glory so filled the Temple that the priests had to withdraw. They couldn't perform their service because of the cloud.

Hundreds of singers and musicians accompanied by 120 trumpets praised Yahweh in song. So many animals were sacrificed that the altar could not hold them. So Solomon consecrated the middle part of the courtyard in front of the Temple and offered sacrifices there.

After Solomon finished his prayer of dedication, fire came down from heaven and consumed the burnt offerings and the sacrifices.

That was the beginning of a grand festival. The dedication of the Temple was celebrated for seven days, followed immediately by the seven-day Feast of Tabernacles.

After the dedication of the Temple, Yahweh appeared to Solomon again just as he had done at Gibeon before construction on the Temple had started.

"I have heard your prayer," Yahweh said. "I have consecrated this temple, which you have built, by putting my Name there forever. My eyes and my heart will always be there.

"But as for you, you must walk before me as David your father did. Do all I command and observe my laws and I will establish your royal throne over Israel forever. But if you or your sons turn away from me and worship other gods, I will uproot Israel from my land and I will reject this Temple. Though this temple is now so imposing, all who pass by will be appalled. They will scoff and say, 'Why has Yahweh done such a thing to this land and this temple?' People will answer, 'Because they have forsaken Yahweh their God, who brought their fathers out of Egypt, and embraced other gods, worshiping and serving them. That is why Yahweh brought all this disaster on them.'"[5]

---

[5] I Kings 9:2-9; 2 Chronicles 7:11-22

29

Solomon's Downward Journey

With the temple completed and dedicated, Solomon turned his attention toward building his palace complex. He spent thirteen years building it, putting more resources into it than into the Temple.

The Temple was spectacular, but only priests and Levites could enter. Gatekeepers made sure that people didn't go further than the courtyard. The people could only imagine what was inside.

The palace complex was a different story. People could enter at the king's invitation. The Palace of the Forest of Lebanon was much bigger than the Temple—almost triple the size. In front of the Palace of the Forest of Lebanon, and equal in area to the palace itself, was a colonnade filled with a 'forest' of cedar columns connected at the top. In front of the colonnade was an open space covered with a roof upheld by more columns.

Included in the palace complex were three other buildings all of the same design. The first was the Hall of Justice from which Solomon judged. The other two buildings were set farther back. One was a residence for the king; the other was for Pharaoh's daughter. When the palace was finished, Pharaoh's daughter moved in.

In spite of Yahweh's warning to observe his laws, Solomon immediately began to break the rules for kings. Even before he started construction on the Temple, he began to accumulate horses. Soon he had 12,000 horses, most of them imported from Egypt.[1]

While building his palace complex, Solomon started accumulating more wives at the rate of a new wife every month. Solomon had

---

[1] 2 Chronicles 1:14-16 and Deut. 17:16-17

convinced himself that if he married every woman he lusted after, it was not adultery or prostitution. Ten years after the Temple was finished, he had sixty queens, eighty concubines, virgins beyond number,[2] and he was courting another.[3] This was against God's rule for kings that they not take many wives.

By the time Solomon finished the construction of the Temple and the royal palace complex, he had achieved all he had desired to do.[4]

With the temple and the palace complex done, Solomon turned his attention to less spectacular projects— constructing supporting terraces around the palace; rebuilding villages; rebuilding cities and fortifying them with walls, gates and bars; and extending the wall of Jerusalem. While working on these projects, Solomon paused, as he had done during the construction of the temple, to sacrifice offerings during the three major appointed feasts of Yahweh—only now he could make sacrifices on the magnificent new altar at the Temple.

Solomon maintained an outward show of piety throughout his life. Three times a year he sacrificed burnt offerings and fellowship offerings on the altar he had built for the Lord, burning incense before the Lord along with them, and so fulfilled the temple obligations.[5] He made sure that the daily sacrifices and all the feasts were celebrated in accordance with the ordinances his father David had put in place. He saw that the priests and singers and gatekeepers were not deviating from David's commands.

In the 24th year of Solomon's reign, shortly after completing the palace complex, Solomon got a visit from a prominent dignitary— the Queen of Sheba. She had heard of Solomon's wisdom and came to test

---

[2] Song of Solomon 6:8

[3] The NIV *Archaeological Study Bible* suggests Song of Solomon was written in the middle of his reign, about 950 BC.

[4] 1 Kings 9:1

[5] 1 Kings 9:25

The Plan

him with hard questions. She arrived with a very great caravan of camels loaded with goods.

Few of Solomon's guests asked such intelligent questions as the queen did. He was happy to answer all her questions. He described plant life, from the cedars of Lebanon to the hyssop that grows out of walls. He explained to her about animals and birds, reptiles and fish.[6] He quoted many of his proverbs and even sang her a song he had composed.

The queen watched Solomon in the Hall of Justice as people brought their cases to him. His wisdom in handling those cases left her with her mouth open in astonishment.

When his day in court was finished, Solomon brought the queen to dinner. There she was amazed at the food on his table and the seating of his officials. The attendants wore robes which indicated their duties. Servants and cupbearers wore different robes.

But what impressed the queen most was the Temple.

She could not go inside, but Solomon took her at sunrise to the Temple to watch the morning sacrifice. Solomon explained to her the significance of everything the priests and Levites did for the daily burnt offering.

"The Temple and the system of sacrifices that go with it are designed by God to show people how they can have fellowship with God," Solomon explained. "This fellowship happens, not as the result of going through the motions, or performing the right ceremonies, but as a result of hearts genuinely seeking a relationship with God. The same heart attitude that God looked for in Moses' time He is looking for today.

"Fellowship with God was initiated by God Himself. The very first verse in Moses' Book of Laws[7] tells us, 'Yahweh called to Moses and spoke to him from the Tent of Meeting.'

---

[6] 1 Kings 4:33

[7] Book of Leviticus

"Can you imagine being in your tent and hearing Yahweh's voice calling to you? 'Come to My tent. Come away where we can talk. I would like to talk with you.'

"That is what God is saying to us today. He is calling to you and me, 'Come. Spend time with me. Let's talk.'

"The burnt offering represents total surrender to Yahweh. Will you respond?"

The queen wanted to know more. She watched the priest pause to put his hand on the head of the lamb.

"Why is he doing that?"

"He is acknowledging that this animal represents us as a sinful nation," Solomon replied. "In particular he is acknowledging that he himself is a sinner. All of us deserve to die for our sins, but an Anointed One is coming. He will atone for wickedness so that we may live."

The queen watched as the lamb was killed and skinned and a pair of Levites took the hide and smelly parts away.

"Where are they going?" she asked.

"The one carrying the hide will give it to the priests," Solomon replied. "Many hides are turned into parchments on which to copy the words of the Law.

"The Levite with the offal will take it to the Valley of Hinnom to be burned," Solomon continued. "Unused parts of the sacrificed animal are not treated like ordinary garbage. They were treated with respect. They will be burned in a special place in a special way.

"The ashes from the temple offerings are holy," Solomon explained. "They are taken to a special place within the Valley of Hinnom. The ashes make that spot in the garbage dump ceremonially clean—holy. The offal is taken to the same place and burned.[8]"

"Are all sacrifices the same?" the queen asked.

"No. There are burnt offerings and sin offerings and guilt offerings. Different situations require different sacrifices and the rules for each

---

[8] Leviticus 4:11-12

The Plan

are slightly different. But one offering is voluntary— the fellowship offering. In that case the fat is burned but the meat isn't. The one making the sacrifice eats the meat while the fat is burning on the altar. In that way the person and Yahweh share a meal together in fellowship."

"The person consumes the meat while Yahweh consumes the fat," the queen guessed.

"Correct. But the fellowship offering is never made in isolation. The person always makes a burnt offering or a sin offering or a guilt offering first. Sin must be dealt with before one can have fellowship with Yahweh."

Solomon and the Queen of Sheba watched as the carcass was washed, cut into pieces and burned—all of it—on the altar as an act of total surrender to God.

The queen sniffed the air.

"It smells nice."

"Exactly," Solomon replied. "Moses' Book of Laws says, 'All the fat is Yahweh's.' The Book tells us over and over that these sacrifices are an aroma pleasing to Yahweh. The most pleasing part of the aroma comes from the burning of fat. In every sacrifice the priest is careful to make sure that *all* the fat is burned."

During the day Solomon showed the queen more of his projects and achievements. At sunset she wanted Solomon to take her to watch the evening sacrifice. As the priest put his hand on the head of the lamb, the queen stretched out her hand toward the lamb. Solomon understood her gesture and approved. She was placing her faith in the One who would atone for her.

Finally the time came for the Queen of Sheba to return to her home.

"Everything I heard in my country about your achievements and wisdom is true!" she exclaimed in parting. "I didn't believe what was said until I arrived here and saw it with my own eyes. In fact, I hadn't heard the half of your great wisdom! It's far beyond what I was told. How happy your people must be! What a privilege for your officials to stand here day after day, listening to your wisdom!

"Praise Yahweh your God, who delights in you and has placed you on the throne as king to rule for him. Because God loves Israel and desires this kingdom to last forever, he has made you king over them so you can rule with justice and righteousness."[9]

Then Solomon and the queen exchanged gifts. He gave her even more than she gave him. Then she left and returned with her retinue to her own country.

* * * *

The dragon was not amused. If the queen went back to her country and bragged about Solomon and explained The Plan, the whole world might turn to Yahweh!

If every king who visited Solomon learned the Plan.... Unthinkable!

The dragon didn't mind when people were awed by Solomon's wealth. That could easily be used for his purposes. It could be twisted into envy. Even Solomon's wisdom was fine—to a point. There was no harm in dazzling people with information about birds and bees and stars and planets. But when it came to The Plan! That could bring his evil kingdom to ruin. That must be stopped at all costs.

Yahweh had promised Solomon wealth, riches and honor, and He delivered on that promise. Solomon's merchants and traders were very successful. As Solomon's fame spread, kings of Arabia and the governors of the land came to visit Solomon as the Queen of Sheba had done. They also brought gold and silver to Solomon.

"Ah ha!" said the dragon to himself. "I can do better." He called his demons around to announce his idea.

"I can make Solomon even wealthier than God can," he said. "Just watch me. I will make sure that in addition to the revenues God brings him, I will add 666 talents[10] of gold annually."

---

[9] 2 Chronicles 9:5-8, adapted from NLT
[10] About 25 tons. 2 Chronicles 9:13

The Plan

All the demons cheered. They understood the significance of that number. It was the dragon's signature number.

"And I will distract Solomon with beautiful women." The demons cheered louder. "He will have more wives than anyone in history. He will have more money than he can spend and more wives than he can name. Riches and women will lure him away from the God he now loves and serves."

The response from the demons was deafening.

So the dragon and his minions went to work to destroy Solomon's legacy. When the gold started to pour in, the dragon whispered in Solomon's ear.

"Your Palace of the Forest of Lebanon is nice, but all that cedar is boring. You need to make it more dazzling. Put your gold on display."

So Solomon made two hundred large shields hammered out of pure gold and put them on display throughout the Palace of the Forest of Lebanon.

"More!" the dragon whispered.

So Solomon hammered three hundred smaller shields out of gold and hung them on the cedar columns of the colonnade in front of the palace, one on each 'tree.'

"More!" the dragon said, louder this time.

So Solomon made all his goblets of pure gold.

"More!"

Up to this point Solomon had been content with the riches in gold and silver that God had given him. But now he considered silver of little value, and those around him began to think the same way. Solomon wanted nothing made of silver—only gold. So he ordered that all silver items be removed from the palace. All the household articles in the palace were made of pure gold.

"How about a great throne in the Hall of Justice," the dragon suggested. "I can give you a few ideas."

Solomon made a great throne inlaid with ivory and overlaid with fine gold. The throne had six steps, and its back had a rounded top. On both sides of the seat were armrests, with a lion standing beside each of them. Twelve lions stood on the six steps, one at either end of each step.

The dragon got most of these ideas from his memories of life before Earth was created, when he was in Heaven in front of the throne of the Holy One. He knew how to stab God in the heart. Solomon was already dabbling with idolatry. Why not break the first of the Ten Commandments?

"*Carve an image into the throne*," the dragon whispered in Solomon's ear.

So Solomon carved a calf's head into the rounded top at the back of the throne—the rounded top which mirrored the rainbow encircling the throne of the Holy One![11] The calf was the symbol of the Ammonite god Molech as well as an echo back to the golden calf that Aaron made while Moses was on the mountain receiving the Ten Commandments.[12] Having the calf's head *above* his throne signaled that Molech was in a position of authority over him.

"That's more like it," the dragon nodded. "There's nothing like it in any other kingdom."[13]

The first few times Solomon ascended the steps of his grand throne to dispense justice, he felt good. But each day after that was less satisfying even though God continued to give him wisdom.

The dragon continued on his quest to destroy Solomon's love for Yahweh. All the kings of the earth sought audience with Solomon to hear the wisdom God had put in his heart. The kings brought gifts of silver and gold. The silver was quickly put out of sight (silver was as common as stones); the gold was put on display. The kings brought other gifts—robes, weapons and spices, horses and mules. And women!

---

[11] 1 Kings 10:19, Gods' Word and ESV margin. Compare Rev. 4:3.
[12] Exodus 32:4
[13] 1 Kings 10:18-20. Compare Rev. 4:2-3.

The Plan

All the kings—from the Moabites, Ammonites, Edomites, Sidonians and Hittites—all wanted to claim a connection to the great King Solomon. So they brought their daughters to him as wives. Hardly a week went by without Solomon adding one or two beautiful women to his harem.

Solomon loved them all and did his best to please them. These foreign wives worshiped their own gods and talked Solomon into building shrines for their gods. Soon Solomon was worshiping with them, burning incense and sacrificing to their gods.

Eventually Solomon began worshiping Ashtoreth, the goddess of the Sidonians, and Molech, the detestable god of the Ammonites. On the Mount of Olives, east of Jerusalem, he even built a pagan shrine for Chemosh, the detestable god of Moab, and another for Molech, the detestable god of the Ammonites.

* * * *

The angels in heaven wept as Solomon's wives turned his heart slowly but surely toward other gods. Even though Solomon went to the Temple three times a year—at Passover, Pentecost and Feast of Booths—to offer sacrifices on the altar he had built, he became less devoted to Yahweh his God.[14]

When faced with temptation, Solomon decided to deliberately step away from what was right. He applied his heart to know madness and folly.[15] He made a conscious decision to "explore" the dark side of life.

Early in life Solomon had devoted himself to study and wisdom. Looking back and reflecting in his old age, that seemed meaningless. He had explored madness and folly. That was meaningless. He had lived for pleasure and thrills. Meaningless. He had undertaken great projects. Meaningless. Married a thousand wives.

"Meaningless! Meaningless!" he said to himself. "Absolutely pointless! Everything is meaningless. A vapor that vanishes. Nothing but smoke. I've been chasing the wind."

---

[14] 1 Kings 9:25
[15] Ecclesiastes 1:17, ESV

The truth was that wisdom had satisfied him until he left God out of his life and pursued other gods. Building the Temple was the height of his many achievements. He had built it to the glory of God and found great satisfaction in doing so. Now, with God absent from his thinking, the Temple was merely another "great project."

As Solomon pondered, he continued to find things meaningless. But gradually bits of godly wisdom returned to him. Finally Solomon was able to come to a wise conclusion.

"Remember your Creator in the days of your youth... Remember him...before the dust returns to the ground it came from, and the spirit returns to God who gave it....

"Here is the conclusion of the matter: Fear God and keep his commandments, for this is the whole duty of man. For God will bring every deed into judgment, including every hidden thing, whether it is good or evil."[16]

Though Solomon returned to Yahweh and to wisdom, he, like his father David, had to suffer the consequences of his sin. God was very angry with Solomon for his idolatry, so He decided to tear the kingdom away from Solomon, leaving him with only two of the original twelve tribes. Graciously, for the sake of David, God delayed that until after Solomon's reign. But Yahweh raised up adversaries who troubled Solomon for the rest of his life. Solomon, whose name means peace, did not die in peace.

The high places Solomon built for Ashtoreth, Chemosh and Molech lasted for almost three hundred years. They were finally destroyed by King Josiah about sixty years before Jerusalem fell.[17] But idolatry was not driven out of the hearts of the people until the Temple was destroyed and the Jews were carried off to Babylon.

Such was the legacy of the wisest man on earth!

---

[16] Ecclesiastes 12:1, 6-7, 13-14
[17] 2 Kings 23:13

30

Idolatry, Judgment and Hope

By the time the Temple was built, the Plan had been told as thoroughly as it could be told without its actual fulfillment by the Son. The Plan was written in the stars, in Yahweh's annual appointed Feasts, in the sacrifices, in the writings of Moses and others, and in the stories recorded in Scripture. But there was one place it was not written consistently—in people's hearts.

Everybody knew that God existed. All they had to do was observe the beauty he had created all around them. They could see evidence of God's eternal power and divine nature clearly in creation. They also knew that God required them to behave in a certain way. Those laws and requirements were written on their hearts. As Solomon wrote in Ecclesiastes, God has planted eternity in the human heart—a sense of divine purpose, a mysterious longing which nothing under the sun can satisfy, except God.[1]

All people had to do was listen. Listen to the voice of God.

But they closed their ears. They did not want to hear what Yahweh was saying to them. They paid lip service to the fact that God loved them, but they didn't believe it in their hearts. They didn't believe that God's way was best. They wanted their own way. They believed that following their own way would bring happiness.

Many people preferred to invent their own religion. They created gods in their own image or in the image of birds and animals and reptiles.

---

[1] Ecclesiastes 3:11, AMP; Romans 1:18-23; 2:15

Idolatry, Judgment and Hope

And the dragon was happy to see them do that.

Solomon followed the worship practices of his foreign wives.

Jeroboam, the first king of the divided kingdom of Israel, invented a new religion patterned after Judaism. It had to be similar enough to the true worship of Yahweh that his subjects would accept it. So he maintained the annual feasts but celebrated them outside of Jerusalem. He made two golden calves, like the one Aaron had made when Moses was on the mountain, and set them up in Dan and Bethel. He proclaimed that they were the gods who brought them out of Egypt. He built shrines on a variety of high places. He installed priests who were not Levites at the high places. And he added another feast week to the religious calendar loosely patterned after the Feast of Tabernacles.

Every king of Israel who succeeded Jeroboam walked in his evil ways and caused the people of Israel to commit the same abominations. In spite of warnings that Yahweh sent through his prophets, the Israelites persisted in all the sins of Jeroboam and did not turn away from them. Finally, Yahweh removed them from his presence. The people of Israel were taken from their homeland into exile in Assyria in 722 BC.[2]

The southern kingdom of Judah did not perform much better. Solomon's son Rehoboam followed in his father's footsteps. He and the people of Judah engaged in all the detestable practices of the nations Yahweh had driven out before the Israelites.[3] Rehoboam's son committed all the sins his father had done before him.

The next two kings did what was right in the eyes of Yahweh. But Jehoshaphat's son Jehoram married a daughter of the infamous King Ahab of Israel and walked in the wicked ways of Ahab.[4]

Jehoram's wife Athaliah, daughter of Ahab, tried to wipe out the royal line of David. But her grandson Joash escaped the coup and was crowned

---

[2] 2 Kings 17:22-23
[3] 1 Kings 14:24
[4] 2 Kings 8:18

king at the age of six. Jehoiada the priest instructed Joash, and the young king did what was right in the eyes of Yahweh as long as Jehoiada lived. Joash collected the prescribed temple taxes and used the money to repair the Temple, maintenance of which had been badly neglected.

For the better part of 130 years Judah was ruled by good kings, but even they did not remove the high places which Solomon had built, so the people continued to offer sacrifices and burn incense to false gods there.

After a series of good kings of Judah, Ahaz came to the throne. He gave himself to doing evil in the eyes of Yahweh. He walked in the way of the kings of Israel and even sacrificed his son in the fire, following the detestable ways of the nations Yahweh had driven out before the Israelites. Ahaz offered sacrifices and burned incense at the high places, on the hilltops and under every spreading tree.[5]

During his reign the northern kingdom of Israel fell. The king of Assyria captured Israel's capital city of Samaria and took the people of Israel into exile, but Ahaz didn't heed the warning that Judah would be next if they didn't mend their ways.

Hezekiah son of Ahaz was the opposite of his father. He did what was right in the eyes of Yahweh. He removed high places, smashed sacred stones and cut down Asherah poles. He broke into pieces the bronze snake that Moses had made because the people had turned it into a fetish, burning incense to it.

Hezekiah was much like his forefather David. He trusted in Yahweh, the God of Israel, and did not cease to follow him. He kept the commands Yahweh had given Moses. There was no one like him among all the kings of Judah before or after him. And Yahweh was with him; he was successful in whatever he undertook.[6]

Sadly, his son Manasseh did not follow his example. Manasseh rebuilt the high places his father Hezekiah had destroyed. He erected

---

[5] 2 Kings 16:3-4
[6] 2 Kings 18:3-7

altars to Baal and made Asherah poles. He personally carved an Asherah pole and put it in the Temple built for the Name of Yahweh. He bowed down to all the starry hosts and worshiped them. He built altars to the starry hosts in both courts of the Temple. He made his sons pass through the fire in the Valley of Ben-Hinnom as an offering to his gods. He practiced sorcery, divination and witchcraft, and consulted mediums and spiritists. And he led the people astray, so that they did more evil than the nations Yahweh had destroyed before the Israelites.

Yahweh told the prophets, "Manasseh has done more evil than the Amorites who preceded him and has led Judah into sin with his idols."

So the prophets brought word to Manasseh, "This is what Yahweh, the God of Israel, says: I am going to bring such disaster on Jerusalem and Judah that the ears of everyone who hears of it will tingle. I will wipe out Jerusalem as one wipes a dish, wiping it and turning it upside down. I will hand my people over to their enemies because they have done evil in my eyes and have provoked me to anger ever since they came out of Egypt."[7]

But Yahweh was longsuffering. He waited a whole century from the beginning of Manasseh's reign before bringing judgment on Judah.

During that time only one king, Josiah, was good. He came to the throne at the age of eight. When he was 15, he began to seek the God of his forefather David. Four years later he began to purge Judah and Jerusalem of high places, Asherah poles, carved idols and cast images. Under his direction the altars of the Baals were torn down, the incense altars above them were cut to pieces, the Asherah poles were smashed, and the idols and carved images were destroyed. After purging Judah and Jerusalem, Josiah went into what was left of the northern kingdom—to towns of Manasseh, Ephraim, Simeon and Naphtali, and the ruins around them—and did the same. Then he went back to Jerusalem.

When he was 25, Josiah began to repair the Temple. While the repairs were being done, Hilkiah the priest found the Book of the Law

---

[7] 2 Kings 21:3-15; 2 Chronicles 33:2-9

The Plan

that had been given through Moses, and the secretary began reading it to the king.

When Josiah heard the words of the Law, he tore his robes. He was alarmed that Yahweh's great anger was about to be poured out on them because they hadn't acted in accordance with what was written in the Book.

The prophetess Huldah brought word to the king, "This is what Yahweh says: 'I am going to bring disaster on this place and its people—all the curses written in the Book. Because they have forsaken me and burned incense to other gods, my anger will be poured out on this place and will not be quenched.'"

Then she had words specifically for Josiah.

"This is what Yahweh says, 'Because your heart was responsive and you humbled yourself before God when you heard what he spoke against this place and its people, … you will be buried in peace. Your eyes will not see all the disaster I am going to bring on this place and on those who live here.'"

For centuries prophets such as Elijah, Isaiah, Jeremiah and more than a dozen others warned the idolaters of their evil ways. They warned that judgment would come upon them and they would be driven from the land God had given them because of their rebellion against Him.

The prophet Isaiah called out to God's people:

Listen, O heavens! Pay attention, earth!
This is what the LORD says:
"The children I raised and cared for have rebelled against me.
Even an ox knows its owner, and a donkey recognizes its
master's care—but Israel doesn't know its master.
My people don't recognize my care for them."

The prophet tried to get the people to see what damage they were doing to themselves.

> *Ah, sinful nation, a people laden with iniquity,*
> *Why do you continue to invite punishment?*
> > *Must you rebel forever?*
> *You are battered from head to foot—*
> > *covered with bruises, welts, and infected wounds—*
> > *without any soothing ointments or bandages.*
> *Your country lies in ruins, and your towns are burned.*
> *Foreigners plunder your fields before your eyes*
> > *and destroy everything they see.*
> *Beautiful Jerusalem stands abandoned.*
> *If the LORD of Heaven's Armies had not spared a few of us,*
> > *we would have been wiped out like Sodom,*
> > *destroyed like Gomorrah.*

Isaiah tried to get the people to see how God viewed them.

> *Listen to the LORD, you leaders of "Sodom."*
> *Listen to the law of our God, people of "Gomorrah."*
> *"What makes you think I want all your sacrifices?"*
> > *says the LORD.*

> *"I am sick of your burnt offerings of rams and the fat of fattened cattle.... Stop bringing me your meaningless gifts;*
> > *the incense of your offerings disgusts me!*

> *I hate your new moon celebrations and your annual festivals.*
> > *They are a burden to me. I cannot stand them!"*

Isaiah told them God wouldn't listen to their prayers.

> *"When you lift up your hands in prayer, I will not look.*
> *Though you offer many prayers, I will not listen, for your*
> *hands are covered with the blood of innocent victims."*

The remedy was repentance.

> *"Wash yourselves and be clean! Get your sins out of my sight.*
> *Give up your evil ways. Learn to do good."*

Isaiah showed them God's desire that they be reconciled to him.

> *"Come now, let's settle this," says the* L<small>ORD</small>.
> *"Though your sins are like scarlet,*
> *I will make them as white as snow.*
> *Though they are red like crimson,*
> *I will make them as white as wool."*

But there was an ultimatum attached.

> *"If you will only obey me, you will have plenty to eat. But if*
> *you turn away and refuse to listen, you will be devoured by the*
> *sword of your enemies. I, the* L<small>ORD</small>, *have spoken!"*[8]

Isaiah urged the people,

> *Seek the* L<small>ORD</small> *while He may be found;*
> *call upon Him while He is near.*
> *Let the wicked forsake his way*
> *and the unrighteous man his thoughts;*
> *And let him return to the* L<small>ORD</small>,
> *and He will have compassion on him,*
> *And to our God, for He will abundantly pardon.*[9]

---

[8] From Isaiah 1:2-20, NLT
[9] Isaiah 55:5-7, NASB

Yahweh sent word to his people through his messengers again and again, but they mocked his messengers, despised his words and scoffed at his prophets. There was no remedy except judgment. In 586 BC the Babylonians, instruments of Yahweh's wrath, brought terrible death and destruction to Jerusalem and Judah. They carried off the Temple treasures, set fire to the Temple, burned all the palaces, destroyed everything of value in Jerusalem, and carried into exile the remnant who escaped the sword.

By that time Isaiah was long dead, but his prophecies gave hope to the exiles in Babylon. Isaiah had encouraged Israel that though destruction would come upon them, the story would not end there. A remnant would return.

> *In that day the remnant of Israel, the survivors of Jacob,*
>   *will no longer rely on him who struck them down*
>   *but will truly rely on the LORD, the Holy One of Israel.*
> *A remnant will return, a remnant of Jacob will return*
>   *to the Mighty God.*[10]

And Isaiah made an amazing prophecy, naming a man who was not yet born, a man who would fulfill God's promise 150 years after Isaiah declared it. Cyrus, a future king of Persia, would be instrumental in the rebuilding of Jerusalem.

> **Thus says the LORD, your Redeemer,**
>   *who formed you from the womb:*
> *"I am the LORD, who made all things,*
>   *who alone stretched out the heavens,…*
> **who says of Jerusalem,** *'She shall be inhabited,'*
>   **and of the cities of Judah,** *'They shall be built;*
> **who says of Cyrus,** *'He is my shepherd,*

---

[10] Isaiah 10:20-22, NIV

> *and he shall fulfill all my purpose';*
> ***saying of Jerusalem****, 'She shall be built,'*
> ****and of the temple****, *'Your foundation shall be laid.'"*
> *Thus says the* L<small>ORD</small> *to his anointed,* **to Cyrus**, …
> *"I will go before you and level the exalted places,*
> *I will break in pieces the doors of bronze*
> > *and cut through the bars of iron,…*
>
> ***that you may know that it is I, the*** L<small>ORD</small>***,***
> > *the God of Israel,* ***who call you by your name****.*
>
> *For the sake of my servant Jacob, and Israel my chosen,*
> *I call you by your name, I name you,*
> > *though you do not know me.*
>
> *I am the* L<small>ORD</small>*, and there is no other,*
> > *besides me there is no God;*
>
> > ***I equip you, though you do not know me,***
>
> *that people may know, from the rising of the sun*
> > *and from the west, that there is none besides me;*
>
> *I am the* L<small>ORD</small>*, and there is no other.*
> *I form light and create darkness;*
> > *I make well-being and create calamity;*
>
> ***I am the*** L<small>ORD</small>***, who does all these things****.*
>
> ***I will raise up Cyrus in my righteousness****:*
> > *I will make all his ways straight.*
> > *He will rebuild my city and set my exiles free,…*
> > *says the* L<small>ORD</small> *Almighty.*[11]

Added to Isaiah's prophecies were the words of Jeremiah—that Israel's exile to Babylon would last seventy years.

---

[11] Isaiah 44:24 – 45:7, ESV; Isaiah 45:13, NIV

> *This entire land will become a desolate wasteland. Israel and her Israel and her neighboring lands will serve the king of Babylon for seventy years. Then after seventy years are completed, I will punish the king of Babylon and that nation, the land of the Chaldeans, for their iniquity, declares the LORD, making the land an everlasting waste.*[12]

Though Jeremiah lamented the judgment upon God's people, he reminded them of Yahweh's great love. And that love brought hope.

> *The faithful love of the LORD never ends!*
> *His mercies never cease.*
> *Great is his faithfulness;*
> *his mercies begin afresh each morning.*[13]

---

[12] Jeremiah 25:11-12, NLT
[13] Lamentations 3:22-23, NLT

31

Restoration

In case the people in exile doubted that the prophecies of Isaiah and Jeremiah would come true, Daniel, who had been exiled to Babylon as a teenager, reminded them of God's sovereignty.

> *His rule is everlasting, and his kingdom is eternal.*
> *All the people of the earth are nothing compared to him.*
> *He does as he pleases among the angels of heaven*
> *and among the people of the earth.*
> *No one can stop him or say to him,*
> *'What do you mean by doing these things?'*[1]

Jerusalem and the Temple had been destroyed in 586 BC. The seventy years of exile would be up in 516 BC, but the exiles would need their Temple in order to worship Yahweh properly. Rebuilding the Temple would take time, so in 538 BC, Yahweh moved the heart of Cyrus king of Persia to fulfill what Yahweh had spoken through Jeremiah and Isaiah. Cyrus made a proclamation throughout his realm and put it in writing:

> "This is what King Cyrus of Persia says:
>
> *Yahweh, the God of heaven, has given me all the kingdoms of the earth. He has appointed me to build him a Temple at Jerusalem. Any of you who are his people may go to Jerusalem*

---

[1] Daniel 4:34-35, NLT

in Judah to rebuild this Temple of Yahweh, the God of Israel, who lives in Jerusalem. And may your God be with you!"[2]

Babylon had fallen to the Medes and Persians the year before, so the Jewish exiles were now under the rule of Cyrus. During the captivity in Babylon, Zerubbabel had been recognized as prince of Judah, so Cyrus made him governor of Judea. Zerubbabel then led the first group of Jewish exiles back to their homeland. Cyrus even sent with them the treasures that Nebuchadnezzar had taken from the Temple in Jerusalem.

Knowing that worship of Yahweh was even more important than the Temple itself, Zerubbabel and his associates began by building the altar on the foundation where Solomon's bronze altar had been. When it was built, they immediately started presenting burnt offerings to Yahweh in accordance with what was written in the Law of Moses. They offered daily sacrifices morning and evening, and they began offering sacrifices for all the appointed feasts, starting with the holy days of the seventh month.

There was plenty of opposition to the rebuilding, so the Temple was not completed during the reign of Cyrus. In 516 BC, twenty-two years after Cyrus made his decree, the Temple was finally completed and dedicated. Priests and Levites were installed for the service of God in time to celebrate Passover.

What a joyful celebration! The seventy years of exile were up, and the Jews were free to return to their homeland. But the majority of them didn't return immediately. Life in Jerusalem and Judah was not easy.

* * * *

458 BC

Fifty-eight years later, Persia's king Artaxerxes made a decree which made it easier for exiles to return:

---

[2] Ezra 1:1-3, adapted from NLT

The Plan

> *Artaxerxes, king of kings,*
> *To Ezra the priest, teacher of the Law of the God of heaven: Greetings,*
>
> *Now I decree that any of the Israelites in my kingdom, including priests and Levites, who wish to go to Jerusalem with you, may go. You are sent by the king and his seven advisers to inquire about Judah and Jerusalem with regard to the Law of your God.*[3]

The decree provided money from the province of Babylon to buy animals for the required sacrifices to Yahweh. It authorized Ezra to set up an administration of magistrates and judges. The decree also instructed Ezra to teach the laws of God to any who did not know them.

What a change from life in Babylon! What freedom to worship Yahweh!

Ezra and a wave of returnees arrived in Jerusalem after a four-month journey from Babylon. Ezra was just what the Jews needed— a teacher well versed in the Law of Moses, who had devoted himself to the study and observance of the Law and to teaching it in Israel.

Ezra soon learned that the people of Israel, including the priests and the Levites, had intermarried with pagan peoples around them who practiced idolatry and other abominations. When Ezra heard this, he tore his clothes, pulled hair from his head and beard, and sat down appalled. At the evening sacrifice he fell on his knees, spread his hands out to Yahweh and prayed.

While Ezra was praying and confessing, weeping and throwing himself down before Yahweh, a large crowed of Israelites gathered around him. Soon they too were weeping bitterly. They knew they had done wrong. As a result, they covenanted before God to send away all the foreign women and children.

---

[3] Ezra 7:12-14

But not all the foreigners were idolaters or evil doers. Some loved and served Yahweh. So a committee was selected to investigate each case. Three months later all the cases had been reviewed and acted upon. In the end only 110 men had to send their wives and children away.

* * * *

444 BC

Fourteen years later Nehemiah came to Jerusalem to supervise the repairing and rebuilding of Jerusalem's gates and walls. He brought with him another wave of exiles. Many of them had taken foreign wives while in Babylon.

After the wall was rebuilt and the people were safely settled in their towns, on the Feast of Trumpets Ezra assembled all who were able to understand Hebrew. The people listened attentively as Ezra opened the Book of the Law and read to them from daybreak to noon.

Those who didn't understand Hebrew also wanted to listen. So, before Ezra resumed reading in the afternoon, he arranged for more than a dozen Levites to translate and explain to various language groups. As people listened to and understood the words of the Law, they began to mourn and weep.

Ezra knew that the people's sins had to be dealt with, but they were entering the very important fall feast season, so repentance would have to be postponed. Instead, he taught the people about the Feast of Tabernacles, which most of them had never celebrated, and which would be upon them in two weeks' time. The people went into the countryside and brought back branches to build booths on their roofs and in their courtyards. They hadn't celebrated like this since the days of Joshua, and their joy was very great.

For seven days they celebrated the Feast, followed by an assembly on the eighth day. Ezra read from the Book every day. For the first time

The Plan

in decades, maybe in centuries, the entire population of Israel really listened to the Word of God.

For three hours on the eighth day Ezra read to the assembly from the Book, and the people came under conviction of sin. The people had been cured of idolatry during their years of exile in Babylon, but many of them still had foreign wives, which put them in danger of returning to idolatry in the future. For the next three hours the people confessed their sins and worshiped Yahweh their God.

But confession wasn't enough. They had to forsake their sins— and put away their foreign wives. The Levites drew up a binding agreement and put it in writing. The priests and Levites and leaders of the people affixed their seals to it. In the agreement they bound themselves with a curse and an oath to follow the Law of God given by Moses.

They promised not to intermarry with the peoples around them. They promised not to buy or sell on the Sabbath or any holy day. They promised to celebrate the Sabbatical year by not working the land and by canceling all debts.

*They promised
to celebrate the annual
appointed feasts and holy days,*

*to bring the first fruits
of their crops to Yahweh,*

to pay their tithes.

*They promised,
"We will not neglect
the house of our God."*[4]

---

[4] Nehemiah 10:28-39

32

Repentance Didn't Last

Promises, promises.

432 BC

"Why is the house of God neglected?" Nehemiah asked the officials. Nehemiah had returned to Jerusalem after twelve years in Babylon only to learn that things were not right at the Temple. The solemn agreement written twelve years earlier and sealed with the seals of the priests and Levites and leaders of the people was not worth the parchment it was written on.

The priest in charge of the storerooms of the Temple had allowed a close friend to live in one of the storerooms! Nehemiah was greatly displeased and threw all the fellow's household goods out of the room. He then gave orders to purify the rooms and put back the equipment, grain offerings and incense that belonged there.

Further investigation disclosed that there were other irregularities. Sabbath was no different from any other day of the week. Nehemiah found men treading winepresses on the Sabbath. Others were loading their donkeys with grain, wine, grapes, figs and all kinds of goods, bringing it all to Jerusalem for sale on the Sabbath.

When evening shadows fell on the gates of Jerusalem before the Sabbath, Nehemiah ordered the doors to be shut and not opened again until the Sabbath was over. Some men parked themselves at the gates, hoping to get inside in the morning, but Nehemiah commanded Levites to guard the gates in order to keep the Sabbath day holy.

Only twelve years earlier, Ammonites, Moabites and anyone of foreign descent had been excluded from Israel. Now Nehemiah saw men of Judah who had married women from Ashdod, Ammon and Moab. Half of their children spoke foreign languages and couldn't speak the language of Judah.

Nehemiah rebuked the men and called down curses on them. He beat some of the men and pulled out their hair. He made them take an oath in God's name saying they would not allow their sons and daughters to marry foreigners.

"Wasn't it because of marriages like these that Solomon sinned?" Nehemiah cried in frustration. "Even *he* was led into sin by foreign women. Must we hear now that you too are being unfaithful to our God by marrying foreign women?"

Obviously the Law was not written on their hearts.

So ended the Old Testament history of Israel. Nehemiah could do nothing but plead, "O my God, show mercy. Remember me with favor, O my God."[1]

Old Testament prophets gave warning after warning, but the people soon forgot. So Yahweh stopped talking.

Four hundred years passed in silence.

---

[1] Nehemiah 13:22, 31

33

The Plan Begins

Father, Son and Spirit were in the Throne Room talking together.

"It is time to start putting The Plan into action," Father said. "Soon you, my Son, will become human so that human beings can understand who I am and what I am like."

"But first we must send someone to prepare the way," continued Spirit without the slightest pause in their flow of thought.

"He must stir up the hope that has died on earth," said Son. "Humans have such a narrow concept of time. They think we are slow in keeping the Promise. They don't understand that to us the Promise was given only the day before yesterday."

"To humans that seems like two thousand years," Spirit reminded Son, though he didn't need reminding. "From their viewpoint it is four hundred years since a prophet last mentioned anything to do with the Promise."

"They don't understand that the Plan was as good as done before we even created Earth and the concept of time," added Father.

"The one we send will convince people that we have not forgotten the Promise—that now it is near even by their finite standards," said Spirit. "Once hope is restored, they will be looking for the Prince of Peace—you!" he said, turning to Son.

"My role will be to redeem relationships," said Son, "to restore the relationship broken by the first disobedience."

"Some people think peace is the absence of conflict," said Father. "They think they can experience peace by ignoring me. They think if

The Plan Begins

they pretend I don't exist, there won't be any conflict between good and evil so they can go on living as they please with no consequences. They think truth is whatever they imagine it to be."

"The way to break down their resistance to the truth is to appear first as a baby," said Spirit.

"No one will be able to resist me when I appear as a cuddly, helpless infant," said Son, knowing this had been in The Plan before creation. "Everybody loves a baby. But when I grow up before their eyes and start speaking the unvarnished truth, many will hate me— especially the self-righteous types. Then I will show them what true love is by dying for them while they are still sinners."

"And those who believe that you are the Way, the Truth and the Life will experience joy like never before," added Spirit. The other two nodded in agreement.

"So who will prepare the way for me to bring peace to replace the hostility that began in the Garden between holy God and sinful man?" asked Son. "Who will prepare the way for me to bring hope to replace their despair, love to dissolve their hatred, and joy to replace their sadness?"

"We will begin to bring light into their dark world by sending a messenger to prepare the way for the Messiah," said Father. "The Messiah, the true Light, will completely dispel the darkness. His messenger will be a voice calling in the desert, 'Prepare the way for the Lord, make straight paths for him.'"[1]

"The messenger must be raised in a special home where he will be prepared for his duties," said Spirit. "His father must be someone who knows the Scriptures—a priest. Priests understand The Plan better than anyone, even if that understanding is limited, though all the hosts of Heaven know we have done our best to make things plain."

"I know the best father for the messenger," said Son.

"And who would that be?" asked Father.

---

[1] Mark 1:3; Luke 3:4

"Zechariah."

"Zechariah!" exclaimed Spirit. "But he is old! And his wife Elizabeth is both old *and* barren."

"That was also true in the case of Abraham and Sarah," Son reminded him, "but we didn't let that stop us from fulfilling our Promise to him."

"I remember that," said Father. "We were going to fulfill the Promise immediately—we announced it to Abraham when he was 75. Then Son said, 'No, let's wait another 25 years so people will be *really* impressed with the miracle of Isaac's birth.'"

"And I said, 'That opens up a whole world of possibilities. Just watch. Abraham will try to figure out a way to fulfill the Promise on his own,'" added Spirit.

"Of course, Abraham did," said Father, "and that gave us the opportunity to demonstrate that nothing can thwart our purposes."

"That's why Zechariah is such a good choice," explained Son patiently. "How else will people know that we sent the messenger unless a miracle draws attention to him? It has been so long since people have seen miracles that they don't know what miracles look like. They must learn to expect miracles from God again."

"I agree with Son," said Father. "Zechariah is a good choice. Not only are he and his wife both descendants of Aaron, the original priest, but both of them are upright, observing our commandments and regulations blamelessly."

"So it's settled," concluded Spirit. "Zechariah will be the father of the forerunner of the Messiah."

"Zechariah and Elizabeth have been praying for a child ever since they were married," said Son. "It's time they learned that we have been listening."

"Won't they be surprised to learn how special that child will be!" exclaimed Spirit.

The Plan Begins

Two archangels had been in the background standing at attention on either side of the Throne throughout the entire conversation, waiting to serve the Holy One at a moment's bidding. Though Father, Son and Spirit spoke and moved as individuals, the angels could not think of them as anything other than the Holy One, so united were they in their character and thoughts.

Now Father turned to the nearest archangel. "Gabriel!" he called in a voice that conveyed both love and authority.

Gabriel stepped forward quickly, eager to do the Holy One's bidding. It was this attitude of eager obedience which had earned him the promotion to archangel ages ago. If this task weren't so important, he would have smiled to be chosen by the Father; but Gabriel's expression was serious. He listened carefully to the instructions, memorizing every detail.

The message would have to be delivered in a time and place that would leave Zechariah no doubt as to its source, otherwise he might not believe it, and that would be a tragedy. That place would obviously have to be at the Temple in Jerusalem.

An annual feast would not be a good time. During the LORD's appointed feasts all priests from all twenty-four of the priestly divisions were there in Jerusalem. Such occasions were often so hectic there was danger of a message getting lost. No, the message would have to be delivered in a quieter time, between the spring and fall feasts, when only one division of priests at a time was needed to serve at the Temple.

The division to which Zechariah belonged would soon be on duty for their semi-annual week of service. There was always plenty for the priests to do around the Temple—much more than in the days of Moses and the Tabernacle. The Temple which replaced the Tabernacle was so much larger that it needed more furniture. It had ten tables of showbread instead of one and ten seven-branched candlesticks instead of one.

Besides the usual duties associated with making animal sacrifices in front of the Temple, priests had duties inside the Temple. Baking fresh bread for the tables of showbread. Twelve flat loaves per table, 120 loaves! Trimming seventy wicks each morning. Keeping seventy lamps filled with oil.

But one duty in the Temple was special. Despite the size of the Temple, there was still only one altar of incense. Every morning and evening at sunrise and sunset, incense had to be burned on the altar of incense. This altar stood in the Holy Place directly in front of the curtain behind which sat the Ark of the Covenant. It was the closest to the Most Holy Place that any ordinary priest ever got.

The altar of incense was a simple box of acacia wood, three feet high and eighteen inches square, with horns in each corner, completely overlaid with gold. No meat offerings were burnt on it; no drink offerings were poured on it. It was used exclusively to burn incense every sunrise and every sunset.

The incense burning on the altar represented the prayers of praise and worship, petition and intercession offered to the Holy One. Though the Jewish priests did not yet understand it, the incense also represented the prayers and petitions of the Son—the Mediator between the Holy One and man. That understanding would dawn after the coming of the Messiah.

Burning incense on the altar of incense was such a prestigious duty that every priest wanted to do it. The only assignment more prestigious than that was the High Priest's duty once a year on the Day of Atonement, when he went into the Most Holy Place and sprinkled blood on the Mercy Seat. The priest chosen to burn incense had to be someone special—someone of high moral character, someone whose heart was devoted to the Holy One. Because only the Holy One himself could know a person's heart, the assignment was filled not by man's choice but by drawing lots. Every priest hoped that at least once in his lifetime the lot would fall on him.

Every morning a priest chosen by lot would burn incense on the altar, where its fragrance would waft up into the Most Holy Place as a

The Plan Begins

pleasing aroma to the Holy One. Every evening another priest chosen by lot would do the same.

Every morning and evening, as the chosen priest entered the Holy Place, worshipers would assemble in the surrounding courtyard praying. By burning incense on the altar, the priest was, in effect, presenting to the Holy One the prayers of all those worshiping just outside the Holy Place.

Zechariah and Elizabeth lived in the hill country of Judah about ten miles from Jerusalem. When his priestly division was due to serve in the Temple, Zechariah kissed his wife goodbye. "See you in a week," he called to her as he walked down the road.

"May the lot fall on you," Elizabeth called back to him as she always did.

"God willing," Zechariah responded, as he always did. He longed with all his being for a chance to burn incense in the Holy Place.

If he couldn't burn incense, Zechariah hoped he could at least serve inside the Temple. Outside, in front of the Temple, animals were sacrificed on a much larger altar. The duties associated with making animal sacrifices were hard work, bloody and messy, and were usually assigned to younger, stronger priests.

Rather than focus on possible disappointment, Zechariah determined to fulfil whatever assignment he was given to the best of his ability.

When the time came to draw lots for a priest to enter the Holy Place and burn incense, the angel Gabriel made sure that the lot fell on Zechariah, who was both surprised and overjoyed.

"Wait until I get back home and tell Elizabeth that the lot fell on me!" thought Zechariah, pinching himself to make sure he was not dreaming.

He could hardly sleep for anticipating his upcoming duties. Mentally he walked through the steps he would take, visualizing the layout of the Temple.

The Plan

The entrance to the Temple was impressive—the doors were decorated with carvings of cherubim, palm trees, and flowers—but inside the Holy Place was even more beautiful. Though the exterior walls were made of stone, the interior, from floor to ceiling, was beautifully paneled with wood. The cedar panels on the walls and ceilings were decorated with carvings of gourds and flowers, cherubim and palm trees. The floor was covered with cypress planks.

The day Zechariah was to serve, he rose very early and hurried to the Temple in the darkness. While the eastern sky gradually got lighter, he went through his purification rituals and put on his priestly garments, making sure he finished well before the sun broke over the horizon. The clouds scattered overhead were painted in glorious colors as he entered the Temple through the front doors.

Zechariah was aware of his heart pounding in his chest as he walked solemnly through the great hall with tables containing bread on either side of him, a candelabra behind each table. While his hands tightly clutched fresh sticks of incense, his eyes were fixed on one spot—the altar of incense.

Zechariah knew the routine. He would replace the burned sticks of incense with new ones, then light them. Then he would take time to pray to the Holy One as the fragrance of the incense wafted up into the Most Holy Place.

Suddenly the angel Gabriel appeared out of nowhere, standing at the right side of the altar of incense. Gabriel did not have the burning fiery appearance of a seraph. Nor did he have great majestic wings like the cherubim who guarded the Most Holy Place or who guarded the Tree of Life in the Garden of Eden. Gabriel, one of four archangels second in rank only to the Holy One himself, looked much like a man only bigger. But there was no mistaking his heavenly source. He radiated authority.

At first, Zechariah was startled to see Gabriel appear before him. Then he was gripped with fear.

The Plan Begins

Gabriel did his best to put Zechariah at ease. After all, he came bearing good news.

"Don't be afraid, Zechariah!" Gabriel assured him. "God has heard your prayer. Your wife Elizabeth will give you a son, and you will name him John. He will be your pride and joy, and many people will be glad that he was born."

Then Gabriel gave Zechariah details about his son's future.

"He will be great in the sight of the Lord. He must never touch wine or other alcoholic drinks. He will be filled with the Holy Spirit even before he is born. He will bring many people in Israel back to the Lord their God. He will herald the Messiah's arrival with the spirit and power that Elijah had. He will change parents' attitudes toward their children and children's attitudes toward their parents. He will cause those who are rebellious to accept the wisdom of the godly, and he will kindle devout understanding among hardened skeptics. In short, he will prepare the people for the coming of the Messiah!"

Gabriel delivered the message with increasing excitement, but Zechariah did not respond in like manner.

"Do you expect me to believe this?" Zechariah asked. "I'm an old man, and my wife is beyond her childbearing years."

Gabriel could not believe his ears. *How impudent humans can be!* he thought. He would gladly have struck Zechariah dead, but he didn't have a sword in his hand. After all, Gabriel had come on a mission of peace, hope and joy. Instead, he drew himself up to his full height and leaned down into Zechariah's face until they were almost nose to nose.

"I am Gabriel!" he thundered. "I stand in the very presence of the Holy One. It was He who sent me especially to bring you this good news! But now, since you won't believe me, you'll be unable to say a word until the day of your son's birth. Every word I've spoken to you will come true at the proper time—God's time."

The Plan

Zechariah opened his mouth to say he was sorry, but no words would come out. He tried a second time to apologize, but it was no use. He couldn't say a word!

Gabriel gave Zechariah a stern look that said, "I told you so," then vanished from sight.

Deeply ashamed of himself, Zechariah looked around. All of the cherubim carved into the walls seemed to stare accusingly at him. Zechariah no longer viewed them as creatures of beauty and majesty but as creatures to be feared. He half expected one of them to come off the wall and strike him dead.

Zechariah looked down at the incense still in his hands and realized that he had not yet performed the duty for which he had come. There were no priests in sight. They were waiting for him to light the incense and exit the Holy Place before entering to perform their duties.

But did he even have the right to burn the incense? Surely he had disqualified himself by his unbelief! But no, a quiet voice inside reminded him that he had been chosen by lot. The Holy One himself had picked him for this duty. He must perform it, unworthy though he knew himself to be.

Yesterday he was patting himself on the back to think that the Holy One had chosen him for this prestigious task. Today he was ready to crawl into a hole, but there was nowhere to hide. He would have to exit the Temple through the front doors, where all the worshipers were assembled. What should have been the best day of his life had turned into something beyond his worst nightmare.

Remembering that people were praying outside, Zechariah offered a prayer of his own. Momentarily forgetting that he was dumb, he wiggled his tongue and formed his lips to make words, but no sound escaped his throat.

What had Gabriel said? "You won't be able to speak until the day your son is born."

The Plan Begins

"Well," Zechariah thought, "here goes! The Holy One will have to listen to my thoughts instead of my voice."

In his heart, Zechariah confessed his sin of disbelief. Then he humbly approached the altar of incense, removed the burned sticks of incense from the previous evening, placed the fresh incense sticks in the altar and lit them.

Meanwhile, the people outside were getting restless waiting for Zechariah to come out of the Holy Place. Why was he taking so long? they wondered.

When Zechariah finally did come out, he couldn't speak to them. He motioned with his hands, but remained unable to talk.

Gabriel, meanwhile, had returned to the Throne Room to give the Holy One a report.

"I followed your instructions to the letter, O Holy One, but that priest didn't believe me. I wanted to strike him dead, but I didn't have a sword in my hand. Besides, if he were dead, he would not be able to father a child."

"Striking him dumb was a nice touch," said Father with a smile.

"That was the only thing I could think of," replied Gabriel.

"That was my idea," said Spirit. "I planted that thought in your head, Gabriel."

"How could Zechariah not believe?" Gabriel asked, turning to Father. "I thought you said he was the perfect father for the forerunner to the Messiah."

"Not perfect," Father corrected him, "just the best of a sorry, unbelieving lot. Even the high priest is more interested in his present power than in The Plan."

"When I go to earth as the Messiah and fulfill The Plan," Son said, "the high priest will be out of a job and will lose the power and prestige that go with it."

"Don't worry about the choice of Zechariah," Spirit reassured Gabriel. "He will make a great father. Nine months from now you won't recognize him. It's amazing what he will learn when he keeps his mouth shut for a while!"

Before the sun set that day, everybody in Jerusalem knew that something had happened to Zechariah while he was in the Temple. They peppered Zechariah with questions, but could get no explanation from the speechless priest. His hand gestures didn't tell them much. The people assumed that Zechariah had seen a vision in the Temple, but didn't understand why he was suddenly dumb.

Zechariah had plenty of time to ponder his actions as he walked the ten miles to his home after his week of Temple service was over.

"Why didn't I believe?" he asked, trying to understand himself.

For decades he and his wife had prayed for a child, preferably a son. The longer he and Elizabeth prayed, the more they were aware that their prayers might not be answered as they hoped. Many couples who prayed for children were unable to have them. Why should God answer Zechariah's prayers and not the prayers of others?

In spite of this, the angel Gabriel had brought news of a direct answer to their prayer. Why was that so hard to believe?

Zechariah knew the messenger in the Temple was an angel. No ordinary person could enter the Temple and live. Anyone not properly consecrated for service in the Temple would be struck dead by God upon entry. Besides, the angel had appeared out of nowhere. So why the unbelief?

Against great odds Zechariah had been chosen by lot to enter the Temple of the Lord to burn incense on the altar. What better place to learn of an answer to prayer than in the Temple of the living God? Why had he not believed?

Maybe the answer to prayer had been delayed so long that he no longer wanted a child, Zechariah speculated. How many people at his age wanted to be changing diapers and feeding babies? How many had the energy to chase after little children? He and Elizabeth should be

The Plan Begins

enjoying other people's little ones smiling and cooing and doing cute things. When the infants cried or threw tantrums, he and his wife should be able to give them back to their parents. At his age Zechariah and his wife should be grandparents or maybe even great grandparents, but not parents!

Maybe he was overwhelmed by the answer, Zechariah thought. God was about to do infinitely more than he and his wife could ever ask or imagine in their wildest dreams! All they wanted was a baby. But the forerunner of the Messiah?! Preparing him for his role in life was a huge responsibility Zechariah hadn't bargained for.

If Zechariah wanted to raise an objection, Elizabeth's barrenness was the greatest obstacle. But Zechariah had not used that as an excuse.

Zechariah couldn't help comparing himself to the patriarch Abraham. Just like Zechariah and Elizabeth, Abraham was old and Sarah was barren. But there were differences. The Holy One had prefaced the Promise to Abraham with a command, "Leave your country." While Abraham was busy obeying, he had time to digest the implications of the Promise. Furthermore, the details of the Promise had been spelled out little by little over twenty-five years. Abraham had the advantage of time—time to adjust to the idea of a child in his old age. And believe!

Zechariah knew he was just rationalizing. The bottom line was, whatever the reason, he had not believed. He had not responded as Abraham had. Now he would have to explain to his wife why he was struck dumb.

It was a humbling experience. Word had reached Elizabeth before Zechariah even finished his week of Temple service that he was dumb, and she was full of questions.

Signs were inadequate to answer those questions. Neither Zechariah nor his wife knew sign language.

Zechariah had to write out the details for her in full. Seeing it on a writing tablet or on parchment was even more humiliating. How could he have done what he had done?

The Plan

But soon the humiliation was replaced with joy when Elizabeth became pregnant.

The Holy One was right. Zechariah changed.

While Elizabeth busied herself with making clothes, diapers and blankets for the baby, Zechariah studied the Scriptures as never before. While Elizabeth knitted a tiny sweater, Zechariah read the story of Hannah, who like Elizabeth was barren and prayed for a son, and whose prayer was answered with the birth of Samuel. When Zechariah showed the story to his wife, they both identified with Hannah's hymn of praise.

Zechariah took seriously his role as father of the forerunner of the Messiah, as the Holy One knew he would. He read in the first book of Moses the story of Abraham and the Promise—the covenant the Lord had made with him. He studied the major and minor prophets, paying special attention to prophecies about the Messiah who would come to fulfill the promises of the covenant. All this information would be passed on to his son John.

Of special interest was any prophecy which spoke directly of the baby growing in Elizabeth's womb. Zechariah pointed out to Elizabeth the words of the LORD Almighty spoken through the prophet Malachi: "See, I will send my messenger, who will prepare the way before me."

"He's speaking of our son," said Elizabeth in awe, holding her hands over her swelling belly.

"There's more," Zechariah wrote to her on a tablet which he kept handy.

Elizabeth followed where he was pointing, and read, "'See, I will send you the prophet Elijah before that great and dreadful day of the Lord comes. He will change parents' attitudes toward their children and children's attitudes toward their parents.'"

Excitedly Zechariah wrote again, "That's exactly what Gabriel said to me—that our son John will herald the Messiah's arrival with the spirit and power that Elijah had." His finger underlined the words on the scroll: "He will change parents' attitudes toward their children and children's attitudes toward their parents."

Three months before their baby was due, Zechariah and Elizabeth learned who the Messiah would be. A visitor from Nazareth arrived at their door, Elizabeth's cousin Mary.

When Mary entered Zechariah's house and greeted Elizabeth, the baby John leaped in her womb. It was not a mild poke, like Elizabeth was used to experiencing, but a full blown dance!

Elizabeth was immediately filled with the Spirit. She gave a glad cry and exclaimed to Mary, "I thought *I* was blessed, not just to have a child at my age but to be the mother of the Messiah's forerunner. But you! God has blessed you above all women, and the child that you will have is also blessed. Why am I so honoured, that the mother of my Lord should visit me? When I heard your greeting, the baby in my womb jumped for joy. You are blessed because you believed that the Lord would do what he said."

For the next three months, Mary stayed with Elizabeth. They talked excitedly together as they did daily chores. Long hours of conversation were interspersed with periods of deep silence as both women contemplated what the Holy One was doing in and through them.

Zechariah watched and listened in silence, marvelling at how well the two women got along. Despite their differences, they had more in common than most. Though Mary was barely into her teens, she had a maturity that belied her age.

Zechariah noted the differences between himself and his wife's humble cousin, and blushed to think how poorly he compared to her. Mary had believed Gabriel immediately, whereas he had not. But the biggest difference between himself and Mary was her knowledge of the Word of God.

In the evening on the day of her arrival in their home, Mary had sung to them a song she had composed on her journey from Nazareth to

The Plan

their town in the hill country of Judah. In a sweet clear voice she sang, "My soul magnifies the Lord and my spirit rejoices in God my Saviour...."

From beginning to end the song was liberally sprinkled with references from the Holy Scriptures. Zechariah, who had been spending a lot of time studying the Word of God in preparation for the arrival of his own son, recognized the references in Mary's song and was impressed. It was obvious that this young woman, though not much more than a child herself, had made a habit of reading and memorizing the Scriptures, especially the Psalms. There was no way she could have acquired that much Scripture knowledge in the short week since Gabriel's announcement to her.

How many adults, let alone teenagers, Zechariah wondered, had such a knowledge of and love for God's Word? No wonder the Holy One had chosen her to be the mother of the Messiah!

Zechariah resolved to follow Mary's example and study the Word diligently. He would soon be setting an example for his own son John. He would also follow Mary's example and compose what he was learning from the Scriptures into a song. He would recite it after John was born and he was able to speak again.

A few days after Mary returned to her home in Nazareth, Elizabeth went into labour and gave birth to a healthy baby boy. Her neighbours rejoiced at the news.

On the eighth day the house was packed as relatives and friends came to celebrate the circumcision and naming of the baby. Since Zechariah couldn't speak, family members spoke for him, naming the baby Zechariah in honour of his father.

Elizabeth was horrified.

"No!" she objected. "He is to be called John."

"No one among our relatives is named John," the guests replied, puzzled at the choice of name. They turned to Zechariah and asked in sign language what he would like to name his child.

"I'm not deaf," thought Zechariah. "You don't have to talk to me in sign language!"

Unable to say so, he motioned for a writing tablet. To everyone's astonishment he wrote with a flourish, "His name is John!"

Surprise followed surprise. Instantly Zechariah could speak again, and he began praising God! The Holy Spirit filled Zechariah, and the song he had composed and memorized flowed from his lips.

A deep, reverential fear settled over the neighbourhood, and the news of what had happened spread throughout the Judean hills. Everyone who heard about it reflected on these events, wondering, "What does the future hold for this child?"

It was clear that the hand of the Lord was upon the newborn in a special way.

Cheers erupted in the Throne Room as Zechariah finished his song of praise. Father and Spirit were well pleased. The archangels in the background laughed with joy, while the Heavenly City echoed with sounds of rejoicing as the good news spread to thousands upon thousands of angels.

Son, now a three-month-old human fetus, did a little dance in Mary's womb. Though physically separated from Father and Spirit, he was never out of communication range. In Nazareth, Mary felt a tiny flutter in her womb and wondered if she was imagining it.

"What a great song!" exclaimed Father. "Almost exclusively drawn from Scripture!"

"I highlighted certain passages as he studied," said Spirit, "but Zechariah did a great job of weaving them into his song."

"As we knew he would," added Father, smiling. "Isaiah, Jeremiah, Ezekiel, Micah—and everybody's favourite—King David!"

"Don't forget Hannah," Spirit reminded Father. "He quoted Hannah's song."

The Plan

"He even quoted me," interjected Gabriel from behind the Throne, hoping he wasn't speaking out of line.

"Yes, Zechariah stumbled and fell at the beginning of his race, but he recovered in spectacular fashion," said Father. "Preparing his son John to be forerunner for the Messiah is a marathon, not a sprint. Just watch what he does over the next few years!"

"The Plan is still on track," remarked Spirit with satisfaction. "No one can thwart it. No one can prevent its accomplishment. Not those who oppose it. Not even those who support it but lapse temporarily into sin or unbelief."

Son agreed, and did another little dance in Mary's womb.

34

The Newborn Lamb

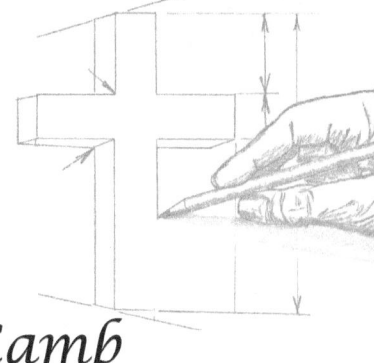

Mary returned to Nazareth, excited to share with Joseph what had happened to her, but Joseph did not believe the woman he loved was still a virgin. Their pledge to marry was legally binding, so Joseph felt he had no alternative but divorce.

Father sent Gabriel to intervene.

"Gabriel! Joseph is planning to divorce Mary! That must not happen! The Son needs a human father. Go quickly and talk to Joseph while he is sleeping. Tell Joseph he must marry her. She was not unfaithful. The child in her womb was conceived by the Holy Spirit. She will give birth to a son. Tell Joseph to name him Jesus."

Joseph woke from his dream convinced that it was from the Lord. He married Mary quickly before her pregnancy was obvious and took her home as his wife.

A few months later Caesar Augustus decided to take a census of the entire Roman world. Everyone in Israel would have to register according to their house and lineage. That meant that Joseph and Mary would have to travel to Bethlehem, the home of their ancestor David. Mary, being close to her time of delivery, tucked a thick roll of swaddling cloths into her travel bag.

Joseph and Mary didn't worry about finding accommodation in Bethlehem. They expected to stay in the home of a relative and bunk in with their uncles, aunts and cousins. The guests in these small towns were typically relatives or friends. At night the guests rolled out their

The Plan

mats and slept on the floor. If everybody squeezed together, they could always make room for one or two more.

Joseph and Mary looked forward to visiting with relatives they hadn't seen in a while. The inconvenience of unexpected travel was brightened by the anticipation of spending time with loved ones.

Imagine Joseph and Mary's shock and pain to be met at the door with stern faces.

"You two were married only five months ago, yet now Mary stands before us ready to pop! You two had sex before marriage.

Shame on you! We don't want you in our house."

This was personal! This was not strangers turning them away. Strangers would not have known how long Joseph and Mary had been married. Strangers would have been sympathetic.

Joseph swore that he and Mary hadn't had sex yet—neither before marriage nor in the few months since. But nobody believed them. Mary tried to explain what the angel said to her and what the Holy Spirit had done in her, but the relatives weren't convinced.

"We have heard lots of excuses, but this is a new one!" they scoffed. "Usually people say, 'The devil made me do it!' but Mary is saying, 'God did it to me!' What nonsense!"

No room in the guest chamber.

They were rejected by family members. That hurt!

Having been turned away by their relatives, Joseph and Mary had to find another option. Mary was showing early signs of labor. They couldn't just sleep in an alleyway.

On the way into Bethlehem, Joseph and Mary had passed a tower called Migdal Eder, meaning 'the tower of the flock.' It was a special watchtower built for the protection of the special temple flocks. It was on the road to Jerusalem and just outside Bethlehem city but still within the region commonly known as Bethlehem. This tower became their only hope for shelter and seclusion, so Joseph took Mary there.

The Newborn Lamb

The angels all held their breath as Joseph stepped into the role of midwife. They let out a sigh of relief when the baby was safely delivered. After Mary had lovingly wrapped her baby in swaddling cloths and laid him in the manger, the angels wanted to tell the whole world.

All heaven was bursting with excitement at the birth of the Son, but nobody on earth except Joseph and Mary knew about it. This could not be!

Lady Wisdom and a band of angels rushed into the throne room.

"Nobody in the palace or the temple is aware of this historic moment," Lady Wisdom lamented breathlessly. "Everybody in Jerusalem is asleep!"

Father understood their concerns.

"I know you think this is a disaster," he said, "but I have everything under control. Some very important people are awake."

"Who?"

"The shepherds."

"Shepherds! Really? Ordinary, smelly shepherds?"

"*Bethlehem* shepherds," Father replied. "And they aren't ordinary. They are royal shepherds, descendants of David, tending sheep destined for the temple in Jerusalem. Bethlehem shepherds are outsourced employees of the temple, specially trained and purified for their role.

"Their sheep aren't ordinary either. They are born for slaughter, destined for Temple sacrifices. Every morning and every evening a lamb is sacrificed at the temple. That's 730 lambs each year! Every Passover thousands more sheep are killed, one per family.

"Lambing ewes are brought to Migdal Eder, the Tower of the Flock. Lambs are born there on the ground floor under the watchful eye of the shepherds. All newborn lambs are inspected for spots and blemishes. Any flaw, no matter how slight, means instant rejection from the temple flock. Swaddling cloths are used by the shepherds to wipe off the newborn lambs prior to their inspection.

"Once the lambs are certified for use as sacrifices in the temple, they are wrapped in swaddling cloths to prevent the lambs from injuring themselves by thrashing about on their spindly legs. Sometimes newborn lambs are placed in a manger or feeding trough, where they can calm down out of harm's way. A lamb wrapped in swaddling cloths is proof that it had passed rigorous inspection."[1]

Spirit continued the explanation.

"The royal shepherds know the Scriptures and are familiar with prophecies concerning the Messiah. . . .

Hear now, O house of David . . . Behold, the virgin shall conceive and bear a Son, and shall call His name Immanuel.[2]

"The shepherds also are aware of Micah's prophecy, more than 700 years ago, that predicted the location of Messiah's birth.

But you, Bethlehem Ephrathah, though you are little among the thousands of Judah, yet out of you shall come forth to Me the One to be Ruler in Israel, whose goings forth are from of old, from everlasting.[3]

"In the preceding chapter Micah pinpointed the location of Messiah's birth even more specifically.

And you, O tower of the flock [in Hebrew, Migdal Eder], *the stronghold of the daughter of Zion, to you shall it come,*

---

[1] Sources: (1) Charles E. McCracken, "Silent Night?", Canadian Communiqué, FOI Gospel Ministry, Inc., Vol. 11.3 Winter 2013; (2) Alfred Edersheim, *The Life and Times of Jesus the Messiah*, 1883, Book 2, chapter 6; (3) Leonard Sweet and Frank Viola, *Jesus, A Theography*, Thomas Nelson, © 2012, pp. 65-67; (4) Gary Stearman, "A Christmas Prophecy—The Tower of the Flock," Dec.1, 2013; http://www.prophecyinthenews.com/a-christmas-prophecy-the-tower-of-the-flock/
[2] Isa. 7:13-14
[3] Micah 5:2, NKJV

even the former dominion shall come, the kingdom of the daughter of Jerusalem."[4]

"Gabriel!" Father called to the archangel standing at attention near the throne. "You have dealt with earthlings before. You can make the announcement. Angels, I know all of you have been rehearsing your part. Be ready to sing when he is finished speaking."

Suddenly the night sky burst open with light above the fields where the Bethlehem shepherds were watching over their flocks, and Gabriel appeared in a blaze of glory. The shepherds were terrified!

"Don't be afraid," the angel said. "I bring you good news that will bring great joy to all people. The Savior—yes, the Messiah, the Lord—has been born today in Bethlehem, the city of David! And you will recognize him by this sign: You will find a baby wrapped in swaddling cloths, lying in a manger."

Suddenly the whole sky was filled with angels.

"Glory to God in the highest," they sang, "and peace on earth to those with whom God is pleased."

Just as suddenly the sky went dark, and the world was silent. When the shepherds recovered enough to talk, their first thought was, "Let's go to Bethlehem and see!"

Though the angel hadn't given directions to the shepherds, there was no confusion or frantic discussion about where to look for the baby. The shepherds immediately understood the implications of the angel's message. The closest manger was at the edge of the fields where they were watching their sheep—at Migdal Eder, the very place Micah prophesied that Messiah would be revealed.

So they hurried off and found Joseph and Mary with her little lamb wrapped in swaddling cloths lying in a manger. Shyly they gathered around the manger.

---

[4] Micah 4:8, NKJV

"What's his name?" one of the shepherds asked when he finally found his tongue.

"His name is Jesus," the parents said proudly.

"The Ruler of Israel," said a shepherd, remembering the words of Micah.

"Our King!" said one and all.

What stories Mary and Joseph and the shepherds exchanged! Stories of dreams and of angel's announcements! When Mary said she was a virgin, the shepherds, knowing Isaiah's prophecy, believed her.

The shepherds marveled that they had been given the high honor of being the first to visit the newborn Messiah. But as they thought about it, they realized how fitting it was. They were not witnessing anything new except who was in the manger.

"See the swaddling cloths? He's perfect! The Lamb of God!"

* * * *

"Truer words were never spoken," said Spirit to the angels who were watching the scene below. "The fact that this Lamb is wrapped in swaddling cloths is proof that he has passed rigorous inspection. He is the perfect Lamb of God!"

"It seems fitting that the Bethlehem shepherds were the first to be notified," commented Lady Wisdom. "It is their holy calling to certify Passover lambs upon birth."

"Migdal Eder was the perfect place for Jesus' birth," Gabriel added. "It is the traditional location for Passover lambs to be born."

"With Yahweh, nothing happens by accident!" said a voice from the choir of angels.

35

Other Witnesses

The shepherds wanted to linger at the manger, but they had sheep to protect and a story to tell. When morning dawned, another shift of shepherds came to take over the watch. The night shift excitedly shared what had happened. Then they scattered throughout Bethlehem to tell the good news.

"The Messiah is born! Angels announced it! We saw him in the manger wrapped in swaddling cloths. Praise be to God!"

All who heard the shepherds' story were astonished, but Mary kept all these things in her heart and thought about them often.

Joseph and Mary registered for the census, but they did not return immediately to Nazareth. Having experienced the rejection of their relatives in Bethlehem, Joseph and Mary knew they would be treated even worse in Nazareth where far more people knew them. Mary was not ready to take the arduous journey back to Nazareth while learning to care for her newborn baby.

Besides, the baby had to be circumcised and officially named on the eighth day. Furthermore, after forty days[1] Jesus, being Mary's firstborn male, must be consecrated to the Lord in Jerusalem. It would be so much more convenient to live in Bethlehem for forty days, maybe even longer.

Fortunately, one of the shepherds knew someone who had believed their story and was happy to take Joseph and Mary and the new baby into their home for a few days. Joseph did some carpentry to earn his

---

[1] Lev. 12:1-4, seven plus 33 days.

keep, and before he knew it, his skills were in demand around town. They decided to put down roots in Bethlehem.

After forty days Joseph and Mary went to the temple in Jerusalem and sacrificed a pair of doves in keeping with the Law. While they were at the temple, they were approached by an elderly man with a question.

"Excuse me, lady, my name is Simeon. May I hold your baby?"

Mary was surprised by the request, but Simeon quickly explained.

"I have been waiting all my life for our Messiah, the consolation of Israel. Some time ago the Holy Spirit told me that I wouldn't die before I had seen the Lord's Messiah. Today he told me, 'This is the day. Go to the temple.' When I saw you, I knew this baby was the one I have been waiting to see all my life."

Mary put her baby into his outstretched arms. Simeon gazed lovingly at the baby then lifted his face toward God.

"Sovereign Lord, now let your servant die in peace, as you have promised. I have seen your salvation, which you have prepared for all people."

As he returned the baby to his mother, Simeon added, "He is a light to reveal God to the nations, and he is the glory of God's people Israel!"[2]

Joseph and Mary marveled at Simeon's words. Then they drank in the blessing Simeon spoke over them. As they parted, Simeon motioned to Mary and spoke quietly into her ear.

"This child is destined to cause many in Israel to fall, and many others to rise. He has been sent as a sign from God, but many will oppose him. As a result, the deepest thoughts of many hearts will be revealed."

Simeon paused and looked Mary directly in the eye.

"And a sword will pierce your very soul."

Just then an elderly woman came up to them and without introduction gave thanks to God for the newborn Messiah. Then just as quickly she turned and spoke to person after person about the child.

---

[2] Luke 2:29-32, NLT, slightly revised.

"Who is that?" Mary asked Simeon.

"That's Anna."

"How did she know our baby is the Messiah?"

"Anna's a prophet. She never leaves the temple courtyard. She worships day and night, fasting and praying. She knows the Holy Spirit told me I would see the Messiah before I died, so she watches me. She probably overheard some of my prayer. That's how she knew your baby is the Messiah. She knows everyone who is waiting expectantly for God to rescue Jerusalem. You can count on her to spread the word."[3]

Life settled into a quiet routine for Joseph and his family as work steadily came his way.

Some people who had heard the shepherds' story were curious to see the baby, but those visits soon stopped. This child of peasants couldn't be their King!

The palace made no announcement that a King was born.

Joseph half expected a visit from some of the chief priests in Jerusalem. Surely they would hear Anna's announcement that the Messiah was born. Surely they would come to investigate. But they didn't.

A little more than a year later, in the middle of the night Joseph was awakened by a commotion outside. Looking out the window, he saw a whole caravan of men and camels! He heard voices, then a knock on the door.

Joseph hurriedly lit a lamp and went to the door. The men standing before him came right to the point.

"We are looking for the one who has been born king of the Jews? Is he here?"

"Mary, we have visitors," Joseph called over his shoulder. "They want to see Jesus."

---

[3] Luke 2:38

The Plan

Mary scurried around to straighten up the house as Joseph lit a few more lamps. There wasn't room inside the tiny house for all the men to enter, but some of them seemed impatient to meet the child and eagerly entered at Joseph's invitation. The hired hands stayed outside with the camels.

Joseph introduced himself to the men, who were strangely but richly dressed, obviously from some foreign land. Then they introduced themselves.

"We are Magi, a priestly caste of astrologers, and we are from the east."

"How did you find us and why did you come in the dark?" Joseph asked.

"We followed the star, the one that indicated the king of the Jews was born," one of the Magi said. "We saw his star in the east and followed it all the way here. We have come to worship the new king."

"We went first to Jerusalem, thinking he would be born in the palace," another Magus said. "But Herod knew nothing about a new king, especially not the Messiah. He called together all the chief priests and teachers of the law, and they told him the Messiah would be born in Bethlehem. Micah prophesied it."

"When darkness fell, we followed the star again," a third Magus said, "and sure enough, it led us to Bethlehem. To find the exact house, we had to travel at night. The star stopped right over your house! Come outside and see it."

Mary lifted her sleepy toddler from his little crib, and she and Joseph went outside with the Magi, who pointed out the bright star in the sky. There it was! Right over their house! They gazed for a while in awe and wonder.

Turning his attention to the child in Mary's arms, one of the Magi asked, "What is his name?"

"Jesus," answered Mary softly, her voice warm with love and pride.

"His name means 'savior'," explained Joseph, "because he will save his people from their sins. That's what an angel told me in a dream. The angel also said, 'They will call him Immanuel,' which means, 'God with us.'"

It was good to be able to speak openly about the child to people who didn't scoff, thought Joseph.

In the chilly night, the toddler began to fuss, so they all went in from the cold. Once back inside, the richly dressed Magi bowed low before the child, taking turns to speak quietly to him in worship.

When one of them clapped his hands, servants approached, carrying gifts. The Magi took the gifts and held them toward the child.

Mary set little Jesus on the floor and the Magi soon squatted in a circle facing him. One by one they presented their gifts, letting Jesus open them, helping him when his tiny hands couldn't manage. As the lids of the treasure chests were lifted, the glitter of gold and the aroma of precious spices filled the room.

Little Jesus babbled and smiled, then toddled around to kiss and hug each of the Magi, who kissed and hugged him back. The Magi were sure Jesus understood what was happening. They were convinced—rightly—that they were in the presence of the Messiah, the King of the Jews.

Mary and Joseph were awestruck by the Magi's visit. Nothing this amazing had happened since the night Jesus was born, when shepherds found him in the manger.

This evening would be like that night over a year ago—an experience to treasure and ponder for years to come.

Gold. Frankincense. Myrrh. Gifts fit for a king! What did it all mean?

And the star! Joseph and Mary were familiar with the story of Balaam, but they had not paid serious attention to his prophecy about a star: "A star will come out of Jacob; a scepter will rise out of Israel."

They had assumed that the star was figurative, but it wasn't. The Magi had followed it all the way to Bethlehem!

Mary didn't have time to figure it all out. Her little one was tired, and she needed to put him to bed. The Magi excused themselves, expressing hope that they would see Jesus when he became king.

That night Joseph had a dream. In it an angel told him to escape to Egypt because Herod wanted to kill the child. The angel would tell them when it was safe to return. Without waiting for sunrise, Joseph awakened Mary, quickly packed whatever they could carry on their donkey, and left Bethlehem for Egypt. The gifts of the Magi would go a long way toward providing for their family of three in Egypt.

Joseph and Mary had lots to talk about on their journey to Egypt. Uppermost in their minds were the events of their last night in Bethlehem. So few had readily believed that Mary's little baby was the long-awaited Messiah, yet these Magi had believed it.

Joseph and Mary could count the believers on their fingers. Other than Mary and Joseph, Mary's cousin Elizabeth was the first. Elizabeth had blessed Mary from the moment she heard Mary's voice call out in greeting before Mary's pregnancy was even visible. Elizabeth liked to claim that her baby John was the first believer. The unborn miracle child of old Zechariah and Elizabeth had jumped for joy in Elizabeth's womb at the sound of Mary's voice.

The first ones to believe after Jesus' birth were the shepherds, who found the baby in the manger as the angel said. Next were the two elderly people whom Joseph and Mary met in the Temple at the time of their purification following Jesus' birth.

Elizabeth and her baby. Her husband Zechariah. Some shepherds. Simeon. Anna. Outside of those few, nobody believed that Jesus was special. Everybody agreed that Jesus was an unusually good child, never throwing a tantrum or screaming in anger, but that didn't prove he was

Other Witnesses

God. What would it take, Mary wondered, to convince people that the Messiah was here?

Yet these Magi – so humble and gentle in spite of their education and obvious wealth – had traveled from afar to worship her child. They obviously took Balaam's prophecy about a star seriously. They had followed it for over a year!

Various priests and rabbis who lived nearby had, from time to time, heard that Mary had given birth to the Messiah, yet they never came to worship him. They simply didn't believe it.

"Why have some believed that our son is the Messiah and some haven't?" Mary asked. "How did the Magi—Gentiles! —pick up on clues about the Jewish Messiah which those who study Hebrew Scriptures for a living have missed?"

"The Holy Spirit must have opened their eyes," Joseph said to Mary.

At that point in their conversation Jesus began to babble, but his parents had no clue what he was trying to say.

Father and Spirit were listening and understood his baby talk.

"Blessed are the pure in heart, for they shall see God."

36

The Voice

John, son of Zechariah, grew up knowing he was special. Over and over again his parents recounted to him the story of his birth.

Zechariah and Elizabeth had prayed for years for a child. The answer was so long in coming that Zechariah didn't believe it when the angel Gabriel told him his wife would bear a son. Gabriel struck Zechariah dumb for his unbelief, telling him he would remain dumb until the angel's words came true.

Eight days after the son was born, the neighbors and relatives gathered for his circumcision and the announcement of his name. Zechariah was still unable to speak. Elizabeth said the baby was to be named John, but the relatives objected. They wanted him to be named Zechariah after his father.

Zechariah would not hear of it. He grabbed a writing tablet and wrote with a flourish, "His name is John!"

Immediately Zechariah's tongue was loosed and he prophesied. He concluded with a prophecy about John.

> *"And you, my little son, will be called*
> *the prophet of the Most High because*
> *you will go ahead of the Lord to prepare his way.*
> *You will tell his people how to find salvation*
> *through the forgiveness of their sins."*[4]

---

[4] Luke 1:76-77

As the son of a priest, John was instructed thoroughly in the Scriptures. He became strong in spirit in spite of being orphaned early in life.

After his parents died, he lived in the desert. He became somewhat of a legend for his austere lifestyle—eating locusts and wild honey and wearing a garment of camel's hair bound with a leather belt.

When he reached the age of thirty, the age at which men could take public office, he began preaching a baptism of repentance for the forgiveness of sins. Soon the whole Judean countryside and all the people of Jerusalem flocked to the desert to hear him preach.

John didn't mince words.

"You brood of vipers! Who warned you to flee from the coming wrath? Produce fruit in keeping with repentance."

To the Pharisees and Sadducees he said, "Don't think you can say to yourselves, 'We have Abraham as our father.' I tell you that out of these stones God can raise up children for Abraham. If you don't produce good fruit, God will cut you down with his ax and throw you into the fire."

When the crowd asked, "What should we do?" John answered, "If you have two shirts, share with someone who has none. Share your food too."

John's message was so compelling that they confessed their sins and were baptized by him in the Jordan River.

To tax collectors he said, "Don't collect any more than you are required to."

They confessed their sins and were baptized.

To soldiers he said, "Don't extort money and don't accuse people falsely. Be content with your pay."

More confession of sins. More baptisms.

The people who were waiting expectantly for the Messiah were all wondering in their hearts if John might possibly be the Messiah.

One day as John was baptizing, one of the strangers who stepped forward to be baptized caught John's attention. The stranger emanated a

The Plan

quiet authority and power. Without knowing exactly why, John objected to baptizing him.

"I need to be baptized by you. Why do you come to me?"

But the stranger insisted.

"Do it. This is the proper way to do everything that God requires of us."

So John did it.

As the man came up out of the water, John saw the heavens ripped open. Then a dove come out of heaven and landed on the man.

This was the sign John was watching for. God had told him, "The man on whom you see the Spirit come down and remain is the one who will baptize with the Holy Spirit." John concluded that the dove was the Spirit of God in visible form.

Then a voice came from heaven: "You are my Son, whom I love; with you I am well pleased."

As the man walked away in the direction of the desert, John called after him.

"What is your name?"

"Jesus."

Jesus! He was the miracle baby born to Mary, his mother Elizabeth's relative! John and Jesus had met a few times as children, but John's parents were elderly and Jesus' parents were poor, so they didn't get together very often. Travel between their towns was not easy. John hadn't seen Jesus since his parents died.

John continued to baptize, but now he had a more complete message.

"Jesus is the Chosen One. Jesus is the Messiah. He is more powerful than I. I am not worthy to untie his sandals. I baptize you with water, but He will baptize you with the Holy Spirit."

Jerusalem was full of people who were watching for the Messiah to appear. The more oppressive Rome was to the Jews the more they longed for their Messiah, or the Christ, as he was called in Greek.

The Voice

When John started preaching and baptizing, news about him spread and some Jews thought he might be the Christ. If not the Christ, he could be the Prophet, or the return of Elijah prophesied by Malachi.[5] But now John was declaring that Jesus was the Son of God, which implied that Jesus was the Christ.

If so, who was John?

The Jews in Jerusalem sent priests and Levites into the desert to interview John and find out. He said plainly, "I am not the Christ. I am merely a voice in the desert as Isaiah prophesied."[6]

The next day after being questioned, John the Baptist spied Jesus and pointed Him out to the crowd.

"Look, the Lamb of God, who takes away the sin of the world! This is the one I have been preaching to you about. I have called you to repent and be baptized in preparation for his coming so that God can reveal him to Israel as their long awaited Messiah."

"How do you know he is the Lamb of God?" someone wanted to know.

"God told me, 'The man on whom you see the Spirit come down and remain is the one who will baptize with the Holy Spirit.' And I saw it happen. I saw the Spirit come down from heaven as a dove and remain on him. It happened right after I baptized him. I testify that this is God's Chosen One."

The next day again John the Baptist was standing with two of his disciples, Andrew and another man named John, when Jesus walked by.

"Look!" John the Baptist said, "The Lamb of God!"

The Baptist's two disciples immediately followed Jesus.

From then on, Jesus' band of disciples grew and John's band of disciples shrank. Jesus and his disciples went out into the Judean countryside, where he spent some time with them, and they also baptized.

---

[5] Malachi 4:5
[6] John 1:19-28

The Plan

Not long after that, one of the Baptist's disciples complained to him, "Rabbi, that man who was with you on the other side of the Jordan—the one you testified about—look, he is baptizing, and everyone is going to him."

John wasn't bothered by the news.

"I told you, 'I am not the Messiah. I am sent ahead of him.' I'm like the friend of the bridegroom. The friend waits and listens for him, and is full of joy when he hears the bridegroom's voice. That joy is mine, and it's now complete. He must become greater; I must become less."

The Baptist's ministry did not last much longer.

He continued to preach boldly, calling all people to repentance regardless of their station in life. He even rebuked Herod the tetrarch, who had married Herodias, his brother's wife. John had told Herod in no uncertain terms, "It is not lawful for you to have your brother's wife."

Herod was furious, and added to his evil deeds by giving orders to have John arrested, bound and put in prison. That wasn't good enough to appease Herodias. She nursed a grudge against John and wanted to kill him. But Herod wouldn't let her.

The situation was complicated. Herod liked to listen to John, knowing him to be a righteous and holy man, but he also feared John. Herod wanted to kill John for rebuking him, but he was afraid of the people, because they considered John a prophet.

So Herod protected him. Herodias bided her time.

Finally the opportune time came. On his birthday King Herod gave a banquet for his high officials and military commanders and the leading men of Galilee. When the daughter of Herodias came in and danced, she pleased Herod and his dinner guests.

Wanting to reward her and to show off to his guests, Herod said to the girl, "Ask me for anything you want, and I'll give it to you. Anything, up to half my kingdom."

The girl went out to her mother and said, "What shall I ask for?"

"The head of John the Baptist," Herodias answered without thinking twice.

The girl hurried in to the king with the request: "I want you to give me right now the head of John the Baptist on a platter."

Herod was greatly distressed, but because of his oaths and his dinner guests, he did not want to refuse her. So he immediately sent an executioner with orders to bring John's head. The man went, beheaded John in the prison, and brought back his head on a platter. He presented it to the girl, and she gave it to her mother.

The Voice was silenced, but not before his mission was accomplished.

John's disciples came and took his body and buried it. Then they went and told Jesus.

37

At the Right Time

When Earth was first created, Lucifer was made the guardian of Eden to rule it as Yahweh himself would. As an imager of Yahweh, Lucifer failed miserably. He wanted to govern Earth for his own purposes, not on behalf of Yahweh. Yahweh cast him out of Heaven due to his rebellion. Lucifer/Satan then trashed Earth in revenge.

Yahweh responded by restoring Eden and creating a new guardian with an expanded mandate. Yahweh commissioned Man to fill the Earth, to govern it as God himself would, and to extend Eden to the whole planet. Yahweh designed his human children to be servant rulers over Earth under his authority as his representatives—while living in close relationship with God.

But Yahweh's adversary interrupted the immediate fulfillment of that design. Yahweh's plan was postponed when the serpent lured Eve and then Adam into partaking of the fruit of the one and only tree God had forbidden them to eat. Adam and Eve, having sinned, could no longer stand being in the presence of the glory of the Holy One. They were driven out of the Garden.

The Holy One foresaw that created beings would make bad choices which would destroy their relationship with him. A plan was needed to restore humanity to fellowship with God.

Plan A—be perfectly holy—was unachievable by created beings, so people came up with variations of Plan A.

Plan A2: Be as perfect as humanly possible.
Plan A3: Be better than others.
Plan A4: Do more good deeds than bad.
Plan A5: Separate sins into categories, then avoid the worst categories.
Surely these plans would meet with God's approval!

No! God did not sign on to variations of Plan A. His Plan A was absolute—be perfect or die! The only other path to life was Plan B: Admit you are a sinner and accept by faith the death of a perfect Substitute in your place.

The substitute used in ancient times—a perfect bull, goat or lamb—only pointed to the perfect Substitute to come.

Every plan has a timeline, and God's perfect Plan was no different. So when the fullness of time had come, God sent forth his Son, born of woman, to buy back those who had been enslaved by sin.[1] The Plan would be fulfilled in Jesus.

For thirty years Jesus lived in perfect obedience to God, fulfilling the Law while laboring in obscurity as a carpenter. Then came the time to reveal the perfect Substitute.

The Voice prepared the way for The Plan to unfold. John the Baptist preached repentance. Then when God showed him that Jesus was the Chosen One, John declared to anyone who would listen that Jesus was the Lamb of God—Jesus was the Messiah.

The secret was now out. The dragon had heard rumors thirty years ago that the Messiah was born. When the entire religious establishment dismissed the thought of a king being born to peasants, the dragon wasn't so sure. But when Jesus was baptized and a voice spoke from Heaven, there was no denying that Jesus was the long awaited Messiah.

Jesus was aware that the dragon was watching for an opportunity to render the Plan ineffective. If he sinned, he would no longer be the perfect Substitute.

---

[1] Galatians 4:4

The dragon followed Jesus into the desert, watching for an opportunity to lure him away from loyalty to his Father. The dragon was pleased to see that Jesus was fasting; that would make his job easier. When Jesus was starved almost to death, the dragon approached and tried to entice Jesus to satisfy his hunger by turning stones to bread.

"*If* you are the Son of God, tell these stones to become bread." Jesus answered, "Scripture says: 'People do not live on bread alone, but on every word that comes from the mouth of God.'"

He was quoting from the words of Moses in Deuteronomy: "Be careful to follow every command I am giving you today. Remember how I led you in the desert to humble you and to test you in order to know what was in your heart, whether or not you would keep his commands. He humbled you, causing you to hunger and then feeding you with manna in order to teach you that people do not live on bread alone but on every word that comes from the mouth of Yahweh. Know then in your heart that as a man disciplines his son, so Yahweh your God disciplines you."[2]

Jesus was making the point that he knew he was being disciplined by his Father. His loyalty was to the Father alone, and he would obey no other.

The dragon tried again. If Jesus could quote Scripture, so could he. He took Jesus to the highest point of the temple and said, "*If* you are the Son of God, jump! For Scripture says: 'He will order his angels to protect you. And they will hold you up with their hands so you won't even hurt your foot on a stone.'"

Jesus again quoted Moses. "Scripture says: 'Don't put Yahweh your God to the test.'" The rest of that Scripture said, "Be sure to obey the command of Yahweh your God and the regulations and laws he has given you."[3]

Jesus' message was: I won't foolishly test the law of gravity. And I won't jump because you order me to. I will obey only Yahweh.

---

[2] Deut 8:1-5
[3] Deut 6:16-17

The final temptation hit directly at the contest between the dragon and Jesus. Because he had lured so many people away from Yahweh, the dragon thought of himself as the ruler of the world. But he wasn't. The ultimate authority still resides in God. The dragon took Jesus to a very high mountain and showed him all the kingdoms of the world and their glory.

"All these I will give you, if you will fall down and worship me."

Jesus' refusal was curt. "Go away, Satan! Scripture says, 'Worship the Lord your God and serve only him.'"

Jesus didn't need Satan's permission to possess the nations. Yahweh would win the nations back by his own means in his own time. Yahweh had his own Plan.

Jesus was time conscious. He knew what "his time" meant. Jesus knew that "his time" was not a time to be popular or to be hailed as King of the Jews. Not yet. "His time" was to die on the cross. In the meantime, he would display the Father's glory.

Little by little, Jesus came out of obscurity. Most of his life he had lived in Nazareth as the carpenter's son. After his baptism he began to show himself as God's Son.

When Jesus went with his disciples to a wedding in Cana and his mother pointed out to him that there was no more wine, Jesus replied, "My time has not yet come."

Jesus then quietly turned water into wine so the master of the banquet could save face. Turning water into wine was a "wow" moment that showed God's miraculous power. Who but God could turn water into wine?

This act, the first of his miraculous signs, revealed his glory, glory which he shared with the Father, and his disciples put their faith in him.[4]

As Passover approached, Jesus showed an even more important trait of his Father—his Father's holiness. Jesus went to Jerusalem. There in the temple courts he found men selling cattle, sheep and doves. Others

---

[4] John 2:1-11

The Plan

were sitting at tables exchanging money and profiting richly from the exchange. Where was the reverence for a holy God? The temple courts were no different from a common market!

Jesus was furious! So he made a whip out of cords and drove all the merchants from the temple area, scattering their sheep, cattle and doves. With a wild swing of his arms, he scattered the coins of the money changers, then overturned their tables.

"Get out of here!" he roared. "How dare you turn my Father's house into a market?"

The Jews were blind to the inappropriateness of merchandizing in the temple. Instead of acknowledging that Jesus had merely pointed out the obvious, they demanded of him, "What miraculous sign can you show us to prove your authority to do all this?"

They wanted to witness a miracle, like turning water into wine!

Jesus had no intention of indulging their desire to be entertained with a miracle. He knew that in two years' time people like this would be crying, "Crucify him!"

Pointing to himself, Jesus replied, "Destroy this temple, and I will raise it again in three days."

After Passover week Jesus and his disciples went into the Judean countryside. There Jesus preached while his disciples baptized. About this time John the Baptist was arrested and locked up in prison for reproving Herod for all the evil things he had done.

When Jesus heard that John had been arrested, he withdrew in the power of the Spirit into Galilee. There he began to proclaim the gospel, saying, "The time is fulfilled, and the kingdom of God is at hand; repent and believe in the gospel."

The Baptist's time was up. Now it was Jesus' turn to "grab the headlines." Reports went throughout all the surrounding country that Jesus was preaching the message John had preached. As a result Jesus ended up teaching in the synagogues in Galilee, being glorified by all.[5]

---

[5] Matt. 4:12; Mark 1:14-15; Luke 4:14-15

At the Right Time

From there Jesus went to Nazareth where he spoke in the synagogue. At first the people spoke well of him and marveled at his gracious words. But then they wanted Him to entertain them with miracles.

"Do here in your hometown what we heard you did at Capernaum."

When Jesus rebuked them, all in the synagogue were filled with wrath. They drove him out of the town and tried to throw him over a cliff. But Jesus passed through their midst unharmed.[6]

So Jesus left Nazareth and went to Capernaum. There he began to teach the people in the synagogue on the Sabbath. They were amazed at his teaching because his message had authority.

The dragon sent someone to challenge Jesus' authority. In the synagogue a man possessed by an evil spirit shouted at the top of his voice, "Stop! Jesus of Nazareth! Why are you interfering with us? I know who you are. You're the Holy One of God and you've come to destroy us!"[7]

"Be quiet!" Jesus ordered the spirit. "Come out of him!"

The demon threw the man down in front of them all and left without hurting him.

The onlookers were stunned.

"What kind of command is this?" they said to one another. "With authority and power he gives orders to evil spirits, and they come out!"

Never had any of them seen or heard of a demon being was cast out of a person.[8] So news about him spread through every place in the surrounding region.

The dragon was just as stunned. He had sent the demon to stop Jesus from interfering with the dragon's kingdom, not to call him the Holy One of God. Nor was he supposed to acknowledge that Jesus had come to destroy evil spirits.

Jesus continued to preach both in Capernaum and throughout all Galilee. He preached John's message, "Repent, for the kingdom

---

[6] Luke 4:14-30
[7] Luke 4:34, MSG
[8] This is the first such case in the Bible.

of heaven is at hand," and more. He taught in their synagogues, proclaiming the gospel of the kingdom. People were astonished at his teaching, for he spoke with authority. He also healed every disease and every affliction among the people.

So his fame spread.

Up to this time, Jesus' disciples were a fluid group, following Jesus as time and work permitted. But Jesus was looking for a team of men he could teach and train full time. He started with the two who had followed him first. Walking by the Sea of Galilee, he found Peter and Andrew casting a net into the sea.

"Follow me," Jesus called to them, "and I will make you fishers of men."

Immediately they left their nets and followed him. A little farther along Jesus found James and John in the boat with their father Zebedee, mending their nets. Jesus called them, and they too immediately left their father Zebedee in the boat with the hired servants and followed him.

By ones and twos Jesus called others until he had a band of twelve who left their careers to follow Jesus. Immediately after he had appointed the twelve, Jesus disclosed to them their mission—to be with Jesus, to preach, and to drive out demons.[9]

Let the holy war begin!

If the dragon thought he was Earth's king, Jesus was about to disillusion him. Miracles were good, but Jesus had come to defeat the dragon, who had attempted to usurp God's authority and establish his own. Jesus would succeed where previous imagers had failed to established Yahweh's rule throughout Earth.

The disciples learned from all the things Jesus taught and did.

For more than a year Jesus proclaimed the good news of the Kingdom, taught to crowds wherever he went, and healed the sick. The common people loved Jesus and flocked to him to be healed. They also

---

[9] Mark 3:14

loved to listen to his teachings. But the religious establishment were not so enamoured of Jesus. He pointed out their pride and hypocrisy, and they began to hate him.

One day Jesus asked his disciples, "Who do people say the Son of Man is?"

That question led to the next one. "What about you? Who do you say I am?"

Peter declared that Jesus was the Christ, the Son of the living God. Jesus immediately commended him for his insight.

"Blessed are you, Simon,[10] son of Jonah! You didn't learn this from a human being. My Father in heaven revealed it to you. You are Peter, a rock. But your confession is an even greater rock. Your confession that I am the Christ is the solid rock foundation on which I will build my church, and the gates of hell will not prove stronger than it. I will give you the keys of the Kingdom of Heaven; whatever you bind on Earth, declaring it to be improper and unlawful, will be bound in Heaven, and whatever you loose or declare lawful on Earth will be loosed in Heaven."

The dragon was horrified at Peter's declaration that Jesus was the Christ. The dragon was even more horrified at Jesus' declaration. It was a stunning announcement with important meaning to both the Greeks and the Romans.

The Greek word *ekklesia* which Jesus used for "church" literally means a "called out" group of people. To the Greeks in Jesus' day an *ekklesia* was an assembly of people "called out" to govern the affairs of a city or a nation. It served much like a city council, parliament or congress. To the Romans, *ekklesia* was a group of people sent into a conquered region to rule it, also altering the culture to make it like Rome. Rome's *ekklesia* changed government, schools, language and social structure

---

[10] Jesus had renamed Peter, but continued calling him by his old name Simon. Everybody else called him Peter, except the disciple John, who called him Simon Peter, using the name Peter for short when his name was repeated in a story.

until the people talked, thought and acted like Romans. The Roman *ekklesia* so transformed people that they considered themselves to *be* Romans. This was the ideal way to control their empire.

When Jesus said He would build His church, his disciples understood him to be speaking of a body of people that would "legislate" spiritually for Him, extending His kingdom rule over the earth. Gates in Jesus' day were often where judges sat to rule or where governing councils met to make decisions. Gates were where they held court. When Jesus said that "the gates of Hades will not overpower it," the disciples understood those "gates" not as physical gates but rather as the governmental plans of hell.

Both the disciples and the dragon understood that Jesus was saying He would raise up a kingdom government on earth over which hell's government would not prevail. Jesus followed this declaration by saying he would give his *ekklesia* "keys",[11] which symbolize authority. Keys lock and unlock in order to close or open. Jesus was declaring his church would have keys (authority) to lock the gates (government) of hell and open the gates (government) of heaven.[12]

The dragon was determined that wouldn't happen. He determined to use Peter to trip Jesus up.

Jesus knew that his disciples were expecting him to set up an earthly kingdom, so he began to explain to them that he must go to Jerusalem, suffer many things at the hands of the chief priests and teachers of the law, be killed, and on the third day be raised to life.[13]

Peter didn't like to hear that. He wanted Jesus to establish his Kingdom immediately. So the dragon put words in his mouth.

"Never, Lord!" Peter rebuked Jesus. "This will never happen to you!"

Jesus recognized the source of that message. Turning to Peter, he said, "Get out of my way, Satan! You are dangerous to me. You have no idea how God works."

---

[11] Matthew 16:19
[12] Dutch Sheets, "The Ekklesia," www.dutchsheets,org, Give Him 15, April 13, 2021.
[13] Matthew 16:21

At the Right Time

Six days later Peter, James and John were with Jesus on a high mountain when Jesus was transfigured before them. His face shone like the sun and his clothes became as white as light. Then Moses and Elijah appeared and talked with Jesus.

Soon the disciples were thinking again of greatness for themselves, but Jesus told them, "Elijah has already come, but people did not recognize him, and he was put to death. In the same way," Jesus added, "the Son of Man is going to suffer at their hands."

Then the disciples understood that Jesus was talking about John the Baptist, but they still didn't seriously comprehend that Jesus must die.

Later that day Jesus repeated his message to all twelve of his disciples.

"The Son of Man is going to be betrayed into the hands of men. They will kill him, and on the third day he will be raised to life."

As a result of all Jesus' preaching and healing, the religious establishment realized they were losing their power over the people. That must not happen! Within a year and a half of Jesus coming to the attention of the public, the religious rulers were plotting to get rid of him. So Jesus avoided Judea, where the Jews were seeking to kill him, and went around in Galilee, where his ministry was appreciated.

When the Feast of Tabernacles was at hand, Jesus, like all Jewish men, was expected to go to Jerusalem for the feast. His siblings, knowing that Jesus claimed to be the Messiah, didn't believe in him, so they taunted him.

"Leave this place and go to Judea so your disciples can see the things you are doing. No one does things secretly when he wants to be known publicly. If you do these things, you should let the world see you."

"My time has not yet come," Jesus replied. "You go up to the feast. I'm not going up to this feast, for my time hasn't yet fully come."

After saying this, he remained in Galilee. But later, after his brothers had gone up to the feast, Jesus went up, not publicly but in private.[14]

---

[14] John 7:1-10

The Plan

For the next six months Jesus continued to teach and do miracles. He also launched an all-out assault on the dragon. He appointed seventy other disciples to go ahead of him in pairs into every town and place where he planned to visit. They were to prepare the way for Jesus by doing what he did—preach the kingdom of God, heal the sick and cast out demons.

The disciples quickly learned how powerful the name of Jesus was. Upon their return they joyfully reported to Jesus, "Lord, even the demons are subject to us when we use your name!"

"I know," said Jesus. "I saw Satan fall like lightning from heaven. He was expelled on my authority. I have given you that same authority to destroy the enemy's power. Nothing will hurt you."

The dragon refused to believe this was the beginning of the end of his power. He stirred up the religious establishment to entrap Jesus. In a number of places the Jews decided that anyone who acknowledged that Jesus was the Christ would be put out of the synagogue.[15]

The tipping point came when Jesus raised Lazarus from the dead after he had been in the tomb four days. Such a miracle could not be explained away. The chief priests and the Pharisees called a meeting of the Sanhedrin and made plans to arrest Jesus and kill Lazarus as well.

The people's reaction was just the opposite. They wanted to hail him as king. Jesus knew it was time to fulfill prophecy:

> *Rejoice greatly, O daughter of Zion!*
> *Shout aloud, O daughter of Jerusalem!*
> *Behold, your king is coming to you;*
> *righteous and having salvation is he,*
> *humble and mounted on a donkey,*
> *on a colt, the foal of a donkey.*[16]

---

[15] John 9:22
[16] Zechariah 9:9

As Jesus and his disciples drew near to Jerusalem and came to the Mount of Olives, Jesus sent two disciples ahead to bring him a donkey's colt. When people heard that Jesus was on his way to Jerusalem for Passover, a great crowd took palm branches and went out to meet him. When the disciples brought the colt to Jesus, he sat on it.

Many of the crowd spread their cloaks on the road. Others cut leafy branches from the trees and spread them on the road. Some people went before Jesus; others followed after him all the way down the Mount of Olives. The whole multitude hailed him with shouts.

"Hosanna to the Son of David!"

"Blessed is he who comes in the name of the Lord!"

"Peace in heaven and glory in the highest!"

"Blessed is the King of Israel!"

"Blessed is the coming kingdom of our father David!"

"Hosanna in the highest!"[17]

The Pharisees were alarmed. "Look, the whole world has gone after him!"

Jesus was not fooled by the adoration of the crowd. He was not interested in any glory that the public bestowed upon him. He was focused on glorifying the Father.

A day or two later, with Jesus approaching the third Passover since his baptism, he knew it was time to fulfill the purpose for which he had been born, and he asked his disciples to prepare to celebrate the Passover meal.

He also directed them to go into the city and say to a certain man, "The Teacher says, 'My time is at hand. I will keep the Passover at your house with my disciples.'"[18]

Three days after the crowd had hailed Jesus as king, Jerusalem was full of people coming to celebrate Passover. Among them were some non-Jews who had come 85 miles all the way from Bethsaida, northeast

---

[17] Matthew 21:8-11; Mark 11:7-10; Luke 19:35-38; John 12:12-18
[18] Matthew 26:18

The Plan

of the Sea of Galilee, to Jerusalem. They had come to worship. And they wanted to see Jesus.

When Philip and Andrew brought them to Jesus, Jesus was aware that he was facing the mission for which he had been born. Before the day ended, he would be betrayed. He must once more tell his followers that things would get much worse before they got better.

"The hour has come for the Son of Man to be glorified," Jesus told his disciples and the visitors from Bethsaida. But he had to disillusion them. Before they saw the glory, they would see him killed.

"I tell you the truth, unless a kernel of wheat falls to the ground and dies, it remains only a single seed. But if it dies, it produces many seeds."

Jesus was quiet for a moment and then continued.

"Now my heart is troubled, and what shall I say? 'Father, save me from this hour'? No, it was for this very reason I came to this hour."

Looking up, he called out, "Father, glorify your name!"

A voice replied from heaven, "I have glorified it, and will glorify it again."

The Passover crowd that was nearby and heard it said it had thundered; others said an angel had spoken to him.[19]

To those who heard it Jesus said, "This voice is for your benefit, not mine. Now the prince of this world will be driven out. But I, when I am lifted up from the earth, will draw all men to myself."

Jesus was talking as plainly as he dared without saying it too clearly. He didn't want the dragon to back out of his diabolical plan at the last moment. The dragon would discover too late that he had fallen into the Holy One's trap.

The crowd said what the dragon was thinking: "We have heard from the Law that the Christ will remain forever, so how can you say, 'The Son of Man must be lifted up'?"

Yahweh had blinded their eyes.[20]

---

[19] John 12:23-29
[20] John 12:34, 40

38

The Dragon Does His Worst

The dragon had come to the realization that Jesus was Yahweh's Anointed One or 'Messiah,' as the Jews called him. Jesus was Yahweh's choice for King.

All previous kings of Israel had failed to rule as Yahweh desired. Saul had been easy to corrupt; he never took seriously the importance of studying the Law of God.

David was a different matter. He loved God with all his heart, and he ruled really well for a long time. But the dragon succeeded in tempting him with Bathsheba and luring him into adultery and murder. The dragon was disappointed to see David turn to Yahweh in repentance so quickly. The dragon was even angrier when Yahweh forgave him so freely. Worst of all, in the dragon's opinion, was the worship system which David established for the priests and Levites, a system which was followed in the Temple for centuries.

Solomon's downfall was his many wives who lured him into idol worship. All of the kings of Israel and many of the kings of Judah were equally disloyal to the Holy One.

The dragon cheered when Yahweh destroyed first the northern kingdom, then the southern kingdom, demolished Jerusalem and sent the Jews into exile.

Looking back over history, the dragon congratulated himself that he had done a pretty good job of spreading evil and chaos throughout Earth. All previous imagers of Yahweh had failed to restore Eden. Now all he had to do was destroy Jesus.

The Plan

So the dragon hatched a plot to get rid of the Messiah and foil Yahweh's plan.

When Jesus first called Judas to join his band of disciples, Judas was delighted. He was captivated by Jesus' teaching and the miracles he did. He was honored to be entrusted with the purse. Early in his walk with Jesus, Judas had heard him say, "You cannot serve both God and Money." But those words soon faded from his memory.

As Jesus grew more and more popular with the people, they gave more generously to the rabbi's band. And Judas started dipping his hand into the purse. The more the people gave, the easier it was to take more for himself.

Now all the dragon had to do was turn Judas against Jesus.

The religious leaders were already jealous of the influence Jesus had over the common people. The Pharisees and chief priests, especially Caiaphas the high priest, sensed that they were losing what limited power they had in a world controlled by Rome. All the dragon had to do was stoke the embers of jealousy and they would take Jesus to the Roman governor and request his execution.

But there was a problem. They didn't dare seize Jesus in public. If they arrested Jesus, the people would riot in his defence— especially if it happened during Passover. The religious leaders would have to find a way of catching Jesus when nobody was looking.

Two days before Passover things began to go the dragon's way. Jesus and his disciples were in Bethany at the house of friends. While Jesus was reclining at the dinner table, a woman came with a jar of very expensive perfume, broke the jar and poured the perfume on Jesus' head. Then she anointed his feet and wiped his feet with her hair.[1]

Judas was indignant. What a waste! Others thought the same thing, and scolded the woman, but Judas spoke most forcefully.

"Why did you waste the perfume? It could have been sold for more than a year's wages and the money given to the poor."[2]

---

[1] Compare Matthew 26:7 and Mark 14:3 with John 12:3.
[2] John 12: 4-6

He didn't say out loud that he wanted some of the proceeds.

But Jesus defended the woman.

"Leave her alone," he said. "Why are you bothering her? She has done a beautiful thing to me. She has poured this ointment on my body to prepare me for burial."

Judas was upset with both the waste of perfume and with Jesus' reaction.

How could Jesus be so self-absorbed as to accept her extravagant act? Judas thought. *How could he call it "a beautiful thing"? How could Jesus not see the waste?*

As soon as he could, Judas excused himself and left the house. He wandered the dark streets alone, mentally fussing about what had happened at dinner. The perfume that the woman had wasted could have gone a long way toward paying for luxuries he would like to enjoy later in life—after he left this itinerant lifestyle behind.

"What a waste!" Judas muttered to no one in particular.

The dragon was listening.

Judas looked up the street and recognized the house of Caiaphas the high priest.

"The chief priests and teachers of the law hate Jesus," the dragon whispered. "They are looking for a chance to arrest him. I'm sure they would pay you handsomely to betray him."

Judas quickened his pace, then paused at the foot of the stairs to Caiaphas' house.

"Do it!" the dragon hissed.

Resolutely Judas climbed the stairs and knocked on the door. The house was full of chief priests and officers of the temple guard. When Judas introduced himself as a disciple of Jesus, they welcomed him gladly.

The chief priests were delighted to hear of Judas' willingness to betray him. As an insider, Judas would know when Jesus was vulnerable and he could tip off the priests or the temple guards as to where to find him. Judas promised to watch for an opportunity to hand Jesus over when no crowd was present.

Caiaphas counted out thirty pieces of silver and put them into a bag. "This will be yours when you deliver him to us," Caiaphas promised.

Two days later Jesus knew that the time had come for him to leave this world and go to the Father. He and his disciples gathered for the Passover feast shortly before sunset. Jesus and his disciples sat down to eat, with Jesus officiating at the Seder meal.

"You've no idea how much I have looked forward to eating this Passover meal with you before I enter my time of suffering," Jesus began. "It's the last one I'll eat until we all eat it together in the kingdom of God."[3]

With those words Jesus led his disciples through a program they had all participated in since childhood—with cups of wine, symbolic foods, questions about the origins of Passover, and comments on the story of the Exodus.

But Jesus also introduced some variations of his own.

Jesus began the Seder as usual by filling each disciple's cup with wine. Lifting his cup of wine, he gave thanks with the traditional blessing spoken over the first cup. Then he said, "I tell you the truth: I won't drink this wine again until that day when I drink new wine with you in my Father's kingdom."

Next in order was the ritual handwashing. His disciples watched as Jesus rose from the table, took off his robe, wrapped a towel around his waist and poured water into a basin. Then Jesus surprised the disciples by beginning to wash their *feet* and drying them with the towel. The first few disciples submitted in silence, not knowing how to react. When Jesus came to Peter, he found his tongue.

"Lord, *you* are going to wash *my feet*?"

Jesus answered, "You don't understand now what I'm doing, but it will be clear to you later."

---

[3] Luke 22:14-16

Peter would have none of it. "You're not going to wash my feet—ever!"
Jesus said, "If I don't wash you, you can't be part of what I'm doing."
That changed Peter's response. "In that case, Lord, don't wash only my feet. Wash my hands and my head too!"
Jesus chuckled, then he turned serious.
"If you've had a bath, you need only your feet washed now and you'll be completely clean. All of you, except one, are clean."
Nobody at the time knew what he meant.
After he had finished washing their feet, Jesus put his robe on again and went back to his place at the table. All eyes were on him.
"Do you understand what I have done to you?" he asked. The disciples were eager for an explanation.
"You address me as 'teacher' and 'Lord,' and rightly so. That is what I am. So if I, your Lord and teacher, washed your feet, you must now wash each other's feet. I've given you an example. What I've done, you must do. I can guarantee you this truth: A servant is not superior to his master; a messenger is not superior to the one who sent him. If you understand what I'm telling you, follow my example—and you will be blessed."
Jesus continued with the Seder ceremony. One plate in the middle of the table contained three pieces of unleavened bread for ceremonial purposes. Jesus took the middle piece, broke it in two, wrapped one of the halves called the *afikomen* in a napkin, and returned the rest of the bread to the plate with the broken piece in the middle. One of the disciples hid the *afikomen*.
Then it was time to tell the Passover story in a way that was meaningful to the age and development, intellectual and spiritual, of each. During this time the disciples, like children, would ask questions.
Jesus was troubled in spirit because he knew what would soon transpire. The disciples noticed his change of mood.
"Truly, I say to you, one of you will betray me."
Those words set off a flurry of questions. John, being the youngest, was expected to ask the first question: "Lord, who is it?"

The Plan

Other questions quickly followed. "Who is it?" "Is it I?"

"It is he," Jesus answered, "to whom I will give this morsel when I have dipped it."

That signaled the next step in the Seder ritual. Jesus dipped a morsel of bitter herbs into salt water and gave it to Judas.

After Judas took the morsel, Satan entered into him, and Jesus said, "What you are going to do, do quickly."

The disciples thought Judas was leaving to give something from the moneybag to the poor. Instead Judas went straight to Caiaphas' house.

Dinner was served, and the disciples soon forgot about Judas and their questions. Jesus began talking about going where his disciples could not come. Then he talked about a new commandment.

"A new commandment I give to you," Jesus told his disciples, "that you love one another: just as I have loved you, you also are to love one another. By this all people will know that you are my disciples, if you have love for one another."[4]

But the disciples weren't thinking about love for each other. They were wondering who would replace Jesus if he went away somewhere. Surely it would be whoever among them was the greatest. So a dispute arose among them as to who that was.[5]

Peter had a different question. "Lord, where are you going?"

While the other disciples were squabbling about who was greatest, Jesus had a quiet conversation with Peter. He told Peter he was going where Peter could not follow.

"Why can't I follow you now, Lord?" Peter objected. "I will lay down my life for you."

Jesus told him otherwise. "Truly, truly, I say to you, the rooster will not crow till you have denied me three times."[6]

For once, Peter was too stunned for words.

---

[4] John 13:34-35
[5] Luke 22:24-30
[6] John 13:36-38

Jesus then returned to the whole group and to the topic of leaving. He comforted his disciples by telling them he was the way to the Father, and he promised to send the Holy Spirit in his place.

After the Passover meal, the Seder ceremony resumed.

It was time to find the *afikomen*. When it was found and brought to Jesus, he took the bread, blessed it, broke it into small pieces and gave it to them saying, "This is my body, which is given for you. Do this in remembrance of me."

Lifting the third cup of the Seder, the cup of redemption, Jesus said, "This cup is the new covenant in my blood, which is poured out for many for the forgiveness of sins."

These last two rituals would be pregnant with meaning for the disciples later.

Jesus then prayed for his disciples, they sang a hymn, and they went out. As usual they went to a place called Gethsemane on the Mount of Olives. It was a quiet garden full of olive trees, one of Jesus' favorite places to retreat from the crowds.

On the way Jesus spoke again to Peter one on one about things he had said earlier in the evening—about being betrayed and dying. Then he added a new piece of information.

"Simon, Simon, Satan has demanded to have you disciples that he might sift all of you like wheat. But I have pleaded in prayer for you in particular, that your faith should not fail. So when you have repented and turned to me again, strengthen your brothers."

Peter would have none of it.

"Lord, I am ready to go with you both to prison and to death."

"I tell you this, Peter," Jesus replied, "the rooster will not crow today until you deny three times that you know me."[7]

Jesus then addressed all the disciples. "You will all fall away from me this night. For it is written, 'I will strike the shepherd, and the sheep will be scattered.'"

---

[7] Luke 22:31-34

The Plan

Peter again denied such a thing was possible. "Even though they all fall away, I will not."

Jesus told Peter the third time, this time in front of all the disciples, "Truly, I tell you, this very night, before the rooster crows twice, you will deny me three times."[8]

Peter emphatically responded, "Even if I must die with you, I will not deny you!" And all the disciples said the same.

By this time they were in the Garden of Gethsemane. Knowing what was ahead of him, Jesus needed to be alone.

"Sit here while I go over there and pray," he said. For the next hour, Jesus prayed desperately while the disciples slept.

"Father, if you are willing, take this cup from me."

In his anguish his sweat was like drops of blood falling to the ground. Finally, he agreed with the Father.

"Not my will but yours be done."

Judas knew Jesus' habits well enough to know he would go to Gethsemane. So that's where he led the arresting force. It was a large crowd armed with swords and clubs, carrying torches and lanterns. Besides a detachment of soldiers, there were representatives from the religious establishment—chief priests, Pharisees, teachers of the law, and elders of the people. Leading the crowd was Judas.

Jesus went out to meet them and was promptly arrested. Initially Peter drew his sword and tried to protect Jesus. But when Jesus healed the man injured by Peter, his bravado collapsed. Then all the disciples deserted Jesus and fled.

Those who had arrested Jesus bound him and took him to Caiaphas the high priest, where the entire Sanhedrin—the Jewish supreme court—had assembled. The men guarding Jesus blind-folded him, mocked him and beat him.

At daybreak the Sanhedrin, with the high priest officiating, looked for evidence against Jesus so they could put him to death. But they

---

[8] Matthew 26:31-34; Mark 14:27-30

didn't find any. Although many people testified falsely against Jesus, their statements didn't agree.

Finally the high priest asked, "Are you the Messiah, the Son of God?" When Jesus replied, "I am," the high priest tore his clothes.

"Why do we need any more witnesses?" he asked. "You have heard the blasphemy. What do you think?"

The Sanhedrin unanimously condemned him as worthy of death. They again blindfolded Jesus, mocked him, spit on him, slapped him and struck him with their fists.

The dragon applauded the abuse, but he was thirsty for more.

The Jewish leaders didn't have the authority to execute anyone, so they took Jesus to the palace of Pilate, the Roman governor. After questioning Jesus, Pilate was not convinced that he was guilty. On learning that Jesus was a Galilean, Pilate sent him to Herod, who had jurisdiction over Galilee.

In Herod's court the chief priests and the teachers of the law vehemently accused Jesus. Herod plied Jesus with many questions, but he answered not a word. Having heard that Jesus claimed to be a king, and seeing this was not a real trial, Herod and his soldiers ridiculed and mocked Jesus. They dressed him in an elegant robe, and sent him back to Pilate.

Pilate called together the chief priests, the rulers and the people and reminded them, "I have examined this man and found no basis for your charges against him. Neither has Herod. Therefore, I will punish him and release him."

But that didn't satisfy the crowd. They were thirsty for blood.

So was the dragon.

Pilate was reluctant to execute Jesus. Then he remembered something. It was the governor's custom at the festival to release a prisoner chosen by the crowd. An infamous criminal named Barabbas was in prison for insurrection and murder.

So Pilate asked the crowd, "Do you want me to release to you the king of the Jews? You have a choice. Barabbas or Jesus?"

The Plan

While Pilate was sitting on the judge's seat waiting for an answer, his wife sent him a message: "Don't have anything to do with that innocent man. I suffered through a terrible nightmare about him last night."

Meanwhile the chief priests were stirring up the crowd, persuading them to ask to have Barabbas released and Jesus executed. Pretty soon the whole crowd was shouting, "Away with Jesus! Release Barabbas!"

"What shall I do then with Jesus, the one you call the king of the Jews?" Pilate asked.

"Crucify him!" they shouted.

Pilate wanted to release Jesus, so he appealed to them again. But they kept shouting, "Crucify him! Crucify him!"

Pilate resisted their cries a third time. "Why? What crime has he committed? I have found in him no grounds for the death penalty."

But they shouted all the louder, "Crucify him!"

"I'll have him punished and then release him," Pilate replied.

But with loud shouts the crowd insistently demanded that he be crucified. Wanting to satisfy the crowd, Pilate released the murderer and surrendered Jesus to the will of the crowd.

The dragon was determined to do his worst. Death was not good enough. He wanted to inflict as much pain as possible before death finally released the object of his hatred.

The elegant robe Herod had used to mock the King of the Jews was removed, and Jesus was flogged. Again and again. Till he was disfigured beyond recognition.[9]

Then the soldiers took Jesus back to Pilate's palace. There a whole company of soldiers gathered around to torment Jesus.

The soldiers tore his clothes roughly from his bloody body and replaced them with a purple robe.[10] They twisted together a crown of thorns and pressed it cruelly onto his head. They put a staff in his right

---

[9] Isaiah 52:14
[10] Compare Matthew 27:28 with Mark15:17 and John 19:2,5.

hand. Then they knelt in front of him and mocked him again and again saying, "Hail, king of the Jews!"

They spit on him. They slapped him in the face. They struck him on the head with a staff again and again.

Once more Pilate came out and said to the Jews gathered there, "Look, I am bringing him out to you to let you know that I find no basis for a charge against him."

When Jesus came out wearing the crown of thorns and the purple robe, Pilate said, "Take a good look! The man!"

Pilate hoped the crowd would have mercy and be satisfied that Jesus had suffered enough. But the chief priests and their officials were unmoved by the bloody spectacle before them. As soon as they saw Jesus, they shouted, "Crucify! Crucify!"

Pilate was still reluctant, maybe even afraid, to have Jesus crucified, especially after he had learned of his wife's dream. When Pilate answered, "I find no basis for a charge against him," the Jewish leaders insisted, "By our law he must die because he claimed to be the Son of God."

When Pilate heard this, he was even more afraid. He hurried back inside the palace and asked Jesus, "Where do you come from?"

Jesus gave him no answer.

"Do you refuse to speak to me?" Pilate demanded. "Don't you realize I have power either to free you or to crucify you?"

Jesus answered, "You would have no power over me if it were not given to you from above."

From then on, Pilate tried to set Jesus free, but the Jewish leaders kept shouting, "If you let this man go, you are no friend of Caesar. Anyone who claims to be a king opposes Caesar."

When Pilate heard this, he brought Jesus out and sat down on the judge's seat.

"Here is your king," Pilate said to the Jews.

But they shouted, "Take him away! Crucify him!"

"Shall I crucify your *king*?" Pilate asked.

"We have no king but Caesar," the chief priests answered.

The Plan

Finally, Pilate handed Jesus over to them to be crucified. The soldiers mocked him once more, "Hail! King of the Jews!" Then they took off the purple robe, put his own clothes on him, and led him out to be crucified.

The soldiers made Jesus carry his own cross. A large crowd followed. Many of those who watched Jesus were appalled. He barely looked human.[11] Women along the way mourned and wailed.

Having been flogged so severely, Jesus was too weak to carry his cross for long, so the soldiers conscripted a bystander and forced him to carry it through the streets of Jerusalem.

Outside the city at a place called Golgotha, meaning 'the place of the skull,' they crucified him. By then it was mid-morning on Preparation Day of the Passover.

The soldiers nailed a notice of the charge against Jesus above his head. The notice in Aramaic, Latin and Greek read: "This is Jesus of Nazareth, the King of the Jews."[12]

The chief priests were upset with the notice and protested to Pilate.

"Don't write 'the King of the Jews.' Write that he *claimed to be* king of the Jews."

Pilate dismissed them impatiently. "What I have written I have written."

Meanwhile the abuse against Jesus continued.

Those who passed by hurled insults at him.

"Ha! Look at you now!" they yelled at him. "You said you were going to destroy the Temple and rebuild it in three days. So show us! Save yourself! If you're really God's Son, come down from that cross!"

The soldiers mocked him by offering wine vinegar for his thirst. "If you are the king of the Jews, save yourself."

The chief priests joined in the mockery. "He saved others, but he can't save himself! Let this Messiah, this King of Israel, come down from the cross so we can see it. Then we'll all believe him! Ha, ha, ha!"

---

[11] Isaiah 52:14
[12] Compare Matthew 27:37, Mark 15:26, Luke 23:38 and John 19:19.

Even the men crucified alongside him joined in the mockery.

About noon the sun stopped shining and a strange darkness fell over the land. For three hours the scene was dark. The crowd was mystified and a hush fell over them. Even the mockers were silent.

Finally, the darkness penetrated Jesus' pain. He interpreted the darkness as evidence his own Father had abandoned him. With a loud voice he cried out, "My God, my God, why have you forsaken me?"

No answer.

A short while later Jesus called out with a loud voice, "Father, into your hands I commit my spirit."

A moment later he cried out again, "It is finished!"

With that, he bowed his head and breathed his last.

At that moment the curtain of the temple was torn in two from top to bottom. The earth shook, rocks split, tombs broke open, and many holy people were raised to life.

When the centurion guarding Jesus saw the earthquake and all that had happened, he was terrified, and exclaimed, "Surely he was the Son of God!"

The dragon didn't know what to make of the strange events, but he rejoiced that his arch enemy was dead. Later that day he watched as Jesus' body was wrapped in linen and placed in a tomb cut out of rock. When a big stone was rolled against the entrance, the dragon and his demons danced over the tomb.

Jesus is dead! God's plan has been thwarted! Eden will never be restored! We won!

Or so they thought!

39

Darkness to Dawn

The disciples went into hiding, fearing for their lives. Their hopes that Jesus was the Messiah who would deliver them from Rome's tyranny were dashed.

Only one man was fearless enough to act. Joseph of Arimathea, a prominent member of the Council, was a secret disciple of Jesus. He had kept quiet about his faith in Jesus because he feared the Jewish leaders.

Joseph went boldly to Pilate and asked for the body of Jesus. Pilate was surprised to hear that Jesus was already dead, but when a centurion confirmed the death, Pilate gave Joseph permission to take the body.

Joseph conscripted his friend Nicodemus, also a member of the Council, to help him. Together they took Jesus' body, hurriedly wrapped it in spices and then in strips of linen, and placed it in the tomb Joseph had cut out of rock for his own burial. They rolled the stone over the entrance and left before sunset when the first day of the Feast of Unleavened Bread, a day of rest, would begin.

The women who had wept as they watched Jesus' suffering and death followed the men and saw them lay Jesus' body in the tomb.

The chief priests and Pharisees remembered that Jesus had promised to rise from the dead after three days, and they feared that Jesus' disciples would steal the body and tell people that Jesus had been raised from the dead. So they asked Pilate to secure the tomb. Pilate agreed to do so. He had the tomb sealed and posted the guard—four shifts of four soldiers each.[1]

For three days and nights there was silence.

After sundown on the third night, when the weekly Sabbath was over, the women went out and bought spices and perfumes to finish preparing Jesus' body. They rose before dawn and started for the tomb. On the way they wondered aloud who would roll the stone, which was very heavy, away from the entrance of the tomb.

Just then the ground shook with a violent earthquake. They looked up to see that the stone had been rolled away. The guards were lying flat on the ground. They appeared to be dead.

Mary Magdalene was the first of the women to recover. She looked into the tomb, saw no body, and went running to report the matter to the disciples. Finding Peter and John, she announced, "They've taken the Lord out of the tomb. We don't know where they have put him!"

Peter and John ran to see. John outran Peter, bent over and saw the sunken strips of linen, but he didn't go in. Peter came along behind him and went straight into the tomb. He saw the empty cocoon of linen, but he also noticed something else. The cloth napkin which had been used to cover Jesus' head was lying separate from the linen. Finally, John went inside the tomb, saw the napkin was neatly folded, and realized what it meant.

At a meal if someone left the table and was finished eating, he left his napkin in a crumpled heap, which signaled to the waiter, "I'm finished here." If he planned to return, he folded the napkin neatly. The message to the waiter was, "I'll be back!"

Jesus has come back from the dead! John realized. *He is alive!*

Meanwhile Mary Magdalene had returned. The guards were nowhere in sight. Mary stood outside the tomb crying. When she

---

[1] Standard procedure. Acts 12:4

The Plan

finally bent over to look into the tomb, she saw two angels there dressed in white.

They asked her, "Woman, why are you crying?"

"They have taken my Lord away," she said, "and I don't know where they have put him."

At this, she turned around and saw a man standing there, but she didn't realize that it was Jesus. He asked her the same question, "Woman, why are you crying? Who are you looking for?"

Thinking he was the gardener, she said, "Sir, if you have carried him away, tell me where you have put him."

Jesus then spoke her name. "Mary."

Recognizing his voice, she turned toward him with a cry of delight. "Teacher!"

The other women at the tomb were sorrowful and weeping, but the angels reassured them, "Jesus is not here. He has risen! Come and see the place where he lay. Then go quickly and tell his disciples."

Word spread quickly. "Jesus is alive!"

At first people didn't believe it. But then they remembered Jesus saying that he would rise again.

* * * *

All Heaven rejoiced to see the empty tomb and the resurrection of Jesus. Yahweh had raised him from the dead! Death could not hold him. The penalty for sin was paid. Jesus had made a way for humanity to be reconciled to God.

The Kingdom of God would be restored! Jesus had started the process with his ministry; now it could be completed as his imagers appropriated that resurrection power.

When the dragon and all the lesser evil spirits saw the empty tomb, they realized that Yahweh had outsmarted them. If they had known that the death of the Messiah was necessary for God's plan to succeed, they never would have crucified Jesus.² Once the powers of darkness understood that they had been outwitted, there was a sense that the timetable of their judgment had been set in motion. It was only a matter of time until the dragon and all his evil angels would receive their just punishment.

For forty days following his resurrection Jesus appeared to his disciples and others, giving many convincing proofs that he was alive. So many hundreds of people saw him that the resurrection was undeniable.³ Jesus told his followers to go and make disciples of all nations, baptizing them in the name of the Father, Son and Holy Spirit, and teaching them to obey everything he had commanded them.

"And surely," Jesus said, "I am with you always, to the very end of the age."

But he added a promise: "I am going to send you what my Father has promised. So wait for it. Stay in Jerusalem until you have been clothed with power from on high."

Saying that, Jesus led his followers out to the vicinity of Bethany, lifted up his hands and blessed them. While he was blessing them, he was taken up into heaven.⁴

* * * *

Jesus stood before the throne in Heaven and addressed his Father.

"Mission accomplished! Father, I have done what I was born to do. I finished my work by dying on the cross. You did your part by raising me from the dead. Now it is up to Holy Spirit to pick up where we left off."

"Well done, Son," said Father motioning to the throne beside him. "Please be seated. Finally, our Plan can be accomplished. We created men in our image, but they didn't have the power to obey us perfectly.

---

² 1 Cor 2:8
³ 1 Cor 15:6
⁴ See Luke 24:49-53 and Acts 1:4-11.

The Plan

They didn't have the power to rule Earth as we wanted them to. But with Holy Spirit indwelling them they will have power to do all that and to witness boldly and spread the Good News around the world."

"My disciples thought I had come to be a political king," said Jesus. "Even though I said it as plainly as I could, they heard only what they wanted to hear. I told them I had to suffer and die, but my words went right over their heads.

"The only one who might have finally believed me at the end was Judas Iscariot. When I first called him to follow me, he was red hot, believing I was the Messiah. When it dawned on him that there were personal benefits to controlling the purse, his love for me cooled. Money became his first love. When he finally realized that I was telling the truth about suffering and dying, his heart went stone cold. He hated me for raising his political hopes. Since I had not come to restore Israel in his lifetime, he made the most of his position by selling me for thirty pieces of silver."

* * * *

Ten days later, on the day of Pentecost, Jesus' disciples were among about a hundred and twenty believers who were praying in an upstairs room, waiting for the Father's promise. Suddenly there came a sound from heaven like the roaring of a mighty wind, and it filled the whole house where they were sitting. Then, what looked like flames or tongues of fire appeared and settled on each of them. Everyone present was filled with the Holy Spirit and began speaking in other languages, as the Holy Spirit gave them the ability.

Jerusalem at that time was filled with God-fearing Jews from every nation under heaven, pilgrims celebrating Pentecost. The sound of the wind was so loud it could be heard even outside the house. Pilgrims gathered to investigate. As they did so, the Spirit-filled believers left the upper room and mingled in the streets with the pilgrims, who were bewildered to hear Jerusalem Jews speaking their own languages.

Utterly amazed, they asked, "How can this be? These people are all from Galilee, and yet we hear them speaking in our own native languages! Here we are—Parthians, Medes, Elamites, people from Mesopotamia and a dozen other countries—and we all hear these people speaking in our own languages about the wonderful things God has done!"

Then Peter stood up and addressed the crowd, "Fellow Jews, let me explain. This is exactly what the prophet Joel prophesied. 'In the last days,' God said, 'I will pour out my Spirit upon all people and they will prophesy. Terrible things will happen before that great and awesome day of Yahweh arrives, but everyone who calls on the name of Yahweh will be saved.'"

Peter then preached a simple straight-forward gospel message. The listeners were cut to the heart and asked, "What shall we do?"

Peter replied, "Repent and be baptized in the name of Jesus Christ so that your sins may be forgiven. And you will receive the gift of the Holy Spirit."

About three thousand accepted his message and were baptized. Those Jews then carried the message of Jesus and the Holy Spirit back to their home countries.

That was the beginning of the remarkable spread of the gospel to the ends of the known world. The Kingdom of God spread relentlessly, one new believer at a time. The gospel transformed men and women who had been held hostage by the dragon into sons and daughters of Yahweh. They met together to encourage each other, forming churches. Every church became a new pocket of resistance to the forces of darkness. Every baptism became another pledge of allegiance to the Most High God.

With the coming of Holy Spirit, believers gained a new understanding of Passover. For the first time, they saw that their annual Seder proclaimed their Messiah's substitutionary death— that Jesus was the Passover lamb, and that those who applied his blood to the doorposts of their lives would be passed over by the death angel.

Every day they excitedly shared this new understanding, breaking the matzo and repeating Jesus' words, "This is my body, which is broken for you. Do this in remembrance of me." Recognizing the truth of the third cup of the Seder dinner, they repeated Jesus' words, "This is my blood of the covenant, which is poured out for many for the forgiveness of sins. Drink of it in remembrance of me."

As believers performed this abbreviated Passover celebration daily, they gave it a name: the Lord's Supper.[5] Every celebration of the Lord's Supper proclaimed the success of Yahweh's mysterious Plan, which was a mystery no longer.

Holy Spirit opened the eyes of people's understanding to see that the gospel had been hidden in the sacrificial system taught to them by Moses. Spirit opened their eyes to truths hidden in Yahweh's appointed feasts, which they celebrated annually. Now they could see from their Scriptures that the Messiah had to suffer and die before being glorified.

The power of Holy Spirit which indwelt each new believer gave them courage which the world had never known. Pentecost began the reversal of the damage done by the dragon in the Garden of Eden. Pentecost marked the beginning of the unstoppable march of the gospel around the world.

---

[5] 1 Cor 11:20

40

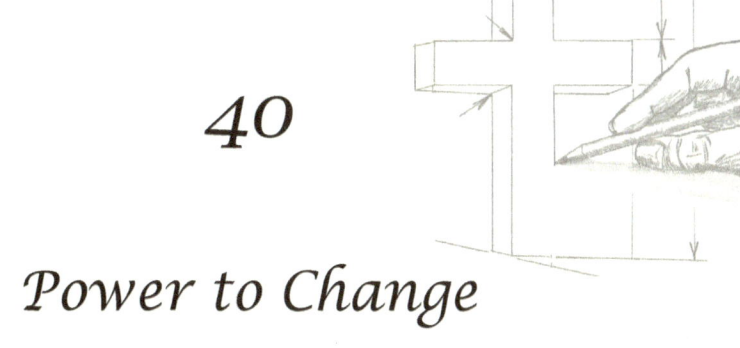

Power to Change

Pentecost was just the beginning. Suddenly the disciples who had been so easily intimidated by those who opposed them were filled with holy boldness, and the world took notice.

Peter's sermon resulted in three thousand Jews accepting his message and being baptized. A few days later, Peter and John were on their way to the temple when a man crippled from birth asked them for money.

Peter said, "I don't have silver and gold, but I have something better to give you. In the name of Jesus Christ of Nazareth, walk!"

Peter then took the man by the hand and helped him up. Instantly the man jumped to his feet and began to walk and jump around and praise God. The people nearby were astonished. They recognized him as the man who begged daily at the temple gate.

Peter seized the opportunity to preach the good news.

"Why are you surprised by this? Why do you stare at us as if *we* made this man walk? This man wasn't healed by us. It is Jesus' name and the faith that comes through him that has given this man complete healing. You killed Jesus, the author of life, but God raised him from the dead. Now, brothers, I know you acted in ignorance, but if you repent and turn to God, your sins will be wiped out."[1]

As a result of that miracle, about five thousand believed Peter's message.

---

[1] See Acts 3:12-26.

The religious establishment, however—priests, Sadducees and the captain of the temple guard—were greatly disturbed by the apostles' teaching. The Sadducees didn't believe in resurrection, and the priests didn't like to see their control over the people slipping away, so they put Peter and John in prison over night. The next day the rulers, elders and teachers of the law met in Jerusalem with the high priest and members of his family and demanded to know by what power Peter and John did this.

Peter was not intimidated. Filled with the Holy Spirit, he spoke boldly.

"It is by the name of Jesus Christ of Nazareth, whom you crucified but whom God raised from the dead, that this man stands before you completely healed. Salvation is found in no one else, for there is no other name under heaven given to men by which we must be saved."

The rulers and elders were astonished at the courage of these ordinary men, and they took note—these men had been with Jesus! The rulers wanted to punish Peter and John, but they didn't dare. Instead they commanded them not to speak or teach in the name of Jesus.

Peter and John replied, "Judge for yourselves whether it is right in God's sight to obey you rather than God. We can't help speaking about what we have seen and heard."

Following their release, Peter and John went to their friends and reported what the chief priests and the elders had said to them. Their friends lifted their voices in united prayer to God. After they prayed, the place where they were meeting was shaken. They were all filled with the Holy Spirit and spoke the word of God boldly.

In the wake of that prayer meeting, believers united as one. They didn't even claim ownership of their own possessions. They shared everything so that not a person among them was needy. From time to time people sold their property—houses and lands—and brought the proceeds from the sales to the apostles to distribute to anyone in need.

Besides preaching, the apostles performed many miraculous signs and wonders. The sick were healed, as were those tormented by evil spirits. More and more people believed in the Lord.

The high priest and his associates put the apostles in jail for preaching, but that didn't stop them. During the night an angel of the Lord opened the doors of the jail and brought them out.

"Go! Stand in the temple courts," the angel said. "Keep preaching! Tell the people the full message of this new life."

In the morning the high priest and his associates together with the full Sanhedrin arrived at the jail to find it securely locked, with the guards standing at the doors—but no one inside!

While they were wondering what had happened, someone came up to them and said, "Look! The men you put in jail are in the temple courts teaching the people."

The high priest dragged the apostles before the Sanhedrin and reminded them, "We gave you strict orders not to teach in this name."

Again the apostles replied, "We must obey God rather than men! You murdered Jesus by hanging him on a tree, but God raised him from the dead. God exalted him to his right hand as Prince and Savior that he might bring Israel to repentance and forgive their sins. We are witnesses of these things, and so is the Holy Spirit, whom God has given to those who obey him."

The Sanhedrin were furious to be told that they were unrepentant sinners who didn't obey God. They were furious at the suggestion that the men before them had the Holy Spirit but they didn't. They wanted to put the apostles to death, but one of their members persuaded them not to.

"Leave these men alone! Let them go! If their purpose or activity is of human origin, it will fail. But if it's of God, you won't be able to stop them. You may even find yourselves fighting against God!"

The apostles were flogged, released, and ordered not to speak in the name of Jesus. But that didn't stop them. Day after day, in the temple courts and from house to house, they never stopped teaching and proclaiming the good news that Jesus is the Christ.

The dragon felt the vibrations when the prayers of God's people shook their house. But he was too proud to give up. He refused to admit defeat. Instead, he redoubled his efforts.

The dragon had been successful in the past by recruiting religious leaders to his side. That strategy had worked in the case against Jesus. Religious leaders had stirred up the crowd to demand that Jesus be crucified.

Now the dragon found a synagogue, the Synagogue of the Freedmen, whose members would cooperate with him. The target was Stephen, a man full of God's grace and power, who did great wonders and miraculous signs. Men from the synagogue argued with Stephen but couldn't stand up against his wisdom or the Spirit by which he spoke. So they charged Stephen with blasphemy and brought him before the Sanhedrin.

When the high priest asked Stephen, "Are these charges true?" Stephen ignored the question. Instead, he launched into a long historical speech pointing out the many times in which leaders in Israel were opposed by their own flesh and blood. Joseph's brothers sold him into slavery in Egypt. Moses was rejected by Israelites who said, "Who made you our ruler and judge?" The Israelites rejected God Himself by worshiping a golden calf.

Stephen quoted the prophet Amos, "Was it to me you were bringing sacrifices and grain offerings in the desert during those forty years, O Israel? Hardly. You carried along your pagan gods— the shrine of Moloch, and the star of your god Rephan, and the images you made to worship them. Therefore, I will send you into exile beyond Babylon."

Stephen concluded by scolding the Sanhedrin and the entire religious establishment.

"You stiff-necked people! You are uncircumcised of heart and deaf to the truth. Must you forever resist the Holy Spirit? That's what your ancestors did, and so do you! Name one prophet your ancestors didn't persecute! They killed anyone who dared talk about the coming of the Righteous One. Now you have betrayed and murdered the Messiah! You deliberately disobeyed God's law delivered to you by angels."

When they heard this, they were furious.

Stephen looked up and said, "Look, I see the heavens opened and the Son of Man standing in the place of honor at God's right hand!"

At this the council members shouted and covered their ears. They rushed at him, dragged him out of the city and began to stone him. His accusers took off their coats and laid them at the feet of a young man named Saul.

Stephen's last words were, "Lord, don't hold this sin against them."

And Saul was there, giving approval to his death.

Saul was a Pharisee of the Pharisees. He put a lot of stock in having been circumcised on the eighth day. He was proud of being an Israelite. Saul hated Stephen's message. He couldn't stand being called stiff-necked, uncircumcised of heart and deaf to the truth.

He "deliberately disobeyed God's law"? Not so! When it came to righteousness, no one kept the law better than Saul.

"A traitor and a murderer of the Messiah"? Preposterous!

Something inside Saul snapped that day.

People like Stephen thought of themselves as belonging to 'the church' rather than to 'the synagogue.' They believed that Jesus was the way, the truth and the life.

"I'll destroy the church!" Saul declared between clenched teeth.

Going from house to house, he dragged off men and women who claimed that Jesus was the Way and put them in prison. Most of the religious establishment joined him. That day a great persecution broke

The Plan

out against the church at Jerusalem, and believers in the Way scattered throughout Judea and Samaria.

At first the dragon was pleased, but he was horrified to learn that those who had been scattered preached the Way wherever they went. Philip, a member of the Way, went to a city in Samaria. There he performed miraculous signs, cast out evil spirits, and healed many paralytics and cripples. Soon there were sounds of rejoicing throughout the city.

People like Philip had to be stopped!

Saul was dismayed to learn that the "sect", as he called it, had spread as far as Damascus. Breathing out murderous threats against the Lord's disciples, he determined to exterminate them even if he had to go to the ends of the earth to find them. Followers of the Way must be rooted out! So at the dragon's instigation Saul went to the high priest and asked for letters to the synagogues in Damascus giving him permission to arrest followers of the Way and bring them as prisoners to Jerusalem.

But Yahweh had other plans. Saul was just the kind of man God wanted on *his* team.

As Saul neared Damascus, suddenly a light from heaven flashed around him. He fell to the ground and heard a voice say, "Saul, Saul, why do you persecute me?"

Saul was confused. He was defending Judaism. He thought he was on God's side.

"Who are you, Lord?" he asked.

The answer stunned him.

"I am Jesus, whom you are persecuting. Now get up and go into the city, and you will be told what you must do."

Three days later in Damascus a man named Ananias came to the house where Saul was staying. Placing his hands on Saul, Ananias said, "Brother Saul, the Lord—Jesus, who appeared to you on the road as you were coming here—has sent me so that you may regain your sight and be filled with the Holy Spirit."

Immediately Saul's sight was restored and he was baptized. Saul joined Yahweh's team, and the dragon lost his top recruit.

Saul stayed with the believers in Damascus for a few days and immediately began to proclaim Jesus in the synagogues. (So much for the letters of arrest in Saul's pocket!)

"Jesus is the Son of God!" he declared.

Those who heard him couldn't believe it.

"Isn't this the man who caused such devastation among Jesus' followers in Jerusalem?" they asked. "Didn't he come here to arrest them and take them in chains to the chief priests in Jerusalem?"

Saul's preaching became more and more powerful, and the Jews in Damascus couldn't refute his proofs that Jesus was indeed the Messiah. Eventually Saul convinced so many that the Jews plotted to kill him. When the murder plot was made known to Saul, during the night some friends lowered him in a large basket through an opening in the city wall.

When Saul arrived in Jerusalem, he tried to meet with the believers, but they were afraid of him. They didn't believe he had truly become a believer. They thought this was a trick to put them all in jail.

A man named Barnabas brought Saul to the apostles and told them how Saul had seen the Lord on the way to Damascus and how the Lord had spoken to him. He also told them how within the city of Damascus Saul had laid his life on the line with his bold preaching in Jesus' name.

Barnabas was convincing, so Saul stayed with the apostles and went all around Jerusalem with them, preaching boldly in the name of the Lord. When the believers heard of another murder plot against Saul, they got him out of Jerusalem and shipped him off to Tarsus, his hometown.

Things calmed down after that. Throughout the country—Judea, Samaria, and Galilee—the church had peace. The believers were permeated with a deep sense of reverence for God, they experienced the comfort of the Holy Spirit, and they grew in numbers.

The Plan

For the next decade or so, the gospel spread throughout the Jewish world. But not to Gentiles. Jewish law forbad Jews to associate with Gentiles.

Yahweh was about to change that. Jesus had died for the whole world, not just for Jews.

So an angel of God appeared in a vision to a Gentile by the name of Cornelius, a centurion in Caesarea. Cornelius and all his family were devout and God-fearing. The angel ordered Cornelius to send men to Joppa to find Peter and bring him to his house. Cornelius promptly sent three of his employees, two servants and a soldier, to fetch Peter.

Knowing Peter would not agree to visit a Gentile, the Lord used a vision to convince him. While Peter was on the roof praying, he saw in the vision a large sheet full of unclean animals, reptiles and unclean birds, and a voice told him, "Get up, Peter! Kill and eat."

"Surely not, Lord!" Peter objected. "I've never eaten anything ceremonially unclean."

"Don't call anything impure that God has made clean," the voice replied.

This happened three times. While Peter was pondering the vision, the men sent by Cornelius arrived at the gate and called out for Peter.

The Spirit then spoke to Peter.

"Simon, three men are looking for you. So get up and go downstairs. Don't hesitate to go with them, for I have sent them."

Peter invited the men into his house as his guests, and they left the next day for Caesarea. When they arrived, Cornelius was expecting them. He had called together a large gathering of his relatives and close friends.

"May I ask why you sent for me?" Peter wanted to know.

"We are all here in the presence of God to listen to everything the Lord has commanded you to tell us," Cornelius replied.

What an opportunity! Peter spoke of Jesus' death and resurrection. While Peter was speaking, the Holy Spirit came on all who heard the message. The circumcised Jewish believers who had come with Peter were astonished to see the gift of the Holy Spirit poured out even on Gentiles. They spoke in tongues and praised God!

Peter responded by ordering the Gentiles to be baptized.

"Can anyone keep these people from being baptized with water? They have received the Holy Spirit just as we have."

The news of what happened at Peter's house quickly spread. When Peter showed up in Jerusalem, the believers, who were all circumcised Jews, criticized him. Peter explained everything to them precisely as it had happened, and they had no further objections.

"Praise God!" they said. "He has granted even the Gentiles repentance unto life."

It took time for believers outside Jerusalem to think of sharing the gospel with Gentiles. Those who had been scattered by the persecution triggered by Stephen's death traveled as far as Phoenicia, Cyprus and Antioch, but they preached only to their fellow Jews. In Antioch, however, some shared the gospel with Gentiles, and a great number of them believed and turned to the Lord.

That many new believers would need a lot of shepherding. News of this reached the ears of the church at Jerusalem, so they sent Barnabas to Antioch.

When Barnabas arrived, he saw evidence that God had done a great work of grace in these new believers' lives. He was glad and encouraged the believers to stay true to the Lord. As more and more people were brought to the Lord, Barnabas realized that he could use help. Whom should he recruit?

The first one to come to his mind was Saul. So Barnabas went to Tarsus to look for him. After finding Saul, Barnabas brought him back to Antioch. For a whole year they met with the church and taught great numbers of people.

Followers of Christ in Antioch were so transformed by the gospel that people gave them a new name—Christians! The believers were flattered to be known as "Christ-like ones."

Saul was so transformed that he changed his name. In new-found humility he changed his name to Paul, a Greek name meaning To the Jews 'Paul' meant something quite different, but it was also very fitting. Anybody with knowledge of Hebrew would have associated the sound of the name Paul with the Hebrew verb *pa'a*. The word is used to describe the bleating of sheep, the rallying cry of a warrior, or the cries of a woman in labor.

Saul, the proud Pharisee, had become a humble sheep. Saul, the warrior who had warred against the church, spent the rest of his life warring for the church and against the spiritual forces of darkness. And the pain Paul suffered in the process of birthing new churches was very much like a woman's labor pains. On several occasions the beatings he received almost killed him.

When giving testimony before King Agrippa, Paul recounted the Lord's words to him at the time of his conversion on the road to Damascus: "Saul, Saul, why are you persecuting me? It is hard for you to kick against the goads."[2]

Jews would have recognized the play on words. The Hebrew word for the final letter of Paul's name, *lamed*, describes a cattle prod or goad![3]

Paul's name is so fitting both in Greek and Hebrew that it is easy to believe he got the idea for his new name from the Lord himself.

No one in New Testament times was more changed by the power of the Holy Spirit than Paul, formerly known as Saul. And no one was more used of God to bring the Kingdom of Heaven to Earth.

---

[2] Acts 26:14
[3] https://www.abarim-publications.com/Meaning/Paul.html

41

Ups and Downs

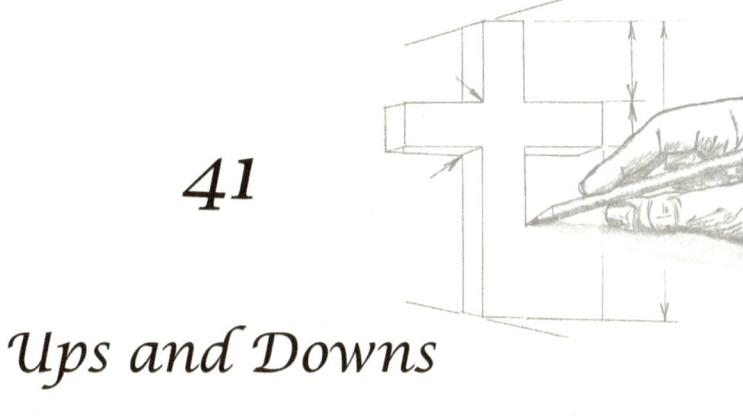

Jesus had told his disciples to go into all the world and preach the good news to all creation. They did that. They didn't sugar-coat the gospel. They preached and let the gospel spread on the merit of its own attractiveness. They also baptized new believers. They drove out demons and healed the sick. Holy Spirit, indwelling every believer since Pentecost, empowered them to do what they had not been able to do in the past—conquer the sin in their lives, live out the reality that they were new creatures in Christ, and speak out boldly for Jesus. Holy Spirit also opened their eyes to understand the Scriptures as never before.

Initially the church grew most rapidly in the synagogues. Devout Jews there were looking for the Messiah. All one had to do was convince them that Jesus was the Messiah and they immediately became Christians. Their knowledge of Scripture and their annual celebrations of the Lord's appointed feasts gave them great insight, which the Gentiles did not have.

Disciples who had followed Jesus during his earthly ministry wrote historical accounts of Jesus' life so it would never be forgotten. Two of those, Matthew and John, had been among the Twelve and had lived with Jesus day and night for almost three years. Apostles such as Peter, James, John and Paul wrote letters to churches and individuals. Those letters, many of them written in prison, are still being read today.

The Plan

The dragon did his best (or worst) to silence Christians. He used both religious and political leaders to denounce them. He used Roman governors and emperors to intimidate them and destroy them.

Christians refused to worship or sacrifice to the Romans gods. This was seen as an act of defiance against Rome's culture and politics and against the very nature of Rome itself. In the Roman empire Caesar was seen as divine. The exclusive sovereignty of Christ clashed with Caesar's claims to his own exclusive sovereignty. Christians could accept only one divinity, and it wasn't Caesar.

Citizens were expected to demonstrate their loyalty to Rome by participating in the rites of the state religion which had numerous feast days, processions and offerings throughout the year. Even attending civic festivals, athletic games, and theatrical performances was dangerous for Christians, since these were held in honor of pagan deities. Christians who did not participate were seen as belonging to an alien cult, an illicit religion that was anti-social and subversive. They lived under the constant threat of being arrested on capital charges.

Life as a Christian required daily courage as they were continually being forced to choose between Christ and the world in countless ways. But Jesus had told his followers they were not of this world.[1] So they did not hide their convictions and pretend to be Romans.

Many pagans believed that bad things would happen if their pagan gods were not properly propitiated and reverenced. By the end of the second century, there was a widespread perception that Christians were the source of all disasters brought against the human race by the gods. The Christian apologist Tertullian wrote, "If the Tiber rises as high as the city walls, if the Nile does not send its waters up over the fields, if the heavens give no rain, if there is an earthquake, if there is famine or pestilence, straightway the cry is, 'Away with the Christians to the lions!'"[2]

---

[1] John 15:19; 17:14
[2] Bart D. Ehrman, *A Brief Introduction to the New Testament* (Oxford University Press, 2004, ISBN 978-0-19-536934-2), pp. 313–314

But the dragon's tactic of widespread persecution against Christians backfired on him. Christians fleeing persecution were scattered around the world. Wherever they went, more people were saved and new churches were formed.

Believers even rejoiced that they were found worthy to suffer for Jesus' name. When they were put in jail and could no longer persuade people in synagogues, they persuaded their fellow inmates in the prison.

Finally, the dragon changed tactics—ease rather than persecution. In 312 AD Constantine the Great issued the Edict of Milan, which established tolerance of all religions including Christianity. Rome adopted Christianity as its official religion and Christians no longer had to live continually in battle mode. Life became easier and Christians let down their guard. They became lax about training their children to love God and hate evil. Little by little, error crept into their teaching. 'Minor' sins were tolerated and ignored. Within a generation or two there was very little contrast between those who called themselves Christians and those who did not. The Catholic Church became more secular and political than spiritual.

Over the centuries the light of the gospel sometimes shone brightly, sometimes faded. Godly leaders would preach and teach the Word faithfully. When they died, other leaders, not so godly, would manipulate the Church for political ends.

The average person was poor and uneducated; many were illiterate. Important documents, such as the Bible, had to be copied by hand, so they were rare and expensive. The organized church controlled what people thought and believed about God. Icons, simple pictures of Bible characters or events, were commonly used as a springboard to tell a Bible story. Church-goers memorized a simple creed which taught them the basics but none of the rich details.

It was hard to make the full gospel known to the masses, but God always had a remnant of people who kept the torch of God's light burning.

The invention and worldwide use of the printing press in the fifteenth century meant a greater distribution of ideas, ideas that threatened the ironclad power structures of Europe. One of the first books to be printed was the Bible, making its contents widely available to ordinary people. When people read the Bible for themselves, they learned how to tell truth from error.

During the middle ages the Catholic Church had developed the concept of purgatory. Rather than being damned to hell eternally after death, the Church said, a person would go to purgatory, a temporary place of torment. After they suffered long enough, they were freed to go to heaven. The more an individual had sinned, the greater the punishment awaited them and the longer they remained in purgatory.

The pope gave bishops the power to reduce sinners' time in purgatory while they were still alive based on the performance of good deeds such as saying prayers, donating to charity, going on a pilgrimage or helping to build a church.

The doctrine of purgatory soon devolved into the practice of buying one's way out of purgatory. By purchasing an 'indulgence', an individual could reduce the length and severity of the punishment for one's sins, or so the Church claimed. Buy an indulgence for a loved one, and he or she would go to heaven and not burn in hell. Buy an indulgence for yourself, and you needn't worry about that pesky affair you've been having.

Basically, the church was selling forgiveness. The wealthy could buy indulgences for anybody—their ancestors, relatives and friends—even those who were already dead. The practice that began in the 13th century was so successful that soon both government and church were taking a percentage of the funds for their own uses.[3]

Early in the sixteenth century a German monk named Martin Luther was profoundly aware of his sin and longed for inward peace.

---

[3] Robert Wilde, "Indulgences and their Role in the Reformation," Indulgences and their Role in the Reformation (thoughtco.com), updated April 28, 2020.

While he was reading Paul's epistle to the Romans, the Holy Spirit illuminated the truth that a person is justified by faith alone.

"Sola!" Luther wrote in the margin.

Later he expanded on that one word: "Sola gratia, sola fide, solus Christus, sola Scriptura, soli Deo gloria." Salvation is by grace alone, by faith alone, through Christ alone, by Scripture alone, and to the glory of God alone. And Luther found peace with God.

About that time, Pope Leo X was building the Church of St. Peter in Hamburg, Germany. To do so he needed a lot of money, not just for the church but for his own personal extravagant tastes. So indulgences were widely advertised. A Dominican monk named Tetzel, a salesman of proven ability, was hawking indulgences in the neighborhood of Wittenberg with patter and buffoonery. Luther overheard his chant:

"No sooner will the pennies clink in the box
Than the keys will clink in purgatory's locks."

That was the last straw for Luther. Outraged, he was determined to expose the gigantic fraud and blasphemous pretensions of the Church. Failing to stir church leaders into action, Luther nailed his protest on the door of the church at Wittenberg. Indulgences, Luther said, can remit neither guilt nor divine punishment. True repentance alone brings pardon, and for the pardoned sinner indulgences are valueless.

Luther's Ninety-five Theses released a flood of pent-up feeling that for generations had been building against papal oppression. Friends printed copies of the Theses and they were distributed throughout Germany. At last someone had been found to express what so many knew, but dared not say.

Luther's five solas summed up the heart of true Christianity. Luther's action emboldened many to challenge the Catholic Church in general and papal authority in particular for what they perceived to be its errors and abuses. Those who identified with Luther's protest became known as Protestants. That was the beginning of the Reformation—the split

The Plan

of the western church into Protestantism and what is now the Roman Catholic Church.

In 1519 Luther took part in a debate held in Leipzig during which he denied the final authority of the Pope and declared that the Councils of the Church were fallible. Luther would bow, not to the Church, but to the direct Lordship of Christ, and His Word would be his sole authority and guide.

Luther followed those statements up with three treatises in which he unsparingly criticised the abuses and doctrines of Rome, demanded radical reform, and upheld the authority of the Scriptures, justification by faith, and the priesthood of all believers. For that the Roman Catholic Church declared Luther a heretic and prepared a papal bull of excommunication.

The papal bull of condemnation arrived, but Luther was one 'heretic' who was not going to be led to the stake easily. A bonfire was arranged outside Wittenberg, but something other than Luther would be burned. Luther, amidst a crowd of sympathisers and arrayed in the robes of his Order, approached the fire holding copies of the Pope's bull and flung it defiantly into the flames. Citizens of Wittenberg looked on with approval. The civil authorities made no move to protest. It was evident that not only Luther but a considerable part of Germany was in a state of ecclesiastical rebellion.

It had taken courage for Luther to bring to light the Scriptural revelation which had made such a mighty impact on his own life, the revelation that each individual is saved through faith in Christ alone. Sadly, his emphasis upon the need for a personal relationship with Christ was lost on many. A few years later Luther said, "The number of those who began with us and had pleasure in our teaching was ten times greater, now not a tenth part of them remains steadfast."[4]

---

[4] John W. Kennedy of India, *The Torch of the Testimony*, Christian Books, Quebec City, Canada, ©1965, p. 143.

The history of the western church, much like the history of the Israelites in the time of the judges, continued on its rollercoaster course. The dragon cheered.

Persecution increased steadily as the dragon attempted to stamp out the Christian church in Europe. Christians wanted to be able to worship God freely and live their lives according to the Bible.

Suddenly there was hope on the horizon. A whole new continent was discovered! In 1620 a shipload of believers headed across the Atlantic to establish a new life. The Pilgrims planned to establish a nation under God with the Bible as their guide. Within 150 years that dream came true. The United States of America was constituted in 1776.

Farther north the same thing happened in 1867. Canada was established as the Dominion of Canada, based on Psalm 72:8: "He shall have dominion from sea to sea."[5]

A dominion is a country where the Lord is sovereign, a territory over which God reigns as King.

The founding documents and laws of both America and Canada were based on the Bible. Sadly, those laws are being revoked one by one. Canada started by revoking the Lord's Day Act in 1985.

---

[5] Psalm 72:8, KJV

42

Authority Restored

All power and all authority belong to God, and he distributes that power and authority as He wills. Initially, when God created Earth, He gave Lucifer authority over Eden to be its guardian. When Lucifer rebelled and aspired to be like the Most High, God revoked Satan's authority and gave it to Adam. When Adam and Eve fell for the serpent's smooth talk and ate the forbidden fruit in the Garden of Eden, Adam forfeited his authority over Earth and Satan regained it.

But God had a plan to restore Adam's authority.

Yahweh's plan was so daring, so bold, so staggering in its ramifications that no one could guess what it was. The dragon and his kingdom could not decipher it, though they certainly tried. Even the angels didn't fully understand it until the Plan was fulfilled.

Satan's authority and power remained unchallenged until Jesus came to earth.

In accordance with the Plan, God had become an *adam*, Hebrew for *man*. Jesus came as the last Adam to regain the first Adam's lost authority. When Jesus showed up on the fallen world scene, He left no doubt as to His ownership of it. He demonstrated authority over nature by such things as walking on water, commanding the wind and the sea to obey him, multiplying food, and turning water into wine. He demonstrated authority over the animal world by using a fish to collect the money needed for a tax. He demonstrated his dominion over disease by healing multitudes. He even displayed power over death by bringing dead people back to life.

Jesus' sinless life qualified him to pay the penalty for Adam's sin and the sin of every person after him. In the process Jesus also won back Adam's lost authority. He now delegates that authority to his children once again, in His name. Holy Spirit backs up and enforces this authority with His power. God's original plan was restored.

There is now a race of humans on the earth filled with God's life and nature, capable of relating to Him as Father and capable of managing Earth well in both the physical and spiritual realms.

The more Christians understand their authority through Christ and His victory, the more Holy Spirit's power is released and Satan's power is bound. God provides His Church, his *Ekklesia*, with weapons against every enemy attack.

People need to realize that when they are born again, they are no longer simply humans; they are a new race of supernatural beings called Christians, "little Christs." They are sons and daughters of the Most High God, filled with His Spirit and anointed to represent Him.

The dragon's strategy to stop the rule of God on earth—to stop evangelism and to stop the spread of biblical morality—is primarily twofold. One is to use fear to overpower faith; the other is to blind Christians regarding the Ekklesia. If the dragon can keep Christians from understanding what it means to be the Church, God will be without a government on Earth. Then, even though the dragon has officially lost his authority there, he can still rule.

Yahweh did not intend the Church to be weak, scared, intimidated and bullied. He didn't intend the Church to be shaken by government tyranny, by the devil's activity or by demon propaganda. Jesus didn't leave heaven and come to earth to be beaten by a reprobate, rebellious, fallen angel. He came to destroy the works of the devil!

Yahweh gave the Church authority to bind the powers of darkness ruling in governments on earth. We can break the hold of the dragon seeking to transform nations through ungodly laws, beliefs, and activities. We can bind the power of Satan in our schools and homes.

The Plan

We can decree that Jesus is Owner and Lord over all the earth. And in His name, we can release the spirit of revival, of holiness, of worship, and the fear of the Lord into our land.

God has given each of us a sphere in which we have influence. We must release our influence as the Ekklesia in our families, our communities, our cities, and beyond. The dragon doesn't mind when the church functions only in the realm of empathy and sympathy, but he does not like us moving into the secular realm with Christ's authority. He becomes nervous when we step out into our responsibility as the Ekklesia of God. That's when we stir up conflict in both the earthly and spiritual realms. That's when kingdoms clash.

When the Ekklesia today behaves like the Ekklesia in the book of Acts—saving the lost, healing the sick, raising the dead, and casting out demons—the power of God will verify our message and people will turn to Christ. The Church will multiply. The world will know we have been with Jesus.

When the Ekklesia of Christ's kingdom exercises its full authority, the dragon will find that he has to deal not just with Jesus—he will have to deal with millions of His followers! Hell won't be able to handle it! The Ekklesia will be unstoppable!

43

The Battle Engaged

For generations the kingdom of darkness was intimidated by the Kingdom of Light. But as the Ekklesia let their guard down, the dragon became more and more bold. His strategy was twofold—to attack in the church and on the streets.

In the church the dragon whispered, "Did God actually say…?" He tried to make God's words sound foolish, unsophisticated, outdated, irrelevant. Even untrue. "Follow the science!"

To those he couldn't deceive, he whispered, "Concentrate on what happens inside the church. Preach the Word. Feed the hungry. Do good. Leave government to the politicians. Don't worry about what happens outside your walls. The rapture will happen soon and you will be out of here. Then good riddance to the chaos!"

On the streets the dragon and his minions went on a rampage. Violent rioters ruled the night, setting cities on fire, looting, and creating mass destruction. The sounds of cursing and gun shots filled the air. The rioters were lawless; their actions were inspired by the demons. They were not afraid of the local police, who were totally helpless in the face of such lawlessness. A strong, demonic force thought they were in control.

"I own these cities!" the dragon shouted.

What the dragon did not see were the riot police. Not the city riot police. The Ekklesia! They had been assigned to restore order and peace in the nation.

The Plan

A mighty angel with a megaphone shouted to them, "Unite! Become as one to hold back the darkness!"

The Ekklesia stood shoulder to shoulder and quickly interlocked their shields. They were dressed in full riot gear—modernized spiritual armor.[1] Their job was to frustrate the dragon's plans.

People in high positions operating under Jesus' authority could use their earthly authority to control unruly crowds, maintain public order, discourage criminality, and protect people and property. Where earthly powers cooperated with the dragon, peace and quiet could be restored by spreading the gospel and allowing Holy Spirit to transform people, and through them transform society.

With each order shouted from the angel, the Ekklesia obeyed. They marched forward two thundering steps, shields interlocked, pressing back against evil.

"Use your voices!" the angel commanded. "Take the authority God has given you!"

In the churches the angel spoke, "Much of this chaos is your fault. You abandoned your cities and schools to those who hate God. You shut your eyes to what was going on outside your walls. You paid no attention to what was being taught in your schools. Those children have grown up, and now they run everything. The media controls what you hear or don't hear. The schools teach your children their values, not yours. The justice system targets good people and lets evildoers out of jail. Take back your authority and speak out!"

Again the Ekklesia obeyed. As they marched, they released declarations of war against the evil one. Their sword was not in their hands; the sword was in their mouths! They prayed and declared victory in the name of Jesus.

"Hold back the darkness!" the order rang out again. On all fronts the Ekklesia marched forward, pushing back evil. The gates of hell could not prevail; the forces of evil were not stronger than God's church.

---

[1] Ephesians 6:11-17

The sound of the Ekklesia's boots echoed in the heavens. The armies of heaven were marching with them! This sound caused the demons to scream in agony and panic as they realized they were not dealing just with humans, God's army on earth; they were also being confronted with the armies of heaven!

Two armies were advancing—one on earth and one in heaven. Two armies were taking authority and dominion in the earth. Two armies were bringing God's kingdom into the land. Two armies were pushing back against the very gates of hell. The power of God was exploding against the dragon's strongholds!

The Lion of Judah shouted to the dragon, "You and your evil hosts are not in control. I have determined that My Ekklesia will live in My victory. They will fight and I will help them prevail."

The Ekklesia heard the deep-throated roar of their Lion King.

"This is MY territory! This is *My* world! You, My Church, will prevail, not fail! You will not run from devils; you will reign with Me! You will not be trembling passive deserters; you will be strong and courageous!

"Hear the roar of the Lion of Judah activating holy fear in the kingdom of darkness. Hear the voice of My power. Hear the words of your Supreme Commander unveiling *His* plans. I am declaring war against cultural evils and government structures of darkness.

"Giants and swamp creatures hidden in gross darkness will not prevail against My warriors, for I will give them night vision. They will find and intimidate My enemies hiding in dark demon territories. Using the spiritual weapons of warfare I have given them, they will tear down strongholds. Do not fear the giants in the land! Hunt them down!"

In a gentler voice the Lion continued, "My people, do not be afraid of the night! The night does not belong to evil. I own the night! The night only coaxes the wicked out of their hiding places; then when the light is turned on, they have no place to run.

"You may feel that you are living in a day in which evil has prevailed. But I say to you, I will uncover evil and corruption. I will expose hidden plans and demonic schemes.

"You may feel you're at the Red Sea and Pharaoh's armies are pursuing. You may even feel trapped and that your plight is hopeless. But it is not! Remember what I did to Pharaoh. I can and will do it again.

"So, hold back the darkness, Ekklesia! This is a time to advance even in the midst of evil. Hold back evil through prayer and intercession. Hold your position with worship that opens the heavens. Hold the line for justice, truth, and righteousness.

"Shake off weariness! Rise up as warriors, empowered by Holy Spirit, and take your land. Press on to victory! I didn't come to lose! I came to expand My Kingdom. Satan is a defeated foe. He may win some battles, but I will win the war. Hold back the darkness!"

Suddenly a different sound came from the people of God. A boldness rose within them. With a fierce, determined voice they cried out in unison:

"Roar over us, Lion of Judah! The demons hiding in darkness will tremble. You will use us to defeat them. We position ourselves to listen for Your voice and instructions. You will tell us exactly where, when, and how to strike the blows. We will shout Your decrees—your battle cries—against rulers of darkness and foes of Your Kingdom.

"If God be for us, nothing can stop us! We are coming forth as a glorious church, capable of representing Christ in all of His authority. The plans of hell will not overcome the Ekklesia!

"We arise in unity, with shields locked and declarations of victory in our mouths. The gates of hell will not prevail against us! We will hold back evil and advance Your Kingdom!"

By the time the dragon realized what was happening, it was too late for him to recover. With the Ekklesia on earth restraining the powers of darkness, the dragon and his followers were rendered powerless. The dragon could do nothing as long as the Ekklesia was present and marching to the orders of God Most High.

44

God Steps In

Meanwhile in heaven Father held in his right hand a scroll which had been written in the days of the prophet Daniel. Daniel had been reading it when God told him to shut the scroll and seal it up until the time of the end.[1]

Daniel had done a very thorough job and sealed it with seven seals. Ever since then, the angels in heaven and people on earth have longed to see what was written in it.

The mighty angel Gabriel,[2] who had numerous encounters with humans—explaining visions to Daniel, announcing the birth of John the Baptist to Zechariah, and announcing the birth of Jesus to Mary—had taken a special interest in that scroll. He wanted to know what was inside. Every time something significant happened on earth, Gabriel wanted to know if it was related to what was written in the scroll.

Finally, he could restrain himself no longer. With a loud voice he cried out, "Who is worthy to open the scroll and break its seals?"

All heaven searched for someone to break the seals. They looked in heaven, on earth, and even under the earth, but no one stepped forward. Some of the searchers began to weep.

Then one of the elders cried out, "Weep no more! Behold! The Lion of the tribe of Judah! He has conquered! He can open the scroll and its seven seals."

---

[1] Daniel 12:4, 9
[2] Gabriel means *hero of God*, from the Hebrew root *gabar*, meaning *to be mighty*.

With that, all heaven rejoiced. The four living creatures, the twenty-four elders and myriads of myriads of angels burst out rejoicing.

> *"Worthy is the Lamb who was slain!*
> *Worthy are You to take the scroll and open its seals,*
> *for you were slain, and by your blood you ransomed*
> *people for God from every tribe and language*
> *and people and nation."*

The Lamb stepped up to the scroll and started opening the seals one by one.[3]

With each seal broken, a rider came out on horseback, each on a different colored horse. A rider on a white horse used his bow to conquer nations and territories. A rider on a red horse swung his great sword and took peace from the earth. A rider on a black horse brought high inflation and scarcity of food. A rider on a pale horse brought death by murder, famine, pestilence and wild beasts.

As war raged on earth, the dragon inflicted many casualties, especially on followers of Jesus. But the Ekklesia were not dismayed. They encouraged each other with words from Jesus, their Supreme Commander.

"Fear not! Our enemies can kill the body, but can do nothing more to harm us. They cannot kill the soul."[4]

In Heaven the martyrs were greeted by Jesus, who took them by the hand and said, "Well done! Enter into my joy!" Behind him a great cloud of witnesses cheered and shouted, "Bravo! Hallelujah!" as the newcomers were each given a white robe.

As the Lamb greeted a seemingly endless line of incoming warriors, he stepped aside briefly to break the fifth seal. This gave a glimpse of those who had suffered a fate similar to the newcomers. The martyrs cried out with a loud voice that could be heard above the cheers:

---

[3] Revelation 5:12, 9
[4] Matthew 10:28 and Luke 12:4

"O Sovereign Lord, holy and true, how long before you judge the people living on earth and avenge our blood for what they have done to us? We long for justice."

"Be patient," they were told. "It won't be long now. Father is keeping count. He knows exactly how many have been killed as you have been. He has set a limit on these martyrs. As soon as that number is reached, the Sovereign Lord will stop the carnage. That number will be written into the charge against the dragon. Meanwhile, rest a little longer and enjoy your reward. Justice is coming."[5]

Shortly thereafter, the Lamb stepped up to the scroll again. As he broke the sixth seal, a great trumpet blast reverberated throughout the universe. All heaven heard it. Most of the inhabitants of earth were deaf to it, but the Ekklesia heard it and rejoiced at the sound.

Instantly heaven was filled as far as the eye could see with new inhabitants. A great multitude that no one could number stood before the throne and before the Lamb of God, who had been slain before the foundation of the earth. There were people from every nation, every tribe, every ethnicity and every language. They were all clothed in white robes, as if for a graduation ceremony. In their hands each held a palm branch—the symbol of victory, triumph, peace, and eternal life. They were the Ekklesia, the Bride of Christ.

With a loud voice the Ekklesia cried out, "Salvation!"

At long last their salvation was complete, and they shouted it to the entire universe. They had been saved from the penalty of sin when they first pledged loyalty to Jesus Christ. They had been saved from the power of sin as they learned to rely on the Holy Spirit to provide a way of escape in times of temptation.[6] Now they experienced the final phase of salvation—being saved from the presence of sin for all eternity.

The Ekklesia raised their palm branches in a toast to the One who had made their salvation possible.

---

[5] See Rev. 6:10-11.
[6] 1 Corinthians 10:13

The Plan

"To our God who sits on the throne, and to the Lamb!"

Then all the angels fell on their faces and worshiped God. They could not shout, "Salvation!" because they had not experienced it. But they could respond to the Bride's words with a hearty "Amen!"

Then they added a toast of their own: "Blessings and glory and wisdom and thanksgiving and honor and power and might be to our God forever and ever!"

The Bride joined them as they said, "Amen!"

Meanwhile on the earth there were sounds which people did hear.

A bone-jarring earthquake shook the earth, moving mountains and islands this way and that. Rocks crashed down, blocking roads. Bridges were destroyed. Buildings fell. The sun turned black as ink; the sky snapped shut like a book. On the dark side of the planet the moon turned blood red. Stars fell out of the sky like figs shaken from a tree in a high wind.

Pandemonium broke out. Everyone ran for cover. They headed for the mountains and hid in caves and among the rocks. One thought was uppermost in their minds: *Almighty God is angry! We must hide from him.*

Panic was evident in their voices as they called to the mountains and the rocks, "Fall on us! Hide us from the face of him who sits on the throne. Hide us from the wrath of the Lamb! For the great day of their wrath has come, and who is able to survive?"

They preferred death to facing an angry God, not stopping to think that falling rocks would instantly bring them face to face with God in judgment.

Death is not annihilation!

Up in heaven the Bride was rejoicing in the presence of the Lamb. No more hunger! No more thirst! No more hardship! No more tears!

Then all eyes turned toward the Lamb as he stepped up to the scroll again to break the seventh and final seal. This time when he opened the seal no horses rode out. There was just silence.

Total silence.

For half an hour.

It felt like forever.

During the silence seven angels lined up quietly in front of the throne of God, and each was given a trumpet.

Then another angel came and stood quietly at the altar in front of God's throne. The martyrs who had been crying out for justice came out from under the altar. One of these martyrs handed a bowl of smoldering incense to the angel.

"These are my prayers," he whispered to the angel, who put the incense into his censer. "Some of us have been crying out for centuries for God to avenge our blood."

One by one, the martyrs filed by and gave incense to be put into the angel's censer. They were followed by the rest of the saints, all bringing their prayers—some asking for justice and judgment, some asking for mercy and for the salvation of their loved ones.

Heaven was spellbound as the smoke from the incense encircled the altar and rose up to the throne of God. Just as the smoke reached God's nostrils, the angel took fire from the altar, added it to his golden censer and hurled it at the earth.

Instantly the silence was broken.

Peals of thunder! Rumblings. Flashes of lightning! An earthquake!

The earth was experiencing the wrath of God.

One by one the angels sounded their trumpets. With each trumpet sound, another disaster hit. Disasters on earth. Disasters at sea. Disasters on rivers and springs. Disasters in the cosmos.

All these disasters happened with minimal loss of life. Yes, many people died, but the death toll could have been so much worse. God designed the disasters to awake people to their need to repent and turn to God.

In his wrath God remembered mercy. The Ekklesia was gone, but God did not leave mankind without the light of the gospel. Shortly before the earthquake which signaled the coming of the wrath of God, an angel had put a seal on the foreheads of 144,000 Jews. These were Jews who knew the Scriptures and were looking for their Messiah, but they had not believed Jesus was that Messiah. When the wrath of God fell, they searched the Scriptures and very quickly realized that Jesus was indeed their Messiah. They read the Bible from cover to cover and figured out what was happening.

The 144,000 soon became evangelists, proclaiming, "Repent! Jesus is the only way to salvation and eternal life."

Not very many people listened, and those who did turn to Jesus were soon persecuted. Many were killed for their faith. The 144,000 were also targets of persecution, but the seal on their foreheads gave them special protection. They could boldly proclaim the gospel without fear of death.

The first four trumpets brought disasters all over the earth indiscriminately. The fifth trumpet had a specific target—those who continued to rebel against God.

This trumpet was worse than the previous "acts of God" for those who experienced the brunt of it. This trumpet was a woe! And God commissioned Satan himself to do the dirty work.

Jesus—the one who declared, "I have the keys of Death and Hades,"[7]—handed the key to the shaft of the bottomless pit to Satan, formerly Lucifer, who had fallen from heaven like lightning before man was created. As usual, God put restrictions on what Satan could and could not do. He could not harm the earth, its grass and its trees—that was God's jurisdiction. And he could not harm God's people—the 144,000 and anyone else on whose foreheads God had placed his seal.

When Satan opened the shaft of the bottomless pit, smoke poured out, darkening the sun, and strange evil beings emerged from the smoke. They looked something like locusts, something like horses, and could sting like scorpions. Their sting brought such torment that people longed to die, but death escaped them. The "locusts"—under

---

[7] Rev. 1:18

the direction of Apollyon, the king of the bottomless pit—stung people relentlessly for five months.

After that, the sixth trumpet sounded, announcing another even greater woe, again targeting human beings. Two hundred million troops were released to drastically reduce the population of earth. Using weapons of mass destruction, nuclear and chemical, they succeeded in killing a third of mankind!

The events ushered in by the trumpets were designed to give people one last chance to turn to God. These people had either ignored God or rejected Him all of their lives. When the Ekklesia disappeared and they realized the wrath of God was being expressed by the disasters happening on earth, some of them repented and turned to God. By the end of the fourth trumpet disaster, people had either repented of their sins or hardened their hearts toward God. During the fifth and sixth trumpets nobody turned to God. They continued doing as they had done before. Murder, idolatry, witchcraft, sexual immorality and stealing were accepted as normal.

People shrugged. "Everybody does it," they said. "No big deal."

Meanwhile, God had a special interest in his people Israel. He had planned long ago and foretold through the prophets that he was going to bring a remnant back to himself. In addition to the 144,000 who were preaching all over the world, God placed two witnesses in Jerusalem to preach the unvarnished truth, "Repent or perish!"

The two witnesses, like the 144,000, were also miraculously protected by God from those who wanted to destroy them. The two witnesses had special powers to go on the offence against their foes. Simply by speaking, they could kill their enemies. They also had power to shut the sky so it didn't rain, to turn waters into blood, and to strike the earth with all kinds of plagues. The vast majority of people hated these two witnesses. They did not appreciate being confronted with their sin.

The Plan

At the end of 42 months Apollyon, king of the bottomless pit, was given permission by God to make war on the two witnesses and kill them. For three and a half days their death was celebrated worldwide. Every TV channel and all social media displayed the pictures, as authorities refused to give permission for the bodies to be buried.

At the end of three and a half days the two witnesses came to life and stood up on their feet. Great fear fell on those who saw it. What happened next frightened them even more.

A loud voice spoke from heaven, "Come up here!" And the witnesses went up in a cloud. Then a great earthquake struck Jerusalem and seven thousand people were killed. That ended the second woe.

The survivors were terrified and gave glory to the God of heaven.

What God won't do to bring people into his kingdom!

Up in heaven a mighty angel roared, "No more delay! Sound the seventh trumpet!"[8]

When the trumpet sounded, loud voices in heaven proclaimed, "The kingdom of the world has become the kingdom our Lord and of his Christ, and he shall reign forever and ever."[9]

Outwardly that didn't appear to be true. The world appeared to be under the rule of the dragon. The antichrist was let loose to make war on the saints[10] and to conquer them, and the false prophet set up a new world religion which forced everybody to worship the image of the antichrist. All commerce was tightly controlled by the antichrist's world government.

But God was reigning. He was giving Satan enough rope to hang himself, he was in control of the time clock, and he was about to fulfill his promise to cleanse the house of David from sin and impurity.

Yahweh had declared concerning Israel, "Two thirds shall be cut off and perish, and one third shall be left alive. This third I will put into the fire; I will refine them like silver and test them like gold. They

---

[8] Rev. 10:1, 6-7
[9] Rev. 11:15
[10] i.e., tribulation saints, both Jews and Gentiles, who had been saved since the rapture.

will call on my name and I will answer them. I will say, 'They are my people,' and they will say, 'The LORD is our God.'"[11]

For the next 42 months God poured out his wrath upon the Jews, destroying two-thirds of them in the process. Those Jews who survived repented of their unbelief and declared Yahweh to be their God.

During those 42 months Satan also demonstrated to the world exactly how evil he was, and all creation had the opportunity to observe and understand what pride leads to. Yahweh was proving to the entire universe that he was perfectly holy, perfectly patient, perfectly merciful, perfectly loving and perfectly just.

When everyone on earth had made a firm decision for or against God, Father declared it was harvest time.

The Son, knowing the end was near, was sitting on a big white cloud wearing a golden crown and holding a sharp sickle in his hand. Father was inside the temple in heaven when he gave an angel a message for the Son. The angel wasted no time exiting the temple and calling with a loud voice to the one sitting on the cloud.

"Put in your sickle and reap. The hour to reap has come. The harvest of the earth is fully ripe!"[12]

With one mighty sweep of his sickle, the Son harvested the earth of those who had conquered the beast and its image and its number. They were brought up to what appeared to be a sea of glass mingled with fire. There with harps in their hands they sang a song celebrating God's justice—justice for which they had longed.

> *"Great and amazing are your deeds,*
> *O Lord God the Almighty!*
> *Just and true are your ways,*
> *O King of the nations!*
> *For you alone are holy,*
> *And your righteous acts have been revealed."*[13]

---

[11] Zechariah 13:1, 8-9
[12] Revelation 14:15
[13] Rev. 15:3-4, abbreviated

The Plan

Meanwhile another mighty angel with a sickle had been dispatched to harvest a different crop. Those who opposed God were like grapes ripe for the picking. The angel swung his sickle and threw them into the winepress of the wrath of God.

The inhabitants of heaven looked toward the temple and saw that it was filled with smoke from the glory of God. No one could enter the temple while God's wrath was being poured out on those who had rejected God and pledged their loyalty to the beast.

Seven bowls of God's wrath were then poured out on the earth.

As God poured out his judgments, a song rose in heaven.

"Just are you, O Holy One, who is and who was,
for you brought these judgments.
For they have shed the blood of saints and prophets,
and you have given them blood to drink.
It is what they deserve!"[14]

Those who had earlier been crying out for justice now responded enthusiastically.

"Yes, Lord God the Almighty,
True and just are your judgments!"

The climax of God's judgment was a battle such as the world had never seen. All the nations gathered against Jerusalem, but God made Jerusalem an immovable rock. Those who tried to destroy Jerusalem hurt only themselves. God defended his people and destroyed all their enemies.

While the nations were gathering for war against Jerusalem and the Lamb, Jesus and his Bride were celebrating their wedding supper. Immediately thereafter, heaven opened and Jesus rode out on a white

---

[14] Rev. 16:5-6

horse as King of kings and Lord of lords. His eyes were like fire and his robe was dipped in blood even before the battle began.

This was not the blood of his enemies. This was his own blood declaring that he had defeated the dragon long ago when he died on the cross!

This was the blood Jesus had taken with him when he entered the Most Holy Place in the temple in heaven, "the more perfect tabernacle that is not man-made," after His resurrection and ascension. This was the blood which obtained for us eternal redemption. This was the blood which "cleanses our consciences from acts that lead to death, so that we may serve the living God!"[15]

This was the blood of the One who "was sacrificed once to take away the sins of many people" and who "will appear a second time, not to bear sin, but to bring salvation to those who are waiting for him."[16]

This was the blood which had defeated the dragon.

Now it was time for the Bridegroom to make his second appearance on earth and to make war on the followers of the dragon. Behind him was the Bride, the Ekklesia, who had become the armies of heaven. They were also riding on white horses, ready for battle. They were not dressed in armor or in battle fatigues but in fine linen, white and clean, knowing that they would not have to lift a finger to obtain victory. They simply watched as the Bridegroom opened his mouth.

His Word was a sharp sword which cut down the kings of the earth and their armies. Within moments they were all dead. An angel standing in the sun called out with a loud voice to the birds to feast on their flesh. The antichrist and the false prophet were captured alive and thrown into the lake of fire.[17]

Thus the King of kings and LORD of lords treaded the winepress of the fury of the wrath of God Almighty.

---

[15] Hebrews 9:11, 12, 14
[16] Hebrew 9:28
[17] See Revelation 19:11-21.

45

Millennium and Judgment

When Jesus set foot on the earth, Eden was restored. The curse on the ground that Adam had brought by his sin was lifted. No more thorns and thistles. The earth produced food without farmers breaking a sweat. The animal kingdom was at peace. Lambs could gambol in the presence of lions without fear of being eaten. Mosquitoes and other insects no longer tormented humans. The dragon was locked up in the bottomless pit, where he could no longer deceive people as he had done in Eden.

Earth was perfect, but human beings weren't. They were still born with a sinful nature, and they could not blame their sins on Satan, because he was locked up.

The earliest inhabitants of this restored earth were loyal to Yahweh. They believed in Jesus and received him. But their offspring were born with Adam's DNA.

They, like every descendant of Adam, were born sinners. They told lies and stole things and punched their playmates without being taught to do so. Many of them chose not to love and follow God. It wasn't long before they committed more serious crimes.

Outwardly society was peaceful, but that was due to Jesus' rule. Together with those who had kept his works to the end[1] and those who had lived through the Tribulation without worshiping the beast or receiving his mark, Jesus ruled the world with a rod of iron. The

---

[1] Revelation 2:26

Millennium and Judgment

Law as written in the Bible was strictly adhered to. The death penalty was meted out for murder and kidnapping—even for cursing one's father or mother.[2] Blasphemers and Sabbath-breakers were stoned to death.[3] Incest and adultery, sexual perversions and homosexual practice, idolatry and witchcraft were punishable by death.[4]

Outwardly society practiced only one religion—worship of Yahweh. All the survivors from nations that formerly attacked Israel now traveled to Jerusalem year after year to worship the King and to keep the Feast of Tabernacles.

But inwardly many people rebelled. They refrained from committing crimes, not because they wanted to please God but for fear of punishment. Nations sent delegations to Jerusalem for the Feast of Tabernacles annually. Not all went because their hearts were overflowing with worship; many went because they knew if they didn't show up, Yahweh would not send rain on their land. Families visited the Holy Land annually. Not all went to worship Yahweh; many went simply because they didn't want to suffer from the various plagues which were punishment for not going.[5]

The Law was not written on their hearts. They did not embrace The Plan of redemption.

For a thousand years peace reigned, but rebellion simmered under the surface. Then Satan was released from his prison. Once more he deceived the nations into thinking following him was better than following God. He promised them the same thing he had promised Jesus in the wilderness: "Worship me and I will give you all the kingdoms of the world. Just think how glorious that will be!"

"We can defeat Jesus," Satan told all who would listen. "He is powerful, but he isn't God. He's just a man like all of you. If we gather a big enough army, we can overthrow him."

---

[2] Exodus 21:12-17; Deut. 24:7
[3] Leviticus 24:16, 23; Numbers 15:32-36
[4] Leviticus chapter 18; note verse 29. Exodus 22:18-19; Deut. 13:6-11; 17:2-5
[5] Zechariah 14:16-19

The Plan

People all over the world were convinced. From the four corners of the earth people gathered for battle, countless in number, like the sand of the sea. Those loyal to Jesus camped around the beloved city of Jerusalem to protect it. Soon they were surrounded by the rebellious army.

But there was no battle. Before Satan's followers could fire a shot, fire came down from heaven and consumed them all. The devil who had deceived them was thrown into the lake of fire, where the antichrist and the false prophet already were being tormented.

Then all those who had rejected God were raised from the dead. They were raised with indestructible bodies, capable of living in eternal torment.

Suddenly there was a mighty roar. All eyes turned to see the entire universe on fire. All the heavenly bodies—stars and planets— were exposed to such heat that they simply melted and disappeared![6] Even the earth on which the people had been standing disappeared, leaving them nowhere to stand, nowhere to hide. They cried out in agony from the intense heat, but they were not consumed in the fire. As quickly as the fire came, it passed.

Everybody was brought before the great white throne of judgment. Some had been confident about this day, sure that the Judge would be impressed with their good works. Others had simply hoped for mercy.

Now the dead, great and small, stood naked before the throne while the books were opened. Being naked physically made most of them realize that they were also naked spiritually.[7]

Deeds good and bad were recorded in infinite detail in the books. None satisfied the perfect holiness of God Almighty. And none of those before the throne had their names recorded in the most important of books, the only book which could save them from the lake of fire—the Book of Life.

---

[6] 2 Peter 3:7-13; Rev. 20:11-15
[7] Rev. 20:11-15; Hebrews 4:13

Great weeping and wailing could be heard as, one by one, those in judgment heard their verdict: "Guilty! Your name isn't in the Book of Life. Your 'good deeds' are filthy rags. Get out of my sight!" Then they were ushered to the lake of fire.

All the angels and all the children of God watched the proceedings with reverential fear. This is what they had escaped by choosing to love and worship Yahweh! There was silence in heaven as the truth sank in.

46

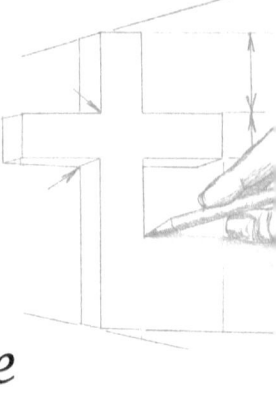

Eternity Future

With evil put away forever, Father made an exciting announcement from his throne:

"Behold, I make all things new!"[1]

The Son spoke a few words, and stars and planets and constellations once more filled the cosmos. The new constellations told a new story, which everybody was eager to hear.

The story made no mention of a dragon or a serpent or a scorpion. He was no longer a factor in their lives. Some constellations—such as the Lion and Gemini the United—were still featured, but their stars were renamed to fit their new story. Some constellations did not need to be changed. The Harp will make music for all eternity. And some constellations were completely new, telling a new story about Jesus, his Bride, and their exciting future together.

Son created a wonderful new earth as the angels sang and the children of God clapped and whistled and cheered. They all laughed with delight to see the Son create some familiar creatures and others that were entirely new. The new earth, like the old one, had a moon, but it had no oceans, no massive bodies of water, only rivers and lakes and streams. Every acre of it was inhabitable and explorable.

When creation was complete, the Ekklesia gasped as they realized they were moving. The entire holy city, the new Jerusalem in which

---

[1] Revelation 21:5

they were residing, was descending toward earth. When it was settled in place, the Father made a declaration from his throne.

"Behold, the dwelling place of God is with man. He will dwell with them, and they will be his people, and God himself will be with them as their God. He will wipe away every tear from their eyes, and death shall be no more, neither shall there be mourning, nor crying, nor pain anymore, for the former things have passed away."[2]

The Holy City shone with the glory of God, with the brilliance of a precious jewel. Its streets were pure gold, as pure as transparent glass; the foundations of its walls were decorated with every kind of precious stone; each of the twelve gates was made of a single pearl.

The most striking feature of the city was the light. The sun and the moon were visible from time to time, but their light was not needed, just as the light of the moon is not needed on earth now during the day. The glory of God gave the city light brighter than anything humans had ever experienced during their life on earth. Their previous bodies would have shrunk from such dazzling brightness, but their new bodies with their new eyes were able to enjoy the light.

The second most notable feature was the river of the water of life. It flowed from the throne of God down the middle of Main Street,[3] with pedestrian traffic on both sides of the river. Lining the street on both sides was what appeared to be two rows of trees. Closer examination showed that this was one remarkable tree connected by its roots and drawing water from the river of life. The tree yielded a different fruit each month—twelve crops of fruit in a year!

The Bride of Christ enjoyed serving God perfectly by reigning with him for ever and ever. Father enjoyed nothing more than to sit on his throne at the head of Main Street and watch his children in their spare time enjoying the beautiful city he had prepared for them. As his children drank from the river and plucked fruit from the tree of life,

---

[2] Revelation 21:3-4
[3] Rev. 22:2, NLT

The Plan

they often looked up to gaze at the Father's face. They never ceased to be amazed that they could do so and live. They loved to see his face and his smile of approval.

Father watched his children ruling over creation as he had designed them to do and turned to the Son.

"This is exactly what I envisioned in eternity past before creation— my family filling the earth and having dominion over it— over the fish of the sea, over the birds in the sky, and over every living thing that moves on the earth. They are doing it just as I would have done. Thank you, Son, for dying to make our dream come true."

Son beamed at his Father's "Well done!"

Holy Spirit agreed heartily. "The Plan was executed to perfection!"

And God saw everything that he had made, and behold, it was very good.[4]

---

[4] Genesis 1:31

Author's Comments

Chapter 2: The Plan Conceived

From the beginning Plan A (salvation by works) has always been strictly theoretical. *If* a man lived a sinless life, he could go to Heaven. But then he would boast about it (Ephesians 2:8-9), and pride is a sin! God knew Plan A was never a serious option for mankind, so He came up with Plan B (salvation as a free gift).

Chapter 6: Chaos

If the angels were created before "the beginning", then Genesis 1 is not a history of the origins of the spirit world, but just of our world. Genesis 1:2 (NIV) says, "<u>Now</u> the earth <u>was</u> formless and empty." The Septuagint translated the first word as "but", showing contrast. Translations which use the word "was" often show the alternate translation "became" in the margin. Thus Genesis 1:2 could, or should, read: *"<u>But</u> the earth <u>became</u> (or "had become") without form, and void."*

There is evidence that the expression "without form, and void" (KJV) from the Hebrew *tohu v'bohu* indicates destruction, not simply primitive creation. Though it is usually translated as "waste and void," "formless and empty," or "chaos and desolation," ancient versions of Scripture render the phrase more strongly. The Aramaic version says, "And the earth had become ruined and uninhabited."

God did not create the earth in disarray. Everything He creates is good. But the earth <u>became</u> formless and empty!

Compare Jeremiah 4:23-26 (KJV), which also uses the phrase "*tohu vav bohu*", as follows:

> "*I beheld the earth, and, lo,*
> *it was without form (tohu), and void (bohu); and the heavens,*
> *and they had no light.*
> *I beheld the mountains, and, lo, they trembled,*
> *and all the hills moved lightly.*
> *I beheld, and, lo, there was no man,*
> *and all the birds of the heavens were fled.*
> *I beheld, and, lo, the fruitful place was a wilderness,*
> *and all the cities thereof were broken down*
> *at the presence of the Lord, and by his fierce anger.*"

These verses describe the Earth as it would have been at the time of Genesis 1:2: The Earth was "formless and void" (or "in disarray and empty"); there was no man; there were no birds. Jeremiah also suggests that being "formless and empty" or "waste and void" is the result of God's anger.

It is possible that there is a considerable time gap between Genesis 1:1 and Genesis 1:2. In that case verse 1 describes the original creation, which was good; verse 2 describes the earth after the fall of Satan; and the rest of the chapter starting at verse 3 describes re-creation.

In Jeremiah 4:23-26 the prophet sees Judah laid waste by conquest and captivity. The cities have received judgment from the Lord. "All the cities thereof were broken down (in disarray) at the presence of the Lord, and by his fierce anger." But the terminology is the same as that used in Genesis 1:2, so following the initial creation of Earth the "cities" may also represent the homes of the angels who had fallen. "The deep" in Genesis 1:2 (Hebrew: *tehown*) is the same word which in Greek is translated "abyss" and used to refer to the home of demons and evil spirits. See Luke 8:31; Rev. 9:1-2; 11:7; 17:8; 20:1-3.

Thus Genesis 1:2 could be read: "***But** the earth was **in disarray, and empty;** and **spiritual darkness** was upon the face of the **demonic realm.**"

Doesn't this sound like a description of hell? It would seem that the Lord created Earth and withdrew his presence from it, but then upon this He created the Earth we know, as is described in Days one to six. Thus Satan and his followers live in the deep, the abyss, the demonic realm, underneath the good but fallen creation we inhabit.[1]

Chapter 8 - 10: The Heavens Declare

The Twins have been known under different names. The Greeks called them Hercules and Apollo. The Latins called them Castor and Pollux. The vessel in which Paul sailed (Acts 28:11) is named after Gemini.

God's redemption plan is written in God's Word and declared in the heavens. Satan, as the master of illusion or delusion, still captivates the gullible. Horoscopes side-track the unsuspecting and superstitious, and endeavor to replace the truth of God with the ideology of man. The modern Latin names which the Constellations bear today in some cases are mistakes, others are gross perversions of the truth, as proved by the pictures themselves, which are far more ancient and have come down to us from primitive times. In some cases the transition from ancient to more modern languages helped to hide the meaning. In other cases, the meaning of constellations has been perverted intentionally.

After the nations had lost the original meaning of the pictures, they invented a meaning out of the vain imagination of their hearts. The Greek Mythology is an interpretation of the signs and constellations after their true meaning had been forgotten (deliberately distorted?). Society would tell us that the Bible is an evolution from, or development of, the ancient religions of the world. But the fact is that certain practices of other religions are a corruption and perversion of original truth!

---

[1]   source: http://ajchesswasbibleblog.blogspot.com/2005/06/genesis-12_20.html

On the fourth day of creation God made the sun, moon and stars. When He set them in the sky, He said, "Let them be for signs and for seasons."[2] 'Seasons' are not merely the four seasons of the year, but *appointed times,* such as the Lord's appointed feasts of Passover, Pentecost and Tabernacles. 'Signs' are *a sign of something* or *some One to come.*

From Creation to the time of Moses the world was without a written revelation from God, but He did not leave man in the dark. The Creator both numbered and named each star, and those names tell the story He wanted us to know.

The Artist Creator first drew pictures around clusters of stars, then identified and named certain stars within them so the pictures could be remembered and their stories handed down to posterity. Those pictures are amazingly consistent throughout all nations and cultures. The stars in the constellations do not form the outline of the figures but are points within a picture. This tells us that the *picture* is the original. Altogether there are forty-eight star-pictures which make up twelve signs, each sign containing three other constellations.

Besides the monthly movement of the sun through the circle of the heavens highlighting a new sign each month, there is an almost imperceptible annual difference. The pole of the heavens is moving ever so slowly, so that the sun begins each year a little behind where it was the year before. Owing to this constant regression, every 2,131 years the sun begins the year in a new sign. Since Creation, the Polar Star has moved through three different signs. At the time of Creation, the Polar Star was the brightest star (the *Alpha*) in the constellation of *Draco,* the Dragon. Now the Polar Star is the *Alpha* in *Ursa Minor,* the Little Dipper!

I think that is where it belongs.

---

[2] Genesis 1:14

Chapter 11: New Creation

Note the verbs used in Genesis 1. Use a translation, not a paraphrased version. Notice when God 'created' and when He 'made.'

The verb translated as "created" (Hebrew: *bara*) means "to bring into existence something new, to make out of nothing." It is used in Genesis 1:1, 21, 27 and 2:3. The verb translated "made" (Hebrew: *asa*) means "to make," with emphasis on fashioning the object.

Exodus 20:11 tells us, "For in six days the Lord made [*asa*] the heavens and the earth, the sea, and all that is in them...." The same thing is said in Exodus 31:17: "for in six days the Lord made [*asa*] the heavens and the earth." This indicates that the six-day creation was not new, though a few things – man and some birds and sea creatures – were new. Mostly, God reshaped and repositioned matter that He had already created.

The verb translated as "formed" (Hebrew: *yasar*) is a technical potter's word, reflecting the basic meaning of "molding" something to a desired shape. *Yasar* is used to express God's "planning" or "preordaining" according to His divine purpose.[3]

---

[3] W.E. Vine, Merrill F Unger, William White, Jr., *Vine's Complete Expository Dictionary of Old and New Testament Words*, Thomas Nelson Publishers, © 1984.

The Cover

First an idea.
　The idea is refined.
　　It becomes a Plan.
　　　The PLAN needs a blueprint
　　　　before the construction
　　　　　can begin.

　　　The lines of the blueprint give perspective.

　　　　　　The lines of God's blueprint
　　　　　　don't stop at the edge of the page.

They extend . . .

　　　. . . from eternity past . . .

　　　　　. . . through Calvary . . .

　　　　　　　. . . to eternity future.

www.ingramcontent.com/pod-product-compliance
Lightning Source LLC
LaVergne TN
LVHW091700070526
838199LV00050B/2224